To:

Sarah

From:

AndRea

Date:

Aug. 10th 2016

365 Devotions

Moments with God

for Moms

Karen Stubbs

christian
art gifts ®

© 2016 Christian Art Gifts, RSA
          Christian Art Gifts Inc., IL, USA

Designed by Christian Art Gifts

Images used under license from Shutterstock.com

Printed in China

ISBN 978-1-4321-1554-8

16 17 18 19 20 21 22 23 24 25 – 12 11 10 9 8 7 6 5 4 3

Her children arise and call her blessed;
   her husband also, and he praises her:
"Many women do noble things,
   but you surpass them all."
Charm is deceptive, and beauty is fleeting;
   but a woman who fears the LORD is to be praised.

~ Proverbs 31:28-30

January

#Hashtag

The Lord is a warrior; the Lord is His name.

Exodus 15:3

What's a hashtag? It's a way people post what they are doing: #loving-life, #home, #lifeofamom. Here's a question: If people were to look at your life, what hashtag would they give you? Would it be #awesome-woman, #gossip, #givingperson, #unfaithful or #servant? That makes you think, doesn't it? God had a hashtag in Exodus. It was #Warrior.

The point of today's devotion is not for you to figure out a cool hashtag for your post today. It's deeper than that. When people look at your life, are there any qualities that stand out? Obviously, we are way more than #hashtags, but sometimes we need to pay attention to our reputations. What do the people in your life feel after they have been around you for an hour? Do they feel like they've lost a debate because you never lose an argument? Are they encouraged or confused?

I want people to be encouraged and feel loved after they hang out with me. It's a good idea to examine the fruits of the Spirit on a regular basis (see Galatians 5:22-23) and allow those qualities to be what you are known for – love, joy, peace, patience, kindness, goodness, faithfulness, gentleness and self -control.

Father, thank You for being a warrior for me!
You go to battle for me against my enemies every day.
I want Your love to shine through my life. I want my life
to be a complete reflection of You, so that when people look at me,
they actually see You. Fill me with Your love and grace.
I give You this day; do with it as You will. Amen.

A beautiful thing

"Leave her alone," said Jesus. "Why are you bothering her?
She has done a beautiful thing to Me."

Mark 14:6

The woman in this story lavishly poured an expensive bottle of perfume over Jesus' head. She did not care about the expense of the perfume or that she was "wasting" it. No, Jesus was far more precious to her than money. She knew, firsthand, of Jesus' love for her. His acceptance and forgiveness in her life had changed her forever; she was free from her sin, her guilt and her shame. She did care how much the perfume cost — that was the point — but she wanted to show her adoration to her Lord and Savior.

Jesus accepted her gift. When everyone else was pushing her away, condemning her for being wasteful and negligent with the perfume, Jesus knew her heart and accepted her lavish gift. The love Jesus had for this woman is the same love He has for you. No matter your past, you have been forgiven. No matter how big a mistake you might have made, you are loved and accepted. Jesus is calling to you today, saying, "Accept My gift of forgiveness, and allow Me to pour My love over you so you can experience freedom and a life without shame."

Father, thank You for loving me.
Thank You for accepting me even though
I don't deserve Your acceptance. I give my life to You
and I gladly accept Your love and forgiveness. Amen.

A different kind of life

*For the grace of God has appeared that offers
salvation to all people. It teaches us to say "No"
to ungodliness and worldly passions, and to live
self-controlled, upright and godly lives in this present age.*

Titus 2:11-12

We have a choice on the kind of life we live. We can live for ourselves or for others. The way of the world and our human nature will always drive us to look out for ourselves. Through the grace of God and His salvation for us, we can choose to live a self-controlled life. A life that is full of godly self-control will strive to put others first, and relationships before material things. Our desire and constant need for more possessions will begin to diminish and be replaced by love for others.

We must choose which road we want to travel. We must ask ourselves, whether we want to try to fill a bottomless pit of greed and selfishness, or whether we want to drink from a well where the water is overflowing and never runs dry? Sometimes we have to look past the here and now to what we will gain in the future.

As you go about your day, be more aware of the road on which you are traveling. It's never too late to change course, but first you must be aware of the path you are on. If the pressures of life consume you and you are always striving to keep up with your friends, then it might be time to start living a life free from worldly passions.

*Father, I want to live a life that glorifies You. I want to
walk away from always wanting more – more material things,
more money, more lavish vacations – just more. God, take away
my lust to keep up with the world and instill in me self-control
and a loving heart toward others. Help me to push past my greed
and turn my heart completely to You and Your ways. Amen.*

A gift

Do not forsake your mother's teaching. This teaching is a light,
and correction and instruction are the way to life.

Proverbs 6:20, 23

Today's Scripture verse is both encouraging and inspiring. Think about it: Moms have the ability to make our children feel safe, to give direction to their days, to guard and protect them. What more would you want for your children whom you love so dearly? We as moms need to rise to the challenge of instructing our children. Our children come into this world with a blank slate. Our teachings and influence have the potential to stay with our children for a lifetime. Don't take this job lightly.

Push past the thought I can't discipline my child because I don't want to break his spirit. You will not break his spirit; you will give him a guiding beacon for his life. If you as the mom can't focus on your child's future and set him up for success, then who else will? Love your child enough to guide and discipline him when needed.

The wisest man on earth, Solomon, wrote Proverbs and he tells us that correction and instruction are the way to life. Don't forget that in your parenting.

Father, thank You for encouraging me as a mom.
I pray that I will accept and embrace Your wisdom like a
warm blanket on a cold night. Give me the courage to discipline
my children in love and to fight the fear that my child might
not love me. Allow my soul to resonate with Your wisdom so that
I may give my child the gift of good teaching. Amen.

A loving home

The LORD is compassionate and gracious,
slow to anger, abounding in love.

Psalm 103:8

⋙ ——— ⋘

God is so compassionate towards us, because we are His children; He is slow to anger and abounding in love. As moms we need to follow after God's example and be gracious and kind to our family. There are so many opportunities we can show compassion every day with our families: we can be compassionate when we are brushing our little girl's hair, when we are tying shoes, or even a small task of hurrying our kids out the door for school. Our attitude and tone usually set the mood of the day.

When we show this type of love we are really passing on the love God has given to us. If love is modeled in the home, more than likely our children will in turn model it in their lives. We learn from God, then model what we learn to our children and pray they will in turn model it in their lives.

•••——————————•••

Father, I pray that my life reflects You in all that I do.
Thank You for being compassionate towards me
and for always giving me love. Show me how to teach love
and grace to my children, because I want my children to know
they are loved by me and, more importantly, by You. Amen.

A mom's prayer

*Show me Your ways, L*ORD*, teach me Your paths.*
Guide me in Your truth and teach me,
for You are God my Savior,
and my hope is in You all day long.

Psalm 25:4-5

As a mom, I need help. The job is too overwhelming and too great to accomplish alone. Who better to look to for help than God? My prayer as a mom should be, "Show me Your way, O Lord, teach me Your path. Guide me in Your truth."

I can believe all kinds of lies that Satan places in my mind, like I don't measure up as a mom; my children give me my sense of worth; my husband should complete me; I must be in control of my child. With every lie that Satan gives, God has a truth to refute it, so I can renew my mind with His truth:

* I don't measure up (see 2 Corinthians 5:17, Romans 5:6).
* My children give me my worth (see Ecclesiastes 2:25-26).
* My husband must complete me (see John 1:12-13).
* I must be in control (see 2 Corinthians 12:9).

My hope is in God all day long. My hope needs to be in God, not in myself. I will fail at times as a mom because I am human. But God does not fail. God is my hope and my refuge. In Him, I will find success.

Father, thank You for teaching me.
Your truth will set me free from the bondage of lies.
Thank You that my hope is in You, that You are trustworthy and
faithful. I pray that I would seek You with all my heart. Amen.

A new heart

"I will give you a new heart and put a new spirit in you;
I will remove from you your heart of stone and give you
a heart of flesh. And I will put My Spirit in you and move
you to follow My decrees and be careful to keep My laws."

Ezekiel 36:26-27

The world can be a cruel place, especially for our children. As moms, we want to shield them from anything harmful. With such good intentions, our hearts often become cold and callous toward others. Protecting our children's safety is paramount, but so is protecting our own hearts.

The condition of our hearts directly affects the way we parent and the way we teach our children to see the world. As a mom, I don't want to teach my children to be afraid of others and not to give love until love is returned. I want to teach my children how to love others the way God loves us – unconditionally. I want to teach my children how to come alongside others and serve them selflessly.

God promises that He will give us new hearts and new spirits; we need only ask Him. He is ready to remove our hearts of stone and give us hearts full of love and grace. Moms who parent with love and grace, and teach their children to live that way, are moms who are worthy to be praised.

Father, give me Your heart. Give me Your love toward others.
Give me wisdom so that I may in turn teach Your ways
to my children. I don't want to parent in fear, consumed by
what the world is doing. I want to parent with a new heart.
Thank You for being my provider of all things. Amen.

A peaceful life

The God of peace will be with you.
Philippians 4:9

Peace is such a beautiful concept. When describing the life of a mom, "peaceful" is not the first word that comes to mind. It's not peaceful when my two-year-old is having a temper tantrum, nor is it peaceful when my 16-year-old is having a temper tantrum. I don't feel at peace when I hear my children fussing and fighting with one another. There is nothing peaceful about being in the car when no one can agree on which fast food restaurant to go to for dinner. Peace is the furthest thing from my family.

God, however, is a God of peace. That's comforting to me as a mom. I can rest in the fact that God is with me at all times, and He will give me peace even when my world is not peaceful. I need to train myself to trust in God's peace and not pay so much attention to my circumstances. Circumstances change; sometimes they are good, and sometimes they are bad. God never changes. He is always good, always loving and always peaceful. I need to remember that.

Father, You are always with me, and I thank You for that.
Because You are with me, Your peace always surrounds me.
Remind me daily that in You I can have peace regardless of my
situation. Teach me to rely solely on You and Your peace. Amen.

A servant's heart

Never be lacking in zeal,
but keep your spiritual fervor,
serving the Lord.

Romans 12:11

So many times, we as moms lose our zeal. Our world can be mundane – cooking, cleaning, carpooling, playing referee between siblings, teaching them right from wrong – day after day, over and over again. It's easy to lose our zeal for life and even more so for spiritual matters.

What is spiritual about making a peanut butter and jelly sandwich? What eternal value is there in changing countless diapers every week? Is there any significance in bath time? Standing alone, these things don't have much value. But add up everything a mom does and multiply it over a child's life, and there is a great deal of value.

You are exhibiting unconditional love: serving, though you know you will not be served in return; giving, when you may or may not be thanked; loving, when you realize your child is only capable of taking.

The win spiritually is that you are being the hands and feet of Christ and demonstrating God's love to your children. They will more easily grasp God's love when they have received that kind of love from you.

Father, remind me always that I am serving You,
and my job is to glorify You in all that I do. When my zeal is
lacking, when I am tired and weary, wrap Your loving arms
around me and whisper in my ear that You will provide what I
need, when I need it. Thank You for taking care of me! Amen.

A weary job

Let us not become weary in doing good,
for at the proper time we will reap
a harvest if we do not give up.
Galatians 6:9

The life of a mom is tiring. Even after the children grow older and are not in that newborn stage of life anymore, the list of chores and "to do's" in a mom's world is never ending. This verse brings hope into my world as a mom. There is a promise attached to this verse. If I don't grow weary in doing good as a mom and I don't give up, I will reap a harvest one day. My work includes teaching my children right from wrong, teaching them manners, teaching them how to love one another, teaching them the right way to walk, talk and treat others – all while doing housework, cooking, running errands and working.

Ladies, I'm on the other side now and I can tell you that when this harvest comes into full bloom, it comes in the form of grandbabies! That is when you reap the harvest of all your hard work and you get to bask in the glory of being a grandmother. You get to love your grandchild and get a full night of rest! It doesn't get much better than that.

Father, thank You for giving me the job of being a mom.
It is a hard job, and one that I do grow weary
in doing day after day, but I am grateful and I love my job!
God, give me Your strength and Your endurance and
help me to see every day as the blessing that it is. Amen.

A wife of noble character

Her husband has full confidence in her and lacks nothing of value. She brings him good, not harm, all the days of her life.

Proverbs 31:11-12

This passage can be a little overwhelming, but do you know what I see when I read these verses? More than anything, this woman is devoted to her husband and her family. Everything this woman does is driven by the love she has for her loved ones, not herself. I think we can all take a lesson or two from the Proverbs 31 wife. If I focus on myself, my needs and my wants, I am going in a different direction than what is ultimately best for me, my husband and my family.

My prayer for all of us moms is that we would aspire to be a Proverbs 31 wife. I want to love my husband and put his needs before my own. I want to be busy doing the work God has given me in raising my children and running my household. I want to be wise and see God's wisdom in His Word. I want to give of my time, talents and money and I want to love everyone. I want to know God and fear Him and feel His love for me.

Will you join me today and focus on being a Proverbs 31 wife?

Father, I want to be a wife of noble character. Teach me what that looks like in marriage. Show me how to put my husband's needs before my own. It sounds so simple, but in life it is hard. I am willing to learn; guide me throughout my day. Help me to be more aware of my husband and not to overlook him because I get busy with life. Amen.

Abide in Jesus

"I am the vine; you are the branches.
If you remain in Me and I in you,
you will bear much fruit;
apart from Me you can do nothing."

John 15:5

Jesus is the key to a joyful life. In order for us to tap into this gold mine of pure joy, we must rest in Him. Picture in your mind trying to teach your child how to float. What words would you use, over and over, to get your child to relax and rest in your arms? The words are usually "trust me." It is the same with Jesus and us: Jesus is calling us every day to rest in Him, to put our faith fully in Him. Jesus is asking us not to fight against Him, but to fully rely on Him. If we do choose to abide in Him, we will begin to bear all the fruit of the Holy Spirit (see Galatians 5:22-23).

What would your life as a mom look like if you reflected Jesus? Your children would be drawn to you like a moth to a flame, because you would be loving, joyful, peaceful, kind, good, faithful, gentle and full of self-control. Who wouldn't want to be around a person like that? Instead of trying to be the best mom on the planet, abide with the One who has it all and start allowing Him to do it for you.

Father, thank You that I don't have to do it all, that all I have
to do is to abide in You. So many times I struggle and fret
and get nowhere … except exhausted. Thank You that I can
rest in You and from it Your fruit will start appearing in my life.
Only You can offer such peace. Thank You! Amen.

Accept one another

Accept one another, then,
just as Christ accepted you,
in order to bring praise to God.

Romans 15:7

We have our children and we all have a desire for them to turn out a certain way: to be model citizens; to be successful in whatever they do; to be kind and compassionate, always thinking of others.

Sometimes, however, our child chooses a different path for their life. It is not that their path is wrong; it is just different from what we had hoped or dreamed for them. What is our role, as a mom, when this happens?

We are called to accept our children and love them exactly as they are, just like Christ loved us. No matter where your child is in their life, they still need your love and acceptance. Your child is different from you – a unique and amazing individual. It is sometimes hard to accept our children just the way they are, but we need to – we are called to.

Accept all of their idiosyncrasies, annoying habits and unusual choices, and love them through it all.

Father, You love and accept me just the way I am.
I pray that I would model this same type of love.
Show me how to love the way You love. Help me to push
aside my expectations and relax as a mom, giving my
children freedom to be who You made them to be. Amen.

Action speaks loud

In the same way, faith by itself,
if it is not accompanied by action, is dead.

James 2:17

Faith alone is not enough in this journey with God. You can believe in God all day long, even the demons believe and tremble (see James 2:19). You must do more than believe, you must take action and obey God.

It is a two-part practice: first, you must believe; and second, you must act. A few practical ways to do this in a mom's world include:

"Children, obey your parents" (Ephesians 6:1) – Act on this command and discipline your child in love, teaching them the importance of this verse.

"Love one another" (John 13:34) – To say you love others is one thing, but to actually love them is another thing altogether. To love others is to put them before yourself, to sacrifice, to not insist on your way, to not have to be heard all the time, and to give grace.

"Trust in the LORD with all your heart and lean not on your own understanding" (Proverbs 3:5) – This verse means to not get caught up in my circumstances in life, but to trust that God will work things out according to His plan, not yours. Keep your eyes focused on God.

Father, I believe in You with all my heart, but when it comes to the action step, I falter. I want to take a step toward action, but doubt enters my mind. Help me to push passed my doubt and fears and just take one step toward You. Thank You for Your endless patience with me. Teach me to push my feelings aside and to boldly trust in You … and act! Amen.

Adored by God

See what great love the Father has lavished on us,
that we should be called children of God!
And that is what we are! The reason the world
does not know us is that it did not know Him.

1 John 3:1

The love of a mother for her child is like no other kind of love. You would do anything to help your child. Amazingly, God loves you even more than you love your child. He has adopted you, and you are now a co-heir with Jesus, a child of God (see Romans 8:17). He wants to lavish you with His love.

Your heavenly Father is the Creator of the universe. He created all things. He is holy, righteous, omniscient, loving, full of grace and mercy, and He calls you His child. Again, you are a co-heir to the one and true God, and you will receive all the benefits that are attached to being an heir.

It is important for you to believe that God truly loves you, because then you will be able to give a greater amount of love to others. Bask in God's love today – soak it in and enjoy it to the full!

Father, thank You for adopting me as Your child.
Thank You for including me as one of Your own and
for lavishing Your love upon me. I pray that I may
be aware of Your love in my life and that I would always
remember that I am dearly loved. God, help me to teach my
children about You and Your great love for them. Amen.

All that I do

Whatever you do, whether in word or deed,
do it all in the name of the Lord Jesus,
giving thanks to God the Father through Him.

Colossians 3:17

Whatever I do as a mom, whether it's tucking my child into bed at night or implementing discipline, I need to do it unto the Lord, giving my best. My purpose as a mom needs to be to glorify God in all my words and actions.

Giving God my best means having a good attitude, a loving spirit and realizing that my job is to glorify Him in all I do. That sounds simple, but in the world of motherhood, it is a constant struggle to keep a positive attitude and a loving spirit. I need to have a good attitude when I am doing laundry and no one even notices. I need to have a loving spirit when my husband is traveling and I am carrying the load of the family by myself. There is no job too small in a mother's world, and I need to do every job as if it were of the highest importance.

I need to remember to thank God daily for the blessings in my life and for the honor of being a mom. It is a privilege to look after the lives that God has entrusted me with. Thank You, Lord!

Father, please bring this verse to my remembrance.
Fill me with Your Spirit, Your love and Your grace.
I pray that I would always be mindful that being a mom has
eternal value. Give me eyes to see from Your perspective. Amen.

Almighty God

He settles the childless woman in her home
as a happy mother of children. Praise the LORD.

Psalm 113:9

Difficult circumstances are part of our lives. Every day we are surrounded by sadness, tragedy, hardship and disappointment. But God is a God of power and glory, and God can bring joy and peace into any circumstance. Maybe as you are reading this devotion, you are in a dark place; maybe you are on bed rest for three months; maybe you cannot get pregnant with your second child and are wondering if you will only be able to have one child; maybe your marriage is in a fragile state and you do not see any hope left. Have hope! God is a God of miracles and He will meet you where you are.

Only God can settle a childless woman's mind and make her happy again. God can restore your life. Cry out to Him and tell Him your need; ask Him to meet you where you are and to give you what you need to get through these dark days.

Accept God's plan and embrace His will, even if it is different from your own. God will bring you peace – submit your life to Him.

Father, You are mighty and powerful! You are sovereign and all-knowing. I am choosing to trust in You. Lord, guide my steps; carry me when I cannot walk. Thank You for getting me through these dark days. I will praise You even when I am sad, lonely or afraid. I give You all my praise and I acknowledge that only through You will I get through this situation. Amen.

Always the same

Jesus Christ is the same yesterday and today and forever.
Hebrews 13:8

In a world that seems to be spinning out of control, we as moms can take comfort in the fact that our Lord Jesus Christ will never change. In a world where we can feel we are losing control daily in our schools, our laws and so many other areas, we can have peace knowing that Jesus is in control. In a world where we feel that bad people get away with everything and good people get trampled on, we can take heart that Jesus has overcome the world (see John 16:33).

The enemy wants us to become discouraged and to lose hope. Remind yourself that your hope has never been in the world – your hope is in Christ. He will be with you and your children. In Christ, you can do all things (see Philippians 4:13); in Christ, you have hope (see Hebrews 6:19). Because of the death of Jesus on the cross, you have victory over this world (see 1 Corinthians 15:57).

Parent the way God instructs you to parent. Be bold! The God you serve, the God you obey, is the same today, yesterday and tomorrow. Stand firm!

Father, I live in a world that changes daily and is not always good. Thank You, Lord, that You never change. Thank You that You are always the same. You are the One I can count on 100 percent of the time. Give me Your boldness to parent my children the way You teach me to parent them. Thank You for Your steadfastness and Your love. Amen.

Amazing gift

For it is by grace you have been saved, through faith –
and this not from yourselves, it is the gift of God –
not by works, so that no one can boast.

Ephesians 2:8-9

It's easy to believe the lie that love must be earned. We strive to perform and to be accepted, which in our minds equals love. The enemy wants you to believe this lie, because if love must be earned, then we are constantly at risk of somehow losing it, which keeps us very vulnerable and insecure.

God, however, wants you to know the truth: His love for you cannot be earned; it is freely given. No one would ever be able to earn His love, because He is a holy God and we are sinners. Through God's amazing love and grace, we can have a relationship with Him and live securely in His love.

People who know they are loved experience life in a deeper, richer way. They are full of life. People who know they are loved also give love more freely. Do you see how your whole family can benefit by the mere fact that you know God loves you? Amazing!

Father, thank You for Your grace and unconditional love.
What a gift! I am forever grateful. Your love changes me.
Teach me to love the way You love. Show me how to model Your
love to my children and anyone I come into contact with. Amen.

Apologizing to others

"Settle matters quickly with your adversary."
Matthew 5:25

If you have more than one child, quarrels are bound to break out at any given point throughout your day. Teach your children from an early age to be quick to apologize to their siblings. In teaching your children the value of humbling themselves and apologizing, you are setting your child up for a life of peace with others.

There is an art to apologizing to another person. First, humble yourself and acknowledge that you have indeed hurt another person. Second, vocalize to the offended that you understand what you did was wrong. Third, move toward the apology and say, "I am sorry; will you forgive me?"

Keep short accounts in your family. This builds strong families. As you teach this principle of short accounts and apologizing to your children, make sure you are living it out in your own life. If you offend your child in some way – maybe by not listening to them, losing your patience or yelling at them – you need to apologize to your child. You will find that your family will grow stronger and be more loving toward each other, with eager hearts toward forgiveness.

Father, remind me throughout my day to keep short accounts, not only with my children, but also with my husband, friends and other family members. God, even when I do not want to apologize, give me the strength and courage to humble myself and admit I messed up. Enable me to teach this life principle to my children and for it to take root in their lives. Amen.

Approval from God

*Am I now trying to win the approval of human beings,
or of God? Or am I trying to please people?*

Galatians 1:10

The main goal in a Christian's life should be to glorify God in every-thing we do. But so many times we lose sight of that goal and we start to focus on pleasing people.

It is the same in a mom's world. A mom's work is all about serv-ing, teaching and placing others before herself. We can get sucked into being such a pleasing mom that we lose sight of who gave us our job in the first place: God. We lose sight of pleasing Him because He is overshadowed by our children.

An example of this behavior is that God teaches us to train our children with discipline and love that will set them up for success, but a child will resist such training. We get caught in the trap of pleasing our children and we lose sight of what God says. If my eyes are focused on pleasing God, I will be at peace with disciplining my child because I will know that in the long run I am doing the best thing for my child. I will not attach my emotions to my child and their reaction to me. Instead, I will keep focused on the end result.

*Father, thank You for my child. Thank You for blessing me in
such a great way with an amazing child. Father, I ask that You
would continue to remind me that You are my top priority.
I need to love and adore my child, but never more than I love
and adore You. You are first and foremost in my life. Amen.*

Are you a helper?

*The LORD God said, "It is not good for the man to be alone.
I will make a helper suitable for him."*

Genesis 2:18

God gave us our spouse so that we could be a companion for them, a helper, someone to "do" life with. We need to constantly remind ourselves of this truth, otherwise we will grow bitter and independent of one another.

The goal in marriage isn't to stay together as long as possible, but to stay together and still like each other after your children leave home. That takes work. It requires you paying attention to your husband, asking him what is going on in his life, asking him how you can help him in any way. Try to resist the desire to keep score. You as the mom will always have changed more diapers, carpooled to more places and sat up more at night with a sick child than your husband. There is no contest or competition – that's a mom's job. Your husband has a job too – providing for your family … and that weight is a heavy burden to bear.

He needs your help, if not for anything else, to encourage him and lift him up to God every day in prayer.

*Father, I do play the comparison game with my husband
and it angers me when I feel like I'm doing all the work.
Forgive me, Lord. Help me to embrace my job as a mom
and not fight against it all the time. I want to be a helper
to my husband. I want to encourage him, pray for him
and help him in any way that I can. Amen.*

Are you angry?

An angry person stirs up conflict,
and a hot-tempered person commits many sins.
Proverbs 29:22

Would you consider yourself to be an angry person? Most people would answer, "No." But when you have children, sometimes anger can come out of nowhere. Therefore, if you do have something boiling deep down inside of you – pain from your past, heartache from a lost love, unforgiveness towards someone – it will begin to boil hotter, until you explode. You think to yourself, *Where is this anger coming from?*

It could come from years gone by when your parents got a divorce and your heart never healed. Your anger could stem from a husband who you feel is not helpful or not in the picture at all. There are many reasons why someone gets angry. It could even be as simple as you not getting your way with your child.

No matter where the anger stems from, you need to deal with it. You owe it to yourself and to your child to figure out what is the source of this anger, to dig it out and begin the healing process. Deal with your anger before you cause damage to the next generation.

Father, give me courage to find the source of my anger.
I am embarrassed to admit that I am angry, but I am.
Forgive me, Lord. Restore my heart and heal me
from my pain, so I may love like You love. Amen.

Are you persecuting Jesus?

He fell to the ground and heard a voice say to him,
"Saul, Saul, why do you persecute Me?"

Acts 9:4

It is easy to see how Paul was persecuting Jesus; he was killing the Jews. In reality we also persecute Him when we are obstinate and demanding. When we stand our ground and refuse to compromise, it hurts Jesus and the Holy Spirit who lives in us.

The fruit of the Holy Spirit is love, joy, peace, patience, kindness, goodness, gentleness, faithfulness and self-control (see Galatians 5:22-23). These fruits are evident in our lives when we walk and abide in Jesus. When there is no evidence of these attributes in our lives, it hurts Him, the Holy Spirit and even God's church, which means we are persecuting Jesus. Think about it: When you insist on your own way, does anyone see Jesus in you? When you demand to be heard, demand to be right, can people see the love of Christ in you?

As you go about your day, be aware of your life and how it affects others. Are you drawing people closer to Jesus by exhibiting love, patience, peace and kindness? Or are you driving people away from you and ultimately persecuting Jesus?

Father, it is hard for me not to insist on my own way.
I acknowledge here and now that I cannot love people
the way You love; it is too much! But You can love people
through me. I submit my life to You and I give up my rights to
You. I want people to see You more than I want to be right. Amen.

Are you thirsty?

As the deer pants for streams of water,
so my soul pants for You, my God.

Psalm 42:1

———

We thirst for many things in life. We thirst for a nice house, a loving marriage, a close family, financial security, satisfaction in our work and significance amongst our peers, but do we thirst for God? Is God on our minds throughout our day? When we run into trouble, is God the first person we think of? When our children are driving us to the point of insanity, do we cry out to God, or do we cry out for our husband to get home quickly?

The psalmist said his soul panted for God the way a deer searches for water. What incredible devotion to God. The psalmist must have learned that only God could quench his thirst – anything other than Him would only be a tease and would never fully satisfy.

God is ready for you to reach out to Him, to cry out to Him and to ask Him to fill your every need. Once you get a taste of His goodness, His love and His mercy, you will begin to want more, and before you know it you will be thirsting for Him.

———

Father, I admit I do not always think of You first.
Sometimes You are the last one I cry out to and
usually it is out of sheer desperation. God, I want to begin
to look to You always, and I want You to be my source of fulfill-
ment. Create a deep desire in me to lean on You always. Amen.

At a loss

If any of you lacks wisdom, you should ask God,
who gives generously to all without finding fault,
and it will be given to you.

James 1:5

The mind of a child can be a mystery at times. So many times we think: What is the reason behind this behavior? Is this a phase? Where is this rebellion coming from? Usually when we find ourselves in those seasons, we go to our parents, our friends, doctors or counselors to ask for advice. Maybe we should start going to God. He is the ultimate Creator of our children and He alone knows all the answers concerning them.

You may not hear God's voice audibly, but start by taking your concerns, your questions and your frustrations to God, and asking Him for His wisdom and His answer to your child's issue. So many times in parenting, we realize we don't have the answer we are searching for and we need complete dependence on God – to trust Him. Have you pleaded with God over the issue you are struggling with? Have you asked your friends or family to pray for this issue as well? Keep an open mind as God directs your path.

Father, I admit that half the time as a parent I'm not sure what I'm doing, and I don't have the confidence I need to carry out my role. I acknowledge today that my confidence does not need to be in me, but in You! Remind me to seek You before anyone else and to be open to Your will for both my life and my child's life. Amen.

Audience of one

Fear of man will prove to be a snare,
but whoever trusts in the LORD is kept safe.
Proverbs 29:25

We tend to be people pleasers. We strive to please our husbands, children, friends, parents, in-laws and even our boss. If making people happy is your ultimate goal, you will fail, because no matter how hard you try, you can't please everyone. However, you can please your heavenly Father and you do please Him.

Our sights should be set on pleasing our heavenly Father as we train up our children in the way they should go (see Proverbs 22:6). It's easy to get off track as a mom, wondering what people will think if my child messes up or behaves in a not-so-perfect way. Instead, we need to be thinking, How would my heavenly Father treat my child in this situation? How would God show love and grace while teaching my child this principle? We don't need to waste time and energy worrying about what others think. Instead, we need to go to the throne of God and ask for advice, concerning ourselves only with what He thinks.

As you go about this day performing your many motherly duties, remember that you have an audience of One.

Father, thank You for loving me. Thank You for always
keeping me safe. I pray that as I go about my day, I will
remember that You are the only One I have to please. Amen.

Be clingy

*That is why a man leaves his father and mother
and is united to his wife, and they become one flesh.*

Genesis 2:24

You must fight for your marriage, especially after your children are born. It is easy to take our husbands for granted and just believe they will always be there for us. But we need to nurture that relationship, just like we nurture our children. There is one fact that we as wives often forget: our husbands were in our lives first.

Force yourself to get away with your husband. Leave your children with a sitter or a family member and get away with your first love — your husband. While you are away, try not to talk about the children, but about things you and your husband have in common. Laugh together, take walks together and hold hands. You need to be gone as long as it takes for the two of you to get back to a younger version of yourselves as a couple.

Your children may resist and cry at the mention of you leaving for a few days, but it is worth it in the long run. Children thrive in a home where Mom and Dad love each other and are committed to each other. Remember that as you are packing and feeling guilty. Don't feel guilty! Go and have fun!

*Father, give me the courage I need to put my marriage
and my husband first. I know my children will miss me
while I am gone, but I need to reconnect with my husband.
I know we still love each other, but it has been a long time
since it was just the two of us. Bless our time away and
bless my children while we are gone. Amen.*

Be gentle

A gentle answer turns away wrath,
but a harsh word stirs up anger.

Proverbs 15:1

It is easy to get pulled into the angry world in which we live. Driving in traffic during rush hour, checking out of a store with a rude salesperson or dealing with another angry parent or coach can be such a battleground. How do we deal with these real-life situations and maintain a loving spirit? We must choose to be gentle.

Gentleness does not come naturally to most of us. When someone is rude, our knee-jerk reaction is to be rude back. Instead, have you ever tried smiling politely back? If you choose to be gentle and loving, the person will usually back down. Being gentle in the face of rudeness or anger is so beneficial in your own life, and even more so for your children to see you modeling this type of self-control.

Children are like little sponges – they soak up all of our habits, good and bad. Think about it: what if your children learned to be gentle to other people and learned how to diffuse a situation instead of stirring it up? I think the world would be a better place.

Father, fill me with Your gentle Spirit today. Teach me how
to look past people's hatefulness and to love them unconditionally.
God, I want to be a good example for my children and to model
for them kindness and gentleness. I cannot do that without You.
Fill me today with Your Spirit and Your love. Amen.

Be humble

*"Whoever takes the lowly position of this child
is the greatest in the kingdom of heaven."*

Matthew 18:4

Being humble is counterintuitive to humans. We are full of pride and self-centeredness. Look at any two-year-old and you will know this is true. One of the first words out of a child's mouth is "No," because they want things done their way, not yours. We must teach our children to be humble, and the best time to teach humility is when they're young.

How do you teach a child to humble themselves? From a very young age, teach your son or daughter to allow others to go first. This act of kindness can be hard for children, especially when they want to go first. By teaching your children to take a step back, they will begin to realize that the world doesn't revolve around them. Throughout their lives, encourage them to humble themselves before the authority figures in their lives — coaches, teachers, bosses, and so on.

Before you can teach humility to your children, you must ask yourself if you yourself are living a humble life — it's hard to preach what you do not practice. Jesus praises those who humble themselves, promising that they will be the greatest in the kingdom of heaven. In order to be great later on, we must humble ourselves now.

*Father, I know that I am a selfish person. I acknowledge that
completely before You. But I don't want to be that way. I want
to be like Christ, who gave up everything, humbled Himself and
became a man. Help me to put aside the false humility I parade;
instead, teach me what godly humility looks like. Amen.*

Be patient

*Be patient, then, brothers and sisters, until the Lord's coming.
See how the farmer waits for the land to yield its valuable crop,
patiently waiting for the autumn and spring rains.*

James 5:7

So many times we as moms try to rush through parenting our children. We get frustrated because we have asked our child at least 10 times to clean up their room and it is still a mess. We ask ourselves, Why won't this child obey? The reality is, it takes time for a child to learn the value of authority and the art of submission. These traits are not learned overnight. A mom deals with another person's heart and no one can change another's heart except for God. We know that God can only do it when that person yields to Him.

What is a mom to do? Give up? No! We must be patient. We must realize that we are in this job for the long haul and there are no short-cuts. We must love unconditionally, love exceptionally and never give up. We need to push past our desire to throw in the towel. We must roll up our sleeves and tell ourselves, Whatever it takes to train up this child is what I will do. It is hard being a mom, but we need to have patience to finish the job well.

There are days, Lord, when I think I cannot wipe up one more spilled drink, stop one more fight between siblings, or listen to my child whine another second. I acknowledge that I must be patient with my children. I need to develop the mindset that parenting is like a marathon. Please give me what I need to finish well. Amen.

February

Be still

"Be still, and know that I am God; I will be exalted among the nations, I will be exalted in the earth."

Psalm 46:10

In a mom's world, being still is usually not a part of our day. Even when our children are taking a nap or at school, there is so much work to do. Being still is a luxury. God, however, wants us to carve out some time in our day to be still and to acknowledge that He is God.

It is important to exalt God and to observe who He is. If we don't force ourselves to slow down and realize who is ultimately in control of everything, we will begin to believe the lie that we are in control. We are not in control, and do not need to be. Our human nature always seeks to control. Therefore, we need to hit the pause button during the day and acknowledge God's sovereignty.

Whether you are in the carpool line at school, nursing a baby in the middle of the night, preparing dinner for your family or folding count-less loads of laundry, hit the pause button. Say out loud, "God, You alone are to be exalted. You alone are Lord over all. I give You this day."

Father, thank You for being God. Thank You that You are in control and that You are Master and Lord over all. Father, I pray that I would discipline myself to pause during my day and to acknowledge that You are sovereign and Lord over all. Amen.

Be strategic

The wise store up knowledge,
but the mouth of a fool invites ruin.
Proverbs 10:14

Wisdom is a mother's friend; she should ask God daily to give her wisdom to know how to parent her children. When a mom is teaching and training a child, a child will usually push back, say no, or disobey. A wise mom will learn how to encourage, motivate and educate her child on the way things should be done. A foolish mom will spew out threats she will not be able to enforce and immediately lose credibility.

If you want to be influential, follow through on what you say. Children know when we are bluffing, so don't throw out rash statements if you aren't willing to follow through. If you see stubbornness in your child, be wise in approaching them. Choose your words wisely. Think to yourself, Can I force my child to do what I'm asking? If the answer is no, then try another approach. Sometimes when we see a child digging in their heels, the best thing we can do is to take a step back and pause. It is better to pause and gather your emotions than to rush in. Remember, it's a journey.

Father, give me wisdom and knowledge concerning
each of my children. You created them, so teach me
how You wired them. Help me to be consistent,
to mean what I say, and grant me the courage to follow through.
Give me love and determination, and fill me with the wisdom
to parent these children You have blessed me with. Amen.

Be wise

Be very careful, then, how you live – not as unwise but as wise,
making the most of every opportunity, because the days are evil.
Therefore do not be foolish, but understand what the Lord's will is.

Ephesians 5:15-17

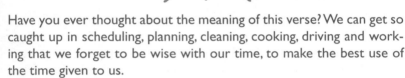

Have you ever thought about the meaning of this verse? We can get so caught up in scheduling, planning, cleaning, cooking, driving and work-ing that we forget to be wise with our time, to make the best use of the time given to us.

What is the best use of your time? Is it looking at Facebook for an hour, dreaming you had another person's life? Is it cramming your schedule so full of activities that you are never fully available to your children or husband? Is it sitting and watching hours of pointless televi-sion that adds nothing to your life but a desire for more?

It's not that these activities are bad or evil – they aren't – but we need to be wise with our time, which is a precious commodity.

Father, as I go about my day, show me how to be wise with
my time. You know my schedule; You know what I need to
accomplish. Help me to make the most of this day that You
have given me. I pray that I may accomplish what I need to
and give myself grace on matters that have to be put on hold.
I give You this day, Father. Do with it what You will. Amen.

Become a great storyteller

Then He told them many things in parables.
Matthew 13:3

$$\Rightarrow\!\!-\!\!\circ\!\!-\!\!\Leftarrow$$

Trying to get your spouse to understand your point of view can be difficult. One effective way to communicate with someone is to use word pictures. A word picture is a modern-day parable. Jesus used parables all the time.

For example, when my children were little, I would work all day on a certain behavior. Then my husband would walk in the door and undo what I had been teaching, and I would get frustrated with him.

I decided to use a word picture with Greg. I would ask him how his day went in the squadron (he was a pilot). He would begin to tell me about his brief and the mission. I would allow him to get all the way through his flight, and then I asked him how he would feel if one of the other pilots came into the room in the middle of his brief and took over. Greg replied that he would not like it at all. I said, "That's exactly the way I feel when you come home at night and allow the children to do whatever they want." For the first time he understood, because I put it in real-life terms.

Father, I want to communicate well with my family.
Please help me to be creative in the way I communicate
so my children and husband will understand my
perspective without me nagging them. I need Your wisdom
and creativity to accomplish this. Amen.

Becoming stronger

The wise prevail through great power,
and those who have knowledge muster their strength.

Proverbs 24:5

This world can drag us down. It appears that people are becoming more mean-spirited and full of rage. In everyday normal experiences, like driving in traffic, if you make a wrong move or change lanes too quickly, other drivers become infuriated. Now, more than ever before, we need strength to cope with everyday life. We need strength to deal with people who are unkind and rude.

A mom's life is no different. She needs strength to deal with all the drama of the younger generation. The pressure that our children face today makes the strongest person cringe in fear. However, we do not need to be fearful; we need to be wise and strong in the Lord God Almighty.

Seek wisdom in God; He is the source of our strength. Jesus knows and understands cruelty. Without a doubt, Jesus was abused, mistreated and mocked, but He stood His ground, strong even unto death.

Jesus found His strength in God. In His last hours on earth, Jesus drew near to God in prayer, asking for strength to get through the devastation that was to come (see Matthew 26:36-45). Seek God in the same way.

Father, so many times being a mom, I have no idea what to do.
I don't feel strong at all; I feel weak and helpless.
God, I look to You to give me wisdom and strength.
I realize that I need You more than ever. Give me what I
need today to parent with wisdom and strength. Amen.

Being a shepherd

"He calls his own sheep by name and leads them out.
When he has brought out all his own, he goes on ahead of them,
and his sheep follow him because they know his voice."

John 10:3-4

What a beautiful picture of how gently Jesus leads us. He is the Shepherd and we are His sheep. In this story, the shepherd calls each sheep by name; it is an intimate relationship – the shepherd knows each one individually. Also note that the shepherd goes on ahead of the sheep, making the path clear for them to follow.

This passage of Scripture is a beautiful picture of how we should be as moms. Christ is our example. He is the picture of a good shepherd. His sheep follow Him because He knows them; they hear His voice and follow.

If you want to have influence with your children, if you want your children to follow your teaching, the best thing you can do is to study them. Take the time to invest in them, learning their likes, dislikes, passions, motivations and disappointments. To be known by your mom is a powerful thing. Don't waste the influence that is at your fingertips.

Thank You for being my Shepherd and for leading me so well.
I pray that I will be an excellent student of my children, that I
will be open to how You designed them, and that I would work
with and not against You. I pray that I would continue to learn
my children's ways. Teach them to listen to my voice. Amen.

Being a student

Show me Your ways, LORD, teach me Your paths.
Guide me in Your truth and teach me,
for You are God my Savior,
and my hope is in You all day long.

Psalm 25:4-5

Moms struggle with the thought of being a "good mom." No matter how great a mom you are, you may feel that you are not doing enough, giving enough or loving enough. Ask God to teach you and direct you on how to be the best mom you can possibly be, and look to Him for fulfillment, not your children. As you mother your children, seek God like you never have before and ask for His wisdom.

In order for us to follow God, we need to pursue Him with all our hearts and "learn" His ways. God's ways are not our ways (see Isaiah 55:8-9). Therefore, we must ask Him to teach us, then humble ourselves and follow Him. As God leads you, obey His commands, even if they feel uncomfortable to you. His ways are always the right ways.

Father, I earnestly seek You with all my heart.
I want to follow You in every aspect of my life,
especially in my role as a mom. God, this job is too big
for me to navigate on my own, and I acknowledge that
You know more than I do. Guide me, teach me, and mold me
into Your likeness. Thank You for Your patience. Amen.

Being content

*I know what it is to be in need, and I know
what it is to have plenty. I have learned the secret of
being content in any and every situation, whether well fed
or hungry, whether living in plenty or in want.*

Philippians 4:12-13

Contentment is learned. We are not born with it; we don't naturally possess it. But through Christ, we can have it. In order to be content, we must begin to look to God and realize that everything comes from Him. Be grateful for what God has given you and learn to be joyful in your circumstances. Choose thankfulness over being discontent.

To give thanks in all circumstances does not mean that you live in a fantasy world where everything is wonderful. You can acknowledge that you are not happy with the circumstances in your life, that you would rather be in a different place, but you can thank God that He is in control. Thank Him for His promise to work all things for our good (see Romans 8:28). Choose contentment.

Father, my natural tendency is to want what others have and to become discontent with what I have. God, give me a grateful heart. Open my eyes so I can see circumstances through Your eyes and not mine. Thank You for meeting all of my needs. Amen.

Being strong

*"My grace is sufficient for you,
for My power is made perfect in weakness."*

2 Corinthians 12:9

Being a mom is hard. The daily grind of teaching, loving, correcting, disciplining and nurturing our children is a lot to bear. Add to those responsibilities the pressures of life – paying bills, making career choices, managing a household – and it is a lot to handle.

So many times we can feel that this burden is too heavy and we just can't keep up. We try to maintain the pace, keep a smile on our faces and push through, but there are days when we just want to get back into bed and forget about it all.

The wonderful, encouraging and inspiring news is that in our weakness, Christ's strength pulls us through every time. When we are weak, He is strong. When we feel like we can't continue, Christ can. Christ's strength is perfect in our weakness.

You don't have to be strong all the time and do everything right. Christ has your back. What a huge relief! As you go about your daily routine, cry out to Him in your moments of weakness. Ask Him to fill you up when you are empty and to give you what you need when you need it.

Father, thank You for this day. Thank You for giving me my children and my many jobs as a mom. Lord, I pray that as I go about my day, I will look to You for strength when I feel weak. God, thank You for equipping me with what I need at all times. Amen.

Best friends

Jonathan made a covenant with David
because he loved him as himself.

I Samuel 18:3

Everyone needs a friend, but a good friend is hard to find. Jonathan and David had a great friendship; one that survived some really hard times. What makes a good friend? The qualities include loyalty, love, trust, and acceptance of others as they are without trying to change them. To have a great friend, you have to be a great friend.

Take time today to think about the kinds of friends you have. Do they seldom call to see how you're doing? Do they only call when they need something from you? If your answer to either question is yes, it might be time to start praying for some new friends.

Ask God to send you a friend like Jonathan was to David. Tell God that you would like a loyal friend who will encourage you and build you up. Seek friends who love God the way you do, so you can encourage one another in your spiritual walk.

Teach your children how to be good friends. Read to them the story of David and Jonathan; explain to them how to put another person above themselves. A child does not naturally know how to be a good friend, but you can teach them.

Father, thank You for being a God who loves relationships.
You know how important they are. God, I do want to be a good
friend. I also desire a true and authentic friendship.
I'm tired of being taken advantage of by my friends.
Teach me, God, how to love others the way You love me. Amen.

Big faith

*Now faith is confidence in what we hope for
and assurance about what we do not see.*

Hebrews 11:1

Our faith can be shaken when we put it in the outcomes of circumstances and not in our heavenly Father. God does not change: He is always good, always loving, always full of grace, always holy and always faithful.

Our views of God can change, however, when we are in situations that cause us to pray for a certain outcome. If that outcome does not happen the way we want, we blame God. We have it backwards. We need to pray as Jesus prayed, "My Father, if it is possible, may this cup be taken from Me. Yet not as I will, but as You will" (Matthew 26:39). Jesus' cup was the cross. He prayed in the Garden of Gethsemane that God would remove His excruciatingly painful death on the cross. Jesus prayed this prayer three times, and all three times, He submitted to God's will.

Often, we cannot "see" God's plan. We pray and ask that God would remove us from the pain and heartache, but we must be willing to pray as Jesus prayed. We must have faith in our heavenly Father, not in our circumstances. God is always good, even when bad things happen. That is big faith.

*Father, I want big faith! I admit I am weak
in this area of my life. I only see the here and now.
I have trouble believing in what I can't see, but God, I want that
kind of faith. Grow me to be more like Jesus, to be able to pray
and really mean, "Yet not as I will, but as You will." Amen.*

Big God

*"Have you journeyed to the springs of the sea
or walked in the recesses of the deep?"*

Job 38:16

God is such a BIG God that our brains cannot completely comprehend His greatness. He is the Creator of all things. He formed the oceans, the stars, the sun and the mountains. He created life for all animals and humans.

Why then do we not trust such a mighty God? He is worthy and deserving of our trust. As Christians, we should never cower or be anxious about what the future holds – our futures are secure in Christ. Our anxiety and worry is pointless.

Think about how much time you waste when you worry. Does your worrying ever change your circumstances? Take that worry and your anxious thoughts to God and lay them at His feet. Ask Him to give you a peace that will carry you through this difficult time.

Start the day by noticing the sun, the mountains and the oceans, and realize how BIG your God is. Look into your child's face and try to comprehend that God is the Creator of this beautiful child. Think about the depths of the oceans and remind yourself that the God you love and serve has walked there.

Father, You are amazing! I don't comprehend all of Your grandness, but today, Lord, I want to declare that You are sovereign, holy, almighty and righteous. When I become anxious, remind me that no problem is too big or too small for You. Gently remind me on a daily basis of Your greatness. Amen.

Birds of the air

"Therefore I tell you, do not worry about your life …
Look at the birds of the air; they do not sow or reap
or store away in barns, and yet your heavenly Father
feeds them. Are you not much more valuable than they?"

Matthew 6:25-26

Anxiety looks different in each of us. One mom may be anxious about discipline, another about the balance of work and home, another about the isolation of being a stay-at-home mom, and another about baby number two on the way and what changes that will bring to the family.

Focusing on our anxious thoughts gets us into trouble and we start to turn away from God. We can't help having anxious thoughts, but what can we do about them?

Peace is the opposite of anxiety. We all want peace, don't we? But how do we get it? We have to trust God and have faith that He loves our children more than we do. Trust that He will show you the next step, tell you how to discipline your children, show you how to prioritize and what you need to remove from your life. Trust God to teach you how to let go of your children, so that they can spread their wings.

Father, thank You that You are a God in whom I can trust.
At times, I am riddled with anxiety and I feel the weight of it on
my shoulders. Lord, teach me how to leave these burdens with You
and to fully trust You. God, I want to be like the birds of the air –
completely dependent on You. Please teach me how. Amen.

Blind faith

*When Jesus saw him lying there and learned
that he had been in this condition for a long time,
He asked him, "Do you want to get well?" Then Jesus said to him,
"Get up! Pick up your mat and walk."*

John 5:6, 8

It's interesting that Jesus first asked the man if he wanted to get well. Jesus first addresses the issue of whether or not the man wanted help. Sometimes people don't want help from their situations, or they don't believe anyone can help them. How many times do we sit and wallow in our frustrated lives, but when someone asks if we need or want help, we don't move?

The disabled man did want help so Jesus gave him a command, "Get up!" Jesus could have touched the man or merely said, "Be healed," but instead He called for an action: "Get up!" Sometimes our faith moves us, but at other times we must take action and move when Jesus says to move.

Are you wrestling with such an issue right now? Is Jesus calling you to release control of your child, but you keep holding on for dear life? Do you feel an urging from God to get your finances in order, even though you don't see how God will deliver you? Do you want to get well? Do you want to find peace? You may need to take action and take that leap of faith.

*Father, give me the courage to follow You wherever You lead me.
Give me the discernment to know when You are speaking.
As I take a step of blind faith, gird me with Your love and grace,
and hold me ever so tightly. Amen.*

Boundaries in your life

When the Most High gave the nations their inheritance,
when He divided all mankind, He set up boundaries
for the peoples according to the number of the sons of Israel.

Deuteronomy 32:8

In a world that seems to be out of control, it's reassuring to know that God set up the nations and "gave them their place on Earth, He put each of the peoples within boundaries."

If boundaries are useful in God's economy, they should be set into motion in my world. We need to push past our fears about what other people think of us and follow God's lead. Boundaries are not meant to hurt, but to help. Everyone needs boundaries in their life, to keep the good in and the bad out.

As you go about this week, take notice of what areas in your life need boundaries. Do you need to set a boundary with your parents or in-laws and ask them not to pop in unannounced? Do you need a boundary where your children are concerned – that they not interrupt you while you are talking with someone? Ask God to give you wisdom in setting your boundaries and then have the courage to execute them.

Father, thank You for leading by example and showing me
that boundaries are important in the economy of life. Give me
the courage to set boundaries and the discipline to enforce them.
Remind me as I go about my day that boundaries are a
good thing and that I don't need to be afraid. Amen.

Bringing God into the ordinary

Submit yourselves, then, to God. Resist the devil,
and he will flee from you. Come near to God
and He will come near to you. Humble yourselves
before the Lord, and He will lift you up.

James 4:7-8, 10

How amazing it is that God will come near to us. It's almost too good to be true, but it is. God will lift us up where we are. We do, however, have a part to play: we must submit and humble ourselves to God.

In everyday terms, what does it mean to submit yourself to God? It means to submit your will to His will and to submit your way to His way. Our will is to push, control and manipulate things. God's will is for us to love, release control to Him and trust that He will work all things together for good according to His glorious riches (see Romans 8:28).

Our way is to argue for our rights. God's way is for us to die to our rights. Our way is to win an argument. God's way is for us to turn the other cheek. By submitting our will and our way, we humble ourselves. There is a promise attached to these verses: "He will lift you up." The God of the universe, the Creator of all things, the Sovereign, Almighty God, will lift you up!

Father, I give You this day. I give You my life –
do with it what You will. God, I want to follow You
and receive Your blessings. Guide me throughout my day
and show me when I am not submitting my will to You. Amen.

Brotherly love

Esau ran to meet Jacob and embraced him; he threw his arms around his neck and kissed him. And they wept.

Genesis 33:4

———

Brotherly love … there is nothing quite like it – when it's good and when it's bad. There is a bond between siblings that no one can duplicate. But with this strong love and devotion comes deep hurt and betrayal when a wrong is committed against one another.

Jacob betrayed Esau and stole his birthright and blessing. In biblical days, a birthright was all a son had. However, despite the betrayal, Esau forgave Jacob. He had every right to stay mad at Jacob, but he chose to forgive him. Jacob didn't deserve forgiveness, but he received it. Esau was genuine in his forgiveness and because of that, the two brothers were united again.

So many times we refuse to forgive someone because it lets them off the hook. After all, they don't deserve forgiveness. They should pay for what they have done. Choose today to forgive the people in your life that need your forgiveness. They may not deserve it, but we didn't deserve to be forgiven either – yet Christ forgave us and paid a very high price to save us.

———

Father, I desire the type of brotherly love that Esau had for Jacob. I know that to forgive is a choice and I want the freedom forgiveness brings. Lord, please give me the courage to forgive. Heal my heart so it doesn't matter if the person "pays" or not. Thank You for Your powerful example of forgiveness in my life. Amen.

Build your house

The wise woman builds her house,
but with her own hands the foolish one tears hers down.

Proverbs 14:1

What does it look like to build a house? You will need to lay the foundation, have a set of house plans and bring in experts like plumbers, electricians and roofers. A builder must be patient to see the project through to the bitter end.

In a mom's world, we need to follow the same plan:

Build your foundation: Your foundation is your walk with the Lord – reading His Word, praying and developing a trusting relationship with Him.

House plan: Have a plan of what you want your family to look like in 10 years. Take time with your husband to discuss values, traditions and qualities that your family will be known for. Throughout the years cross-reference your plan to make sure you are on track.

Experts: Bring in the experts your family needs when they are needed. Whether the expert is a financial advisor, a mentor, a tutor to help with school or a counselor, don't be afraid to ask for help.

Remember, you are building your house, your family. Be wise with your time and resources to build up the best family you can.

Father, thank You for telling me how to be a wise mom.
As I prepare the foundation with You, show me if there is
anything in my life that I need to get rid of, to prepare my heart to
be dedicated to You alone. Give my husband and I wisdom as we
map out our plan. I'm ready to start building my house! Amen.

Carry your load

Each one should carry their own load.
Galatians 6:5

God gives each of us a load that we should carry. The life of a mom has a lot of responsibility that comes with the job. Not only are we supposed to take care of the children, but also cook, clean, manage and carpool. Moms can often feel like our loads are too heavy and we look to our husbands or other family members to lighten it. We can easily place expectations on others that they need to "help"; and when they don't help, we get angry. That is when we know our expectations are unbalanced.

God will give us the strength we need to carry what He has placed in our lives. Look to God and ask Him to give you what you need each day to carry out His plan. There have been times in my life when I felt my load was too heavy to bear, but once I invited God into my world and asked Him for strength, endurance and courage, He always came through for me. Invite Him into your world and ask Him to help you carry your load.

I pray, Lord, that I will be forever dependent in every aspect of my life on You. You have placed me in the circumstances in my life and You will give me what I need to get through them. Please continually remind me of Your faithfulness and love for me. Amen.

Celebrate the little things

The whole assembly then agreed to celebrate the festival seven more days; so for another seven days they celebrated joyfully.

2 Chronicles 30:23

Celebrating is sometimes lost in the rush of life. We get so busy rushing from here to there, trying to accomplish the next task or goal that we forget to hit pause and celebrate what we have just accomplished. Celebrating is needed in our lives. We need to celebrate the family members in our homes.

When your child achieves an "A" on a test that she's been studying hard for, it needs to be celebrated. We should celebrate Dad and Mom when they get a job promotion or are recognized in their field. We need to celebrate life! Hit the pause button and have a celebration for the fun of it, because you are healthy, breathing and growing.

These celebrations do not have to be elaborate or expensive. Keep them simple: Buy a gallon of ice cream and celebrate that it's a hot summer's day. Make hot chocolate and gather around the fireplace in the winter to celebrate the end of a hard week. Life is short, so it should be enjoyed and celebrated. Be the family that is known for celebrating life well.

Father, give me joy. Open my eyes to all the things in my life that I need to celebrate and not take for granted. As I go about my day, show me all of my blessings so I can give You the glory. I want to be a joyful person and someone who celebrates life – this life You have given to me. Amen.

Celebrate you

They celebrate Your abundant goodness
and joyfully sing of Your righteousness.
Psalm 145:7

As moms, we celebrate so many things. We celebrate our children, our families, our children's accomplishments, and every holiday to the fullest. But do we ever truly celebrate ourselves? When was the last time you celebrated yourself and who God made you to be? You are worth celebrating. You need to be celebrated on a regular basis.

Celebrating yourself is hard for most women. But you should do it, because you are amazing! God created you in such a beautiful way – your talents and gifts add to the body of Christ. Without you, the body would not be complete. So, what is one thing about yourself that you can celebrate today? Are you an accomplished cook, an amazing encourager? Do you have a humble heart? Do you think of others before yourself? Are you a beautiful singer? Whatever your talents or gifts, make a point of celebrating them.

You can't teach your children to celebrate themselves without learning how to do it yourself. God made you just the way you are – even the traits you don't like. You are beautiful! Embrace your beautiful self today and thank God for creating such a treasure – you!

Father, I see the beauty and talent in my children,
but when it comes to me, I feel overweight, unattractive
and not good enough. But, Lord, that is wrong of me,
because I know You created me and You don't make mistakes.
Thank You for loving me. Help me to love myself, if for no other
reason than to teach this principle to my children. Amen.

Cheerful heart

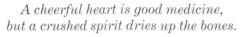

A cheerful heart is good medicine,
but a crushed spirit dries up the bones.

Proverbs 17:22

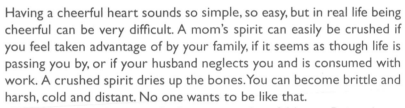

Having a cheerful heart sounds so simple, so easy, but in real life being cheerful can be very difficult. A mom's spirit can easily be crushed if you feel taken advantage of by your family, if it seems as though life is passing you by, or if your husband neglects you and is consumed with work. A crushed spirit dries up the bones. You can become brittle and harsh, cold and distant. No one wants to be like that.

The antidote for a crushed spirit is a cheerful heart. Being cheerful is a choice. God promises us that if we choose joy, it will be like good medicine to our bodies: we will stay young in spirit and be loving toward others. Instead of being harsh, we will be kind. Instead of being cold toward others, we will be warm.

Don't allow your circumstances to steal your joy. You are too beautiful a woman to have dry, brittle bones. Choose joy today. Choose joy when you are helping your children with homework. Choose joy when your husband comes home late from work. Choose joy when your infant wakes up in the middle of the night for a feeding. Choose joy!

Father, thank You for giving me the choice to be cheerful
or to allow my spirit to be crushed. As I go about my day,
point out things that I need to be cheerful about. Give me a
cheerful heart and help me to teach this to my children. Amen.

Child of God

*To all who did receive Him, to those who believed
in His name, He gave the right to become children of God.*

John 1:12

When your child is hurting in any way, what do you do? You wrap your arms lovingly around them and you hold them, saying, "I am here. I love you." Sometimes, that's exactly what your child needs – those warm hugs can make all their problems fade into the distance.

Did you know your heavenly Father wants to love you in the same way? When God looks at you, He sees His child. Just as a mother would never turn her back on her child, God will never turn His back on you. He loves you more than you can ever imagine. He wants to wrap His loving arms around you and hold you through your difficult days.

Today or any time you may be hurting, weak or in need of love, go to God like you would want your child to come to you. Ask Him to wrap you in His arms and love you. Not only is God willing to hold you, He wants you to realize that He is all you need. Allow Him to be your strength when you are weak – your rock and your foundation. His love will carry you through anything life may throw your way. God is waiting for you to reach out to Him, just like we wait for our children to come to us when they need comfort and love.

*Father, thank You that I am Your child. It is amazing that,
through Jesus, I have the right to be Your child, receiving
all the privileges that come with being a daughter of the King.
But, most importantly, I get Your love. You are the
perfect Father and I am so grateful. Amen.*

Choices in life

There is a proper time and procedure for every matter,
though a person may be weighed down by misery.

Ecclesiastes 8:6

A mom's life is all about making wise choices. There are only 24 hours in a day and about eight of those are for sleeping. What are you going to do with the other 16? You need to decide on the wisest use of your and your family's time. Not everyone will be happy with your decisions. For instance, family members might be upset if you ask them to travel to you for the holidays. Or your children could be unhappy if you tell them you are limiting them to one sport or activity per season. We must decide what we feel is best for our family in every season of life.

What season are you in right now? Each one has different challenges. Ask God to show you the areas in your life where some tough choices need to be made and then to give you the courage to implement the change.

Ask God for boldness to stand up for the right use of the time He has given you with your children. Many times, God's ways go against what culture teaches, but His ways are the right ways. Ask God to direct your path.

Father, I pray that I would have the courage to parent
my family in accordance with Your ways. Teach me;
I want to learn from You. If my decisions cause problems, give
me the strength to stand alone. I want to parent the right way –
Your way. Thank You for guiding me on my journey. Amen.

Choose love

God is love. Whoever lives in love
lives in God, and God in them.

1 John 4:16

Marriage pushes us to our limits as women. How is it possible to love a person so much and at the same time to get angry with them? For a marriage to be successful, you must put your spouse's needs above your own.

The problems arise when you don't think your husband is putting your needs before his. We then develop the mindset of, "If he, then I." If he loves me, I will love him. If he changes, then I will change. This way of thinking can be devastating to a marriage. You will find yourself in a crazy cycle of sarcasm, anger, unforgiveness, bitterness and blame.

How do you break out of the cycle? You must begin to take responsibility for your part and realize that the only one you can control is you. Your mindset needs to be, "I will love you even if you don't love me, and I will change even if you don't change." You can only accomplish this when you realize you cannot, but Christ can do it through you. Remember, God is love and His love lives in you.

Father, thank You for my husband. I do love him,
even though he does things that make me mad at times.
Father, I need to take my eyes off trying to change my husband
and focus on You. You will guide my steps. Fill me with
Your love and grace. Thank You for always loving me. Amen.

Chosen by God

You are a chosen people, a royal priesthood, a holy nation,
God's special possession, that you may declare the praises
of Him who called you out of darkness into His wonderful light.

1 Peter 2:9

We all want to be wanted. In grade school, we wanted to be one of the first picked on the dodge ball team. As we grow up, we want to be in the popular group, for a guy to ask us to the dance. Things haven't changed. Even though you're now a mom, you still want to be wanted, to feel special.

Well, you are special! The Lord God Almighty, Master and Creator of the universe, has chosen you. He has chosen you to be an heir with Jesus and to share in His glory for eternity. It doesn't get more special than that!

So often this world blinds us. We belong to God and we are a royal priesthood. We will celebrate for eternity with God. The next time you don't get asked to go to the park with the other moms or don't get invited to lunch, tell yourself it's okay, because God has chosen you and you are wanted by the King of kings!

Wow! To be chosen by You, Lord,
is almost too much to take in. Thank You!
Thank You for loving me even though I am a sinner.
Thank You for giving me mercy and grace.
Create in me, Lord, what You want me to be.
I am Your chosen daughter and You love me. Amen.

Comfort from God

Shout for joy, you heavens; rejoice, you earth;
burst into song, you mountains! For the LORD comforts
His people and will have compassion on His afflicted ones.

Isaiah 49:13

Praise be to God that the Lord comforts His people. Moms need to be comforted all the time. Being a mom is a great job, a job worthy to be praised, but it is hard. A mom gives of herself all day long, usually with no one pouring back into her. We sacrifice and love unconditionally because we love our children and we want to take care of them. But at the end of the day, we grow tired.

How amazing that our heavenly Father understands exactly where we are. He will comfort us. He will fill us up when we are empty if we seek Him. He promises to restore our souls (see Psalm 23:3).

Throughout the day, as you feel yourself being drained of energy, drained of patience and drained of love, cry out to God and ask Him to meet you where you are and to comfort you. Ask Him to fill you with energy, patience for your family and unconditional love toward others.

Father, thank You that You are the God of comfort.
Thank You that You look after Your children and love them.
I admit that I need You more and more every day. Fill me when I
am weak. Fill me with Your power and love. I need You. Amen.

Commitment and dedication

*Ruth replied, "Don't urge me to leave you or to turn
back from you. Where you go I will go, and where you stay
I will stay. Your people will be my people and your God my God."*
Ruth 1:16

Commitment takes loyalty and dedication. You probably didn't realize how much commitment was required to be a mom until you became one. There are many times when you must sacrifice. This can come in many forms: your schedule, time at the gym, your finances, your job or even your friendships. You are required to sacrifice in many ways.

Through your sacrifice and commitment, your children will hopefully witness what commitment looks like and start to mimic your behavior. Don't miss opportunities to teach your children how to stay committed, even when they are tempted to give up.

One easy way to teach commitment is to insist that your children finish an activity once they start. A child can become easily discouraged when practices start to become time-consuming or when music lessons require more practice. We moms can use these situations to teach our children that they must finish what they start. Your children need to learn what commitment means – in sports, school, music, art and relationships.

*Father, I need to be committed to my family. I know
I do get frustrated and sometimes I feel like life is passing me by.
Help me to see the importance of my commitment.
Help me to model commitment for my children. Amen.*

March

Competence from above

Not that we are competent in ourselves to claim anything for ourselves, but our competence comes from God.

2 Corinthians 3:5

Pride has many forms and we can be very prideful when it comes to our children – pride in their accomplishments, appearance, personality, talents and intelligence. But we shouldn't be prideful concerning our children. They are gifts from God and we are simply their steward. God is the Creator of our children and He is the one who has made them who they are.

There is no need for us as moms to take credit for our children's accomplishments; God should get all the credit. We can and should be happy for them, but we would be conceited to think that our children's successes are due to our parenting skills. God gives us wisdom if we seek Him, and He guides our steps. He deserves all the glory and the praise.

Be thankful for your children; be proud of what God is accomplishing through them. Pray daily that they would seek God with all their hearts. Children are blessings from God. Resist turning those blessings into an issue of pride.

Father, thank You for my children. I pray, Lord, that I would always parent them in a way that is pleasing to You. I pray that my parenting would always point my children to You as their loving heavenly Father. God, I am incredibly proud of my children. Please keep me forever mindful that my children are what they are because of You. Amen.

Comrades for life

In all my prayers for all of you,
I always pray with joy because of your
partnership in the gospel from the first day until now.

Philippians 1:4-5

Don't ever underestimate the importance of friendship. Moms need friends. Moms can become isolated and feel they are alone on their journey. Take heart – you are not alone! First and foremost, God is with you and He will provide all of your needs (see Philippians 4:19). Sometimes He provides your needs in tangible ways and one way is through friends. Friends can encourage you, laugh with you, cry with you and pray for you.

A mom's world can be lonely, but if you push past the fear of being rejected, you might be surprised at how wonderful friendships really are. When you choose your friends, find those who are like-minded and walking with the Lord. The Bible says, "As iron sharpens iron, so one person sharpens another" (Proverbs 27:17).

If you are having trouble finding the right friends, ask God to send a friend your way. God is all about relationships and He doesn't want you to walk this journey alone.

Lord, will You find a friend for me and send her my way?
Please send me a friend who will always point me to You; who
will not judge me, but will encourage me. God, teach me how to be
a good friend. Thank You for being a relational God. Amen.

Confidence in God

So we say with confidence, "The Lord is my helper;
I will not be afraid. What can mere mortals do to me?"

Hebrews 13:6

So many times in our "mommy realm," we lack confidence. We often feel ill-equipped. Keep in mind, however, that we have a secret weapon at our disposal: the Lord God Almighty. He is our helper and He will guide us through our days. With God on our side, we can't lose. We should be confident, knowing that God has our back.

When you become overwhelmed, feeling as if you are about to drown, remember that God is your helper. Cry out to Him and seek His counsel and guidance. Ask Him to give you confidence, not necessarily in your own ability, but in His.

Pretend you are recruited to play basketball for an NBA team and you feel overwhelmed. You find out that Michael Jordan is on your team. Suddenly, you are not alone to carry the team, you have Michael to help you win. Well, in life you have someone better than Michael; you have God on your team. Therefore, you can say with 100 percent confidence, "I will not be afraid." You can rest assured that God knows exactly how to handle every situation; He will guide you every step of the way.

Father, thank You for being on my team.
I need You in so many ways and You are faithful,
walking beside me every step of this journey.
Please give me confidence as I parent my children. Show me
what to do and how to handle every situation that comes my way.
I will not be afraid because You are with me. Thank You. Amen.

Constant companion

My help comes from the Lord,
the Maker of heaven and earth.
He will not let your foot slip –
He who watches over you will not slumber.

Psalm 121:2-3

God is with us all the time. He never leaves us. Even when we don't feel He with us, He is with us – working, protecting and watching over us. All of Psalm 121 is devoted to this truth. If you doubt that God is near you, read Psalm 121, and renew your mind with His truth. The enemy wants you to believe that you are alone in this world and that God is too distant to care about your needs. The reality is just the opposite: God cares about your every need, and He is all you need.

Your help as a mom comes from the Lord. God has everything you need to parent your children. In God, you will find all the patience, love, compassion, discipline and self-control you will ever need. Lean into Him. Cry out to Him when you are uncertain which direction to take with your children. Ask God to give you wisdom. He is listening and He is always there. So often we try to parent in our own strength and we fall short. We need to remember that "Our help comes from the Lord." You can't do it all, but God can through you. Let Him help you.

Father, thank You for never sleeping and for always watching over me. Lord, I need Your help! I am crying out to You, because I am weary and I realize that I fall short in this role as a mom. Watch over me, guide me, protect me, and give me what I need to be the mom You designed me to be. Amen.

Cornerstone

*Together, we are His house, built on the foundation
of the apostles and the prophets. And the
cornerstone is Christ Jesus Himself.*

Ephesians 2:20 (NLT)

Who is the center of your family? For most of us, if we are honest, it would be our children. As moms we don't set out to put our children in the center of the family, but they naturally squirm their way in. Before you know it, your whole family revolves around your children's schedules, sports practices, exams, likes and dislikes.

For so many reasons, this is not a healthy way to live. Children naturally believe that the world revolves around them. We are not doing them any favors by supporting this belief. When this is not corrected, children will grow up feeling entitled and self-serving.

Instead, Christ should be the center of your life, the center of your marriage and the center of your home. Jesus is the one true cornerstone. In order to have a Christ-centered life, it must start in the heart. There are many things that force their way to the center of our hearts and most days Jesus is squeezed out. We have to be very cognizant of who or what is truly at the center and fight for Christ to be there. Just acknowledging that there is a battle going on is the first step to being aware of where Christ is in your life.

*Father, thank You for Your precious Son, Jesus Christ.
I do struggle with keeping Jesus in the center of my life
and I ask for forgiveness for that. My heart's desire is for Him
to be number one, but then life happens and He inadvertently
gets pushed aside. Lord, please give me the awareness
and the discipline to keep Him at the front and center. Amen.*

Courage to stand strong

Jesus immediately said to them:
"Take courage! It is I. Don't be afraid."
Matthew 14:27

We teach our children to be courageous and to stand strong, but we don't always apply it ourselves. We moms need courage too. It takes courage to go against what other families are doing. It takes courage to be consistent in disciplining our children. It takes courage to say no to outside commitments so that we can stay focused on our families.

Courage is also needed when God asks you to take a step of faith toward Him. It's scary to get out of the boat and walk into the unknown. Jesus tells us not to be afraid because He will be with us with every step.

Maybe right now God is tugging on your heart to quit your job and be a stay-at-home mom. Your mind has been racing, bringing up every argument as to why that wouldn't work. How would you manage financially? Where would you get your identity? Or maybe the opposite is true: God is opening a door for you to go to work to help pay off some bills, and you are afraid of leaving your children. Whatever your situation, be courageous!

Father, I do need courage on this journey
of motherhood. I am so afraid
I will mess up. Please remind me that You are with me,
and even if I do mess up, You will get me through it.
Thank You for never leaving me and always
equipping me with what I need. Amen.

Creator God

You created my inmost being;
You knit me together in my mother's womb.

Psalm 139:13

God designed each of our children uniquely. No two children are alike; therefore, one size does not fit all. God designed your child's blueprint. Ask Him to teach you how to parent that child. This verse teaches us that God knit each of us together; He knows our deepest desires, passions and inspirations because He created us.

Don't be afraid to parent each child differently. Also, don't be surprised if your children don't understand why you don't treat everyone the same. Teach your child that you are the authority and you have to decide what is best for each child. Explain to your children that ultimately you answer to God and it is Him who you are trying to please.

If you want to be the best mom you can possibly be, ask God every day to teach you about your children. God knows what kind of discipline will work, which love languages your children speak and what type of personality your children have. Seek Him and ask Him to guide you.

Father, thank You for being the Creator of my children
and for making each one unique. I pray that I would view
my job with excitement and joy. What a privilege that You
have given me these children! I ask that You teach me how to
parent them the way they need to be parented. Amen.

Critical nature

"Why do you look at the speck of sawdust in your brother's eye and pay no attention to the plank in your own eye?"

Matthew 7:3

It is extremely hard not to be critical toward people, even in our own families. We can justify our criticism by using the excuse, "I am the mom and I need to share with my son/daughter the need for work in this area." But we need to be careful how many times we choose to go down that road.

The next time you begin to point out an obvious weakness in your child, ask yourself the question, Would my child see this attribute in me as well? If the answer is yes, hit the pause button and go work on yourself before addressing the issue in your child's life. Then, when you approach your child, you can add helpful solutions such as, "I understand this is an area of weakness. I've struggled with this issue myself. Maybe you could try …"

In this Scripture, Jesus is teaching us a lesson about our critical natures. We need to be more tolerant of others and think before we speak. Your job is to guide your children. But remember that a loving tongue goes further than a critical spirit.

Father, thank You for my children. I understand that I need to teach my children and discipline their actions throughout the day. Please teach me how to do that in a loving way. I don't want to be harsh or critical. Instead, I want to be loving. Guide me as I teach them. Amen.

Daily bread

Give me only my daily bread. Otherwise, I may have too much and disown You and say, "Who is the LORD?" Or I may become poor and steal, and so dishonor the name of my God.

Proverbs 30:8-9

Relying on God for our daily bread keeps us dependent on Him and that is where we need to be. I should be dependent on God for my finances, material things, my wisdom, my knowledge of how to parent my children, and for my love toward my husband and children. I need to depend on God for everything in my life.

God knows our human nature. He knows that the more we have, the less we will look to Him to meet our needs. That's why God only gave the Israelites manna one day at a time, to keep them dependent on Him.

Don't look too far into the future. Instead, keep your eyes focused on the here and now and God's provision. He will take care of your future. Trust in Him.

Father, thank You for my daily bread. I pray that I would rely on You for all things. I ask that You would teach me how to become less independent and more reliant on You. Amen.

Daily prayer

I pray that out of His glorious riches He may strengthen you
with power through His Spirit in your inner being,
so that Christ may dwell in your hearts through faith.

Ephesians 3:16-17

We need the strength of God daily in our lives. As moms we can't do our job well unless God is giving us His strength. The job of a mom is too hard to do by yourself, in your own strength. Children demand so much from us – they deplete us. If we do not look to God to fill us up again, to give us strength and wisdom, then eventually we will be empty inside.

God doesn't want you to be hollow inside or a slave to your children. God loves you and wants to empower you with His strength in your inner being. Wow! That's amazing. It's like a huge energy pill to start your day, every day.

Are you receiving what God is so freely giving? Or are you trying to do the motherhood thing in your own strength? Take advantage of the gift that is being offered; you will never regret it.

Father, thank You for Your Spirit that gives me strength.
I need Your strength. I am weary, empty, tired and I need You!
God, fill me up from my innermost being to the point of
overflowing. I thank You for this amazing gift today. Amen.

Days are numbered

Teach us to number our days,
that we may gain a heart of wisdom.

Psalm 90:12

You have a maximum of 6,570 days with your children from the day they are born until they turn 18. You have a limited amount of time to influence your children, to guide and love them.

What are you going to do with this time? Are you going to wish the days away? Dream about a time when your children are out of the house? Try to keep your children with you as long as possible? All three of these options are unhealthy for you and your child.

To make the most of your time, pray and ask God to give you wisdom. Ask Him to teach you about each child. Pray for His direction each day of that child's life and that He will keep you focused on the present.

Ask God to help you stay "in the moment." Leverage your influence with your children; model for them the type of life you would like them to live; guide them each day (resisting the urge to control them); equip them with God's truth; reflect Christ in all that you do; and pray for them every day.

Father, I rush through life wishing my children will sleep through the night and get through the terrible twos. I can't wait until they go to school. I look forward to them being older so I can watch them play sports and enjoy deeper conversations. I can't wait for them to drive to give me a break from carpooling. God, help me to use my time with them wisely. Amen.

Dearly loved

*"I have loved you with an everlasting love;
I have drawn you with unfailing kindness."*

Jeremiah 31:3

Moms pour out love all day long. From the moment our feet hit the floor in the morning, we are serving and loving our families – feeding them, clothing them and cleaning for them. Even during the night, we wake up to care for sick children, or we wait up till the wee hours of the morning for our teenagers to arrive home safely.

As we constantly pour out our love, it is easy for us to start feeling empty inside and soon we get to the point where we have nothing left to give. Take heart! God loves us and He has drawn us with kindness. He will fill us up; He will take care of us; He will clothe us in His love. He wraps His arms around us when we are heartbroken. He will heal our weary souls and fill us up so we can start anew tomorrow. You need to know: you are dearly loved by your heavenly Father, you are His child, and He wants to take care of you the way you take care of your own children. Allow God to love you. Allow Him to help you when you are in need. God wants to be there for you. His love is everlasting; it never fails nor falters. Embrace it.

*Father, thank You for Your love for me. I need You and
I need Your love. I do not deserve such unconditional love,
but I am grateful for it. I thank You that You know and understand that I get tired and weary and yet You don't judge me,
but pour out Your love on me. Thank You! Fill me up today,
so I may in turn pour out Your love onto my family. Amen.*

Deep roots

*Blessed is the one who trusts in the L*ORD,
*whose confidence is in Him. They will be like a tree
planted by the water that sends out its roots by the stream.*

Jeremiah 17:7-8

We are always putting our confidence and trust in something. How many times have we put our confidence in someone, only to be disappointed? Or how many times have we put our faith and trust in something? You can put your confidence in your job and then lose it. You can put your confidence in the church and then find out about a huge scandal, which then destroys your faith in the church. You can put your confidence in your health and fitness only to succumb to illness.

God blesses those who trust in Him; God blesses those who say, "I'm all in, no matter what!" This type of confidence in God is unmistakable, not because of the person's declaration, but because of their actions. When a woman trusts in God with all her heart, mind and soul, there is no denying God's presence in her life. When the drought comes, she does not wither and die. This person is calm because they have learned to trust in God and not their circumstances. Circumstances will come and go – pain is inevitable – but there is peace, love and power with God, even in the storm.

*Father, You are faithful. You are worthy of my trust,
and I pray that I would put all my confidence in You.
God, I want my life to reflect You in all things – in the good
and bad times. I know a drought will come, but keep me
close to You and I will make it through. Amen.*

Designed by God

Start children off on the way they should go,
and even when they are old they will not turn from it.

Proverbs 22:6

Train up your children in the way they should go – not how you would respond or what makes you feel comfortable, but the way they should go. You must realize that God designed your children and He has plans for them. Ask Him today to show you how to parent each child in the way he or she was designed. Learn their ways instead of trying to create little versions of you.

God has wired your children the way He wants them to be, so study them. Celebrate the ways your children are different from you. One child may be a strong leader with a strong will. Ask God to instruct you on the best way to parent this child and thank God for entrusting you with a leader of the next generation.

Father, give me the wisdom to train up my child
in the way they should go. I tend to parent the way that
would work best for me, but teach me how to view each child
individually. Thank You for blessing me with my children;
give me what I need to parent them in a godly way. Amen.

Desire for God

I desire to do Your will, my God;
Your law is within my heart.

Psalm 40:8

We desire many things in life – a new home, a new car or a job promotion. We want a wayward child to come home, eight hours of sleep or even to move closer to our family. These desires are not wrong and God longs to give you the desires of your heart. But what if our first desires were for God? Think about how different your life would be if you thought of Him first – going to Him before calling your best friend or your mom. Your life would be different. Your faith in God would deepen and your trust in Him would not be penetrated by the world.

God would love our desire to be after Him first. He is looking for those who will throw all caution to the wind and follow Him no matter what the outcome might be. But He will never force you into a relationship. He will wait patiently for you to come to Him. It's hard to fathom the type of love that is never-ending and unconditional. But He loves us more than we can imagine and He wants us to love Him in return.

Father, I want You to be number one in my life.
I want You to be the first one I think about in the morning
when I wake up and the last one I think about when
I go to bed. My desire is for You! Amen.

Dinnertime plans

While Jesus was having dinner at Matthew's house,
many tax collectors and sinners came
and ate with Him and His disciples.

Matthew 9:10

Most of us want to have close-knit families where the children enjoy being home, where they want to bring their friends, where home is a safe place. How do we create such an environment?

Children need a place to be themselves, to know they are loved and accepted, and where they can totally let their guards down and know, beyond a shadow of a doubt, their families are on their side.

One way to create such a secure place is to, on a regular basis, eat dinner together as a family. Turn off the TV, set aside the cell phones, put away your work problems, and sit together as a family and have dinner. Listen to your children. Laugh with them. Ask them about their day – the good and the bad. Talk about what their week looks like and share with them what's going on in your life. The dinner table has always been a place where community is built and love is shared, even in the life of Jesus. He took time out of His busy schedule to have dinner with the people He loved. We should do the same.

Father, thank You for showing me how to love
my family and others. I tell myself we don't
have time to sit around the table on a regular basis
and eat dinner, but if I want a close family, I need to make my
family a priority. Give me the courage to rearrange a few things
in my life to make time for what is most important. Amen.

Discipline is important

*No discipline seems pleasant at the time,
but painful. Later on, however, it produces a harvest
of righteousness and peace for those who have been trained by it.*
Hebrews 12:11

As hard as discipline is to put into practice and as painful as it can be for both you and your child, the end goal must be kept in mind. If your end goal is to raise a child who is well adjusted, loving and has a healthy outlook on life, then discipline is not only needed, it's required.

This verse in Hebrews tells us that even though discipline is painful, it brings a harvest of righteousness and peace. Do you want to give your child the gifts of righteousness and peace? Righteousness actually means excellence. Every mom wants her child to have an excellent and peaceful life. Discipline is needed to accomplish such a goal. Think of a professional athlete. They did not accomplish their success without a lot of discipline and training. The same is true for our children. Choose to push past the fear of discipline and remember your end goal.

Father, give me the strength to discipline my children even though it's difficult. Give me discernment to see the ramifications of my children's actions while they are young and how they will play out in the future. I pray, Lord, that I will love my children so much that I won't skip over this important part of being a parent. Amen.

Do not fear

*"For I am the L*ORD *your God who takes hold of your right hand and says to you, Do not fear; I will help you."*
Isaiah 41:13

This verse calms my weary soul. The thought that Almighty God, the God of the universe, Creator of all, the God who has no beginning and no end, sovereign Lord, all-knowing, all-seeing … that very God will take my hand and "help" me seems too good to be true! But it is true.

Fear is always creeping right outside my door. When children are babies, we fear they may die in their sleep. We fear they are in pain and we don't know how to make their pain go away. As our children grow, the fears don't stop.

Take heart! The Lord, our God, will take you by the hand and help you. He will guide and direct your path and show you how to navigate these tumultuous roads. You must choose to listen to Him, to sit at His feet and gain His wisdom. God will take your fears away. In His shadow you will find peace. Whatever circumstances you are dealing with today concerning your children, give them to God. Allow Him to take you by the hand and help you through this fearful, uncertain time.

Father, thank You for wanting to help me and for not expecting me to know what to do. So many times I feel uncertain and ill-equipped to do my job, but You know exactly what I need to do. Thank You for that assurance. Thank You for Your love and compassion. Amen.

Do what is right

Learn to do right; seek justice. Defend the oppressed.
Take up the cause of the fatherless; plead the case of the widow.

Isaiah 1:17

In our society, fatherless children, widows and single mothers surround us. We as the church are called by God to do right by this growing population. We are not called to judge them, to look differently on them or to say, "What a sad situation," and pity them. No! We are called to love them, include them in our families and to encourage them.

Open your eyes and look around – fatherless children are all around you. Single mothers are growing in numbers due to the increase in divorce rates. These people need your help, your love and compassion, not your pity. Invite a divorced family to join you for a holiday meal or to watch a movie. Yours could be the only version of a "normal" family those children will know.

Do right by the people God has placed in your life. Don't just pray for them. Get involved and do something.

Father, I realize that I have a responsibility to those around me –
to do right by them, not only in my prayer life, but also in my
actions. God, give me Your eyes to see people the way You
see them and give me Your love so I can love them well. Amen.

Do you have any fruit?

*The fruit of the Spirit is love, joy, peace, forbearance,
kindness, goodness, faithfulness, gentleness
and self-control. Against such things there is no law.*

Galatians 5:22-23

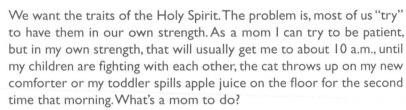

We want the traits of the Holy Spirit. The problem is, most of us "try" to have them in our own strength. As a mom I can try to be patient, but in my own strength, that will usually get me to about 10 a.m., until my children are fighting with each other, the cat throws up on my new comforter or my toddler spills apple juice on the floor for the second time that morning. What's a mom to do?

When I abide in Jesus, spending time with Him and connecting with Him on a regular basis, then I will begin to see fruit. My day will not change. I will still have children that fight, cats that throw up and toddlers that spill juice, but the difference will be me. I will handle the situations better – more lovingly and more patiently – because the Holy Spirit will be oozing out of me. In fact, it won't be me at all – it will be Jesus. However, this type of life only comes through abiding. If you want to have fruit, you must be connected to the Source of the fruit and that is Jesus.

*Father, thank You for the Holy Spirit. My desire is to abide
in You and have the fruit of the Spirit at all times. Teach me how
to abide in You, even in this crazy world of being a mom. God,
show me how to abide in You while I am cooking dinner, nursing
my child or talking to my teenager. I want to learn. Amen.*

Do-gooders

Therefore, as we have opportunity, let us do good to all people,
especially to those who belong to the family of believers.

Galatians 6:10

◦━━━━━◦

Paul challenges us in Galatians to take opportunities to do good for all people. All people include strangers at the grocery store, people pumping gas, people driving next to me on the highway, my neighbor, my cell phone carrier when my bill isn't right. God gives us opportunities every day to reach out to people and show kindness.

I can give the cashier at the grocery store a smile and a greeting instead of staring past her thinking of what I'm going to make for dinner. I can let the person coming into my lane of traffic merge … and smile. Little acts of kindness throughout my day add up to "doing good" to the people around me.

Be creative. Have you ever paid for a cup of coffee for the car behind you in the drive-through at your local coffee shop? That's a nice gesture, a random act of kindness. Today, go throughout your day thinking, *Who could I bless today?* You might be surprised how much you are blessed by these good deeds and how contagious they will become.

◦◦•━━━━◦◦◦◦━━━━•◦◦

Father, remind me throughout my day to do good deeds
and to be kind. I get so busy rushing everywhere,
I forget that the people I am surrounded by all day have lives too,
and they just might need a simple smile and a
"Good morning!" Open my eyes to see the people in my
world who seem to be invisible to me right now. Amen.

Don't forget about you

After He had dismissed them,
He went up on a mountainside by Himself to pray.
Matthew 14:23

Moms take care of their children and families from sunrise to sunset and sometimes through the night. We are constantly tending to the sick, mending and washing clothes, cooking meals, wiping tears, giving hugs and kisses, breaking up fights, fixing broken toys, drawing stick figures on paper, helping with homework – the list goes on and on. If you aren't careful, you will continue to pour out until there is nothing left and you will dry up. To prevent this from happening, you must take time for yourself.

Follow Jesus' example. He saw the importance of getting away by Himself to pray and be revived. Being a caretaker is draining, but we need to be wise and take care of ourselves. What is one thing you used to love to do for yourself that you no longer do? Make a point to do that special thing this week. Some ideas could be: take a long walk, grab a cup of coffee at your local coffee shop and look through a magazine or book, go to a movie with a girlfriend, take a bubble bath, or go to your local flower shop and buy yourself a bouquet of flowers!

Father, I need to push past any guilt I may have around taking time away for myself and just do it – invest in me. I realize now that it's important. If Jesus did it, I can do it. Give me the courage to tell my family, "I'm going out tonight with some friends, and I'm doing it because I love you and me." Amen.

Empathy builds bridges

*For we do not have a High Priest who is unable
to empathize with our weaknesses, but we have one who
has been tempted in every way, just as we are – yet He did not sin.*

Hebrews 4:15

Having empathy with your child is a powerful tool for a mom. Empathy is not agreeing with the complaint; it's agreeing with how your child is feeling. By empathizing we are able to build bridges. When children feel understood, they are more willing to accept guidance. We often try to parent without ever really listening or understanding where our children are coming from in their struggles.

When we come to Jesus with our struggles and our weaknesses, He truly understands, because He has experienced being human and was tempted in every way. It helps me to connect with Him more as my Savior, knowing that He understands my struggles. I may not be able to withstand the temptation in my own strength, but Jesus can. His power is in me.

Christ is our example, and we need to learn to pass grace and love on to our children. As you go about your day, try to have empathy with your children by remembering that Jesus has empathy for you.

*Father, thank You that Jesus has complete understanding of my
struggles and my weaknesses. Thank You that I have Jesus in me
and through Him the power of sin is broken. I pray I will be
able to give my children this same kind of understanding. Amen.*

Empty words

"But I tell you that everyone will have to give account
on the day of judgment for every empty word they have spoken."
Matthew 12:36

We talk all day long every day, but have you ever thought that we will be held accountable for the words we speak? That's a scary thought. To think we will be held accountable for gossiping about someone, for trash-talking about a person, a business or even a teacher at your child's school. What? That's crazy! Words are powerful and Jesus takes them very seriously ... so we should too.

You may have never known that your words were so powerful, but now you do. So from this point forward, choose your words carefully. Have your words be uplifting and positive? If you need to give criticism, think about your words before you blurt them out, and try to have it help, not hurt. Realize the importance of your words during your everyday activities. Don't allow them to be empty. Let them be full of wisdom and love.

Wow! I admit I have never really given my empty words a second thought. Sometimes I am so happy to be talking to an adult that I talk about anything and everything. From this point forward, I want to watch my words and make sure they are pleasing; not only to You, but also to the people I do life with each day. Amen.

Endless love

*I pray that you, being rooted and established in love,
may have power, together with all the Lord's holy people, to
grasp how wide and long and high and deep is the love of Christ.*

Ephesians 3:17-18

There is no way we can humanly fathom the love God has for us. That's why we must accept this type of love by faith. God's love for us is beyond the knowledge of man. There is true beauty in the thought that our heavenly Father loves us beyond our knowledge and understanding.

Ask God daily for the understanding of His love for you. Moms need to realize the depths of His love more than anyone, because moms are in the position to teach God's love to their children. Think about it: if the next generation was told every day about the depth of love that God has for them, how would that change our culture?

You, as the mom in your house, doing your chores every day, could start a revolution – a revolution that has eternal consequences and would set your children on a course that would change their identities forever. Your children would be rooted in God's love, so that even when they fail, they would still know they are loved. The ramifications are endless.

*Oh, how I want to embrace this deep, everlasting love You
have for me. Please open my eyes. God, I want to take hold
of Your love, so that I may in turn teach my children.
I can't teach what I don't know. I'm asking You today to
give me the faith I need to accept Your deep love for me. Amen.*

Enjoying life

I commend the enjoyment of life,
because there is nothing better for a person
under the sun than to eat and drink and be glad.

Ecclesiastes 8:15

We teach so many things to our children on a daily basis. We teach them everything from manners, how to share, schoolwork and chores, to how to have a good attitude, and more. One thing that we sometimes forget to teach them is how to have good, clean fun. We get so wrapped up in how to teach our children all the "important" stuff, we forget to have fun. Fun is a necessity in life. You don't want to be the mom that never has fun, do you? No!

Sometime this week, throw a dance party in your home. Crank up the music, grab your children, get in the middle of the den and dance the night away. Allow your children to pick some of their favorite songs (they will love that), and give all of them permission to let their hair down a little and be free. You might surprise yourself as to how much fun you will have. Life is serious, that is for sure, but don't forget to have fun along the way.

Father, thank You for the gift of life. So many times
I get bogged down with all I have to do in life that I forget
to have fun. I take life too seriously and end up taking myself too
seriously. I want my children to enjoy life and I want them to
learn that from me. Help me to loosen up and celebrate the
wonderful life You have blessed me with. Amen.

Entitlement mentality

Sitting down, Jesus called the Twelve and said, "Anyone who wants to be first must be the very last, and the servant of all."
·Mark 9:35

Our culture has a "me-first" mentality. We push and shove to be the first in line, to win the race, to be the best, to rise to the top. The result is a very self-centered society. There are different times of the year, like Thanksgiving and Christmas, when we think of others and go the extra mile to serve them. But overall, we take care of ourselves first. Our children are no different. Human beings are selfish creatures, to be sure, and the thought of voluntarily becoming last and serving others is not appealing.

God's way is not the way of the world. His way is different. Jesus said that if we want to be first in His kingdom, then we must put ourselves last and take on a servant's heart. We moms need to teach this to our children. There are some practical ways to teach this in your home: allow others to go first in serving their plates for dinner; shuffle the order in which you get in the car; take turns with who will have the honor of sitting in the front seat. Teaching humility is never easy, but these are practical ways your children can learn what Jesus is talking about in this Scripture.

Father, my tendency is to look out for myself first. I don't like this selfish side of me, but I am being honest. Create in me a love for others so that I would choose to put them first. God, give me Your servant's heart and attitude. Go before me today and give me opportunities to serve my family and friends. Amen.

Envy damages

"You shall not covet your neighbor's house."
Exodus 20:17

"Covet" is another name for "envy." Envy is a pervasive tendency in our lives, especially envy of another person's house. It's easy to not be content with your house. Maybe it's too small for your family and everyone is on top of each other. Maybe it's old and ugly and your friend just bought a beautiful new home and has hired a professional decorator. Maybe you like your house, but you long for a new bathroom, a new kitchen or a pool. God tells us not to covet these things.

Isn't it amazing that God put that commandment in the top 10? Why did He do that? He knows that envy sows the seeds of disillusionment and strife, and He wants to protect us from those things. God wants us to live lives of freedom and joy in Him, not bound up by jealousy and envy. Coveting another person's house not only damages your friendship with that person, it also damages you. Be happy with what you have and if you don't like it, ask God to prepare a way for you to find peace with where you live or to provide a way for you to move on.

Wow! I have been so envious of my friend's house. How did You know? It eats at me. I walk into her home and I'm filled with envy. I want what she has and I hate what I have. It makes me miserable to be around and imprisons me. Forgive me. Help me be content with what I have. I give You this burden. Amen.

Everyday life

Commit to the LORD whatever you do,
and He will establish your plans.

Proverbs 16:3

❧ ——◦—— ❧

Solomon was known to be the wisest man and he tells us in this verse that if you want your plans to succeed, you need to commit them to the Lord. This week, as you go about your daily activities, whether it's driving the carpool, changing diapers, working a 40-hour week or squeezing in baseball tournaments all weekend, commit those plans to the Lord. If God is at the top of your list, your plans will succeed.

What does that look like in everyday terms? Before you start your day, share with God what is on your agenda, but before you set out to accomplish your goals, tell God, "This is what I have on my agenda, what is on Your agenda for me today?" Then be open. Your plans may not change, but at least you are inviting God into your world and holding your hands open to what He may have for you.

As you learn to give your day to God, begin to tell Him your struggles, your anxious thoughts or your concerns about your children. He wants to hear and be involved in every aspect of your life.

••• ——◦⊰⊱◦—— •••

God, I commit my desire to be a good mom to You today.
I pray You will bless my efforts and go before me in all I do.
I pray I will always keep in mind that my success is not
attached to my children's actions, but how I respond to them
and love them. Thank You, Father, for my children
and the blessings they bring to our family. Amen.

Excellent life

"Blessed are those who hunger
and thirst for righteousness, for they will be filled."

Matthew 5:6

❧ ⎯⎯⎯ ❧

When we delight in God, He fills the desires of our hearts (see Psalm 37:4). What better desire than to hunger and thirst for righteousness, or excellence, in our lives? Think about what that would look like as a mom – to hunger after an excellent life; a healthy, happy marriage; a great relationship with your children; and being able to work alongside others without strife. Who wouldn't want that kind of life?

Jesus tells us in Matthew that if we hunger and thirst for righteousness, He will give us righteousness or a right standing with God. In order for that to happen, I must put all my focus on my heavenly Father and not on the worldly things around me – the things that continually tug and pull at my attention.

In order to refocus our attention on God, we must discipline ourselves. As you feel the weight of the world on your shoulders, make a conscious effort to submit your thoughts to God, and ask Him to meet your needs. It will take practice, but it will be worth it.

•••⎯⎯⎯⎯⎯⎯⎯•••

Thank You, Lord, that You will fill my life with righteousness.
Thank You for that promise. At times, the pressures of this
world feel overwhelming and I struggle to "fix" my life
the way I see fit. I commit today to start hungering and
thirsting after You. You alone can fill my every need. Amen.

Faith in God

"I am the Lord's servant," Mary answered.
"May your word to me be fulfilled." Then the angel left her.

Luke 1:38

Mary had a tremendous amount of faith in what Gabriel was telling her (see verses 28-38). Mary was a young girl. She was a virgin betrothed to Joseph. Gabriel was an angel sent by God, who told Mary that she would give birth to the Son of God and she would name Him Jesus. Her response was, "I am the Lord's servant. May your word to me be fulfilled." Amazing faith.

Has God given you a vision for your life? Does it feel too great? Has He placed on your heart the desire to stay in your marriage that you feel is dead and to love your husband, whether he loves you in return or not? Is He asking you to forgive your child for shaming your family and to accept your prodigal child back into your family? Is He whispering in your ear to trust Him in this difficult time, even though you don't see any way it will turn out well? What if your response was like Mary's? Think about that today: what would it look like to have faith like Mary, to say, "I am the Lord's servant."

Father, I look at Mary and I am so far away from
that kind of faith. But I want that kind of faith. I want
to do whatever You ask of me. Be patient with me; grow me
to that grand faith. I know if I follow You, my faith will grow.
Help me to take one step of obedience at a time. Amen.

April

Faithful God

The LORD said to Abram after Lot had parted from him,
"Look around from where you are, to the north and south,
to the east and west. All the land that you see
I will give to you and your offspring forever."

Genesis 13:14-15

Abram gave Lot, his brother-in-law, first pick of the new land God had given him. Lot picked the best land for himself. Abram did not care because Abram's trust was in God, not the land. God blessed Abram far greater than Lot because of his deep faith.

Where or who is your faith in at this moment in time? Is your faith and trust in your job, marriage or life with your family? Abram is a perfect example to us all – our faith needs to be in God. He is faithful even when the circumstances don't appear to be in our favor. God is always in our favor. It's not that God will change what we're going through, but He will get you through it, and when you come out on the other end, you will be a stronger, better person.

Place your faith in God. Don't hold back. Receive His full blessings. God wants to bless you. You need to choose to trust Him.

Father, create in me a faith so strong that regardless
of my circumstances, I will trust You. God, I want to
be able to "see" Your faithfulness even in the dark times.
I trust You and I believe that Your love and strength
will sustain me through all of life's difficulties. Amen.

Family of God

*Consequently, you are no longer foreigners
and strangers, but fellow citizens with God's people
and also members of His household.*

Ephesians 2:19

When you think of family, what pops into your mind? Do you think of a Norman Rockwell picture – a mom and dad welcoming you home for the holidays, a home where love is overflowing and never runs out? Family should be a place where you can be yourself and know you are loved and accepted just the way you are. That sounds wonderful. Who wouldn't want a family like that?

Not everybody has a family. Some people are all alone in this world. Maybe you're one of those people. Maybe your parents died in a tragic car accident, or you were born an orphan. Perhaps you have family, but they live thousands of miles away and you feel very alone, especially in this journey of motherhood.

If you're a Christian, you do have family – you're a part of God's family. You're not alone. God loves you and accepts you just the way you are. His door is always wide open for you to come and sit with Him and ask Him any of your questions. God created your children. He is the Father of all. Celebrate your being a part of God's family today and enjoy all the blessings that come with that.

*Thank You for being my heavenly Father and for
accepting me into Your royal family. God, I don't know
what I would do without Your guidance and love for me. Teach
me to create a loving family that is full of Your presence. Amen.*

Fasting for today

*"When you fast, do not look somber as the hypocrites do,
for they disfigure their faces to show others they are fasting."*

Matthew 6:16

Jesus said, "When you fast …" Not if, but when. Therefore, we need to fast. There are all kinds of fasting. It doesn't have to be fasting from food. Sometimes food is an easy item to give up and it means nothing for us to sacrifice eating. When you fast, it should be something you choose to give up that you will miss, something that may be painful to live without. Then you use that time of void to reflect back to God, pray and ask Him to fill your need.

In our culture, we should consider taking a time to fast from social media. Instead of looking at our smart phones multiple times a day to check the latest Instagram post or Facebook message or tweet, we should turn our attention to God. Social media has a way of taking over if we don't establish guardrails to protect ourselves.

There is nothing wrong with social media, just like there is nothing wrong with food. But sometimes we can allow a good thing to get out of control. Perhaps the time has come for you to hit the pause button with social media and step away for a little bit.

*Father, I need to fast in my life,
if for no other reason than because You
instruct me to do so. God, show me the area in my life
that I should fast from and show me how to do it.
Give me the courage to step out in faith
and follow You in this area of my life. Amen.*

Father to the fatherless

*The LORD watches over the foreigner
and sustains the fatherless and the widow,
but He frustrates the ways of the wicked.*

Psalm 146:9

If you're a single mom, you can feel the weight of this heavy world on your shoulders all day, every day. You must do it all: earning the money, paying the bills, driving the carpool, handling the stress of raising the children, doing the grocery shopping, the PTA – all of it. Do you feel overwhelmed and hopeless? Do you feel as if you may not be enough for your child?

God is with you. He will take care of you, the widow, and your children, the fatherless. Your husband may not have died, but he is no longer providing for you, giving you moral support, and he is no longer a father living in the home for your children. God will fill the gap. He promises to watch over you. Trust Him. When you feel so overwhelmed and defeated, cry out to God and ask for help.

For moms reading this devotional today who are not single, your homework today is to buy a single mom a cup of coffee, a flower, make a meal or offer to carpool her child. Who knows? You could be the answer to a prayer a single mom lifted up today!

*Father, You will meet all my needs, even the need
for a husband and a father for my children. God,
I know You will be the Father to my precious children
and my helper. Help me to never doubt that and never to forget
that. With You alone, I will survive and thrive as a mom. Amen.*

Fear not

"So do not fear, for I am with you; do not be dismayed,
for I am your God. I will strengthen you and help you;
I will uphold you with my righteous right hand."

Isaiah 41:10

It's easy to allow fear to creep into your mind because life with children is uncertain, at best. Fear is a powerful four-letter word. "What If?" And fear has the ability to alter how you would normally make decisions and live life. Mothers tend to be fearful creatures. We play the "What if?" game concerning our children, and suddenly our minds are engulfed in fear. When this happens, we become consumed with anxious thoughts and worry. What does worrying accomplish? Nothing. Worrying about life does not change your life; it only gives you ulcers!

Living in fear robs us of peace. We must make an extra effort not to give in to fear. We must place our thoughts on God and realize that He is with us and with our children. God is very capable! Remember this Scripture verse: "So do not fear, for I am with you." Lay your fear at the feet of the Lord. Ask Him to give you strength and to hold you in His arms. A peaceful life is so much better than a life filled with fear and worry.

Father, thank You for promising to hold me in Your hands.
I need Your strength. I need You to take my fear away. I admit
my mind can easily go to the worst-case scenario concerning my
children and then I worry. Honestly, I am tired of worrying. The
thought that You will give me strength and You will hold me is so
comforting. I willingly accept Your offer. Amen.

Firm confidence

Should not your piety be your confidence
and your blameless ways your hope?

Job 4:6

Where do you place your confidence? We all anchor ourselves to something and usually whatever we are anchored to is where we feel the most secure and confident. But when a storm comes and your anchor is moved, you feel vulnerable. Is your confidence tied to your looks, social standing, finances, job, children, marriage or talents? Will those things stand the test of time when storms hit us?

The only anchor that will stay true even during a mighty storm is God. Our looks will fade, social standing is always fickle, money is easily lost, jobs are lost, children grow up and leave, people die and your talents will diminish with time.

God is the same yesterday, today and tomorrow (see Hebrews 13:8). He is faithful and if He is your anchor, you will be secure. Resist the urge to be tied to the things of this world. Tie yourself to God who stays the same.

Father, I want to be confident in You.
I want to be able to walk into a room with other women
and not compare myself to everyone in the room.
God, help me to find my confidence in You and not myself. I
usually come up short. But in You, I know I will be strong. Amen.

Flesh vs. spirit

The acts of the flesh are obvious … hatred, discord,
jealousy, fits of rage, selfish ambition, dissensions, factions.
But the fruit of the Spirit is love, joy, peace, forbearance,
kindness, goodness, faithfulness, gentleness and self-control.
Galatians 5:19-20, 22-23

There is a war raging every day inside each of us – the war between our sinful natures (or flesh) and the life of a Spirit-filled Christian. Our sinful natures tend to give in to jealousy and discord, whereas a life walking after the Spirit seeks peace. Every day we have to make a choice as to which path we will walk: the path of the flesh or the path of the Spirit.

It sounds like an easy choice, until life smacks you in the face. When your in-laws give unwanted advice, it's so easy to walk toward discord instead of choosing peace. You falsely believe that if you choose peace, you're "giving in" and allowing them to walk all over you.

Walking after the Spirit, however, does not mean you're rolling over. You are acknowledging that God's way trumps the flesh, even when it doesn't make sense. You can walk in peace with others and still have boundaries. The next time your in-laws offer unwanted advice, your reply could be, "I will keep that in mind when making my decision." You have not given in and you are maintaining peace.

Father, I need You. No matter how hard I try,
no matter how hard I work, I cannot live the Christian life the
way I should without You. I need to walk with You every day, to
learn from You and to obey You. Then, and only then, will I bear
the fruits of the Spirit. From here on out, I choose You. Amen.

Focus on Jesus

Let us run with perseverance the race marked out for us,
fixing our eyes on Jesus, the pioneer and perfecter of faith.

Hebrews 12:1-2

Moms have so much to do. The list is like your laundry … never-ending. No wonder we burn the midnight oil on projects that should have been finished a month ago or wake up in the middle of the night thinking about the next day's events. We are easily distracted by one "emergency" after another. How in the world do we stay focused? How in the world do we tell one child we can't listen to her complaint because we are listening to her sibling's problem?

Moms have to focus or we will surely get lost in the black hole of mommy world. So how do you decide what to focus on? Certainly not the ever-changing world in which we live, since one minute we're heroes and the next we're zeroes. Do we focus on our friends, families, or the church?

Our only focus should be Jesus. He is the same yesterday, today and forever. Jesus can calm a storm, heal the sick, and bring peace and comfort. Jesus is the answer. Fix your eyes on Him as a ballerina fixes her eyes on her focal point when she spins so as not to become dizzy.

Father, teach me how to stay focused on Jesus. I want to learn
how to stay focused on Christ and do my job as a mom. I know it
can be done, but only through You. You are my Teacher and I am
Your student. Teach me; I am ready and willing to learn. Amen.

Focused attention

*The work is extensive and spread out, and we are
widely separated from each other along the wall.*

Nehemiah 4:19

There are seasons in a mother's life when she must push the distractions of the world aside and truly focus on her job as a mom. The world is constantly pushing us to cram more and more into our calendars. But there are certain times in a child's life that demand and deserve more focused attention.

Some of these seasons include potty training, disciplining in the early years and being "present" for your children in the teenage years. This means putting your wants and needs aside and focusing on the teenagers in your home, showing them you are available.

Staying home with toddlers to potty train them isn't fun, but once you make time and give up that week of your life, your sacrifice will be worth it in the long run. The same is true in the teenage years. As a parent of a teenager, you will need to be more physically available. Leaving a group of teens in your home with no adult supervision is never a good idea. But supervised teens can be delightful. This sacrifice will take longer than a week, but it is worth it in the end!

*Father, thank You for giving me this important job as a mom –
to nurture, love, guide and direct my children. Father,
I pray You will give me wisdom and show me the times in my
child's life when I need to give more focused time and attention.
I pray that I will not resent the hard work,
but that I will realize its importance. Amen.*

Forever together

For I am convinced that neither death nor life,
nor anything else in all creation, will be able to separate us
from the love of God that is in Christ Jesus our Lord.

Romans 8:38-39

If you have accepted Christ as your Lord and Savior, then no one or nothing will ever separate you from Christ. There is no sin you could commit that will separate you from Christ or Him from you. That type of love is mind-blowing. We almost cannot fathom it; our human minds do not love that way or that much. If people hurt us, we either attack or ignore them.

When we hurt Jesus, He keeps loving us. Jesus never gives up on us, even when we ignore Him. Jesus never stops loving us, even if we push Him aside. Jesus never stops pursuing us, even when we run away.

Whatever your day looks like, wake up knowing that you are forever a child of God. Praise God this morning for His amazing love for you!

Thank You for Jesus. Thank You for sending Your one and only Son to die for me. Even saying that is crazy, because I would never sacrifice my child. But You did and it was to save all humankind. God, thank You that I am Your child forever. Amen.

Forgive yourself

Therefore, there is now no condemnation for those who are in Christ Jesus, because through Christ Jesus the law of the Spirit who gives life has set you free from the law of sin and death.

Romans 8:1-2

Christ asks us to forgive others and sometimes, we need to forgive ourselves too. This verse is helpful when I am trying to forgive myself. I need to remind myself that there is no condemnation for those who are in Christ Jesus. Jesus took away all condemnation when He died on the cross. The sins that I have committed and will commit are forgiven, if I am a follower of Christ. Even if I "feel" guilty, I need to trust that I am forgiven.

In the life of a mom, this truth is essential. If you carry around guilt from your past, it will taint every aspect of your life and you will, in turn, pass that sense of unworthiness on to your children. Accept the gift of forgiveness that Jesus paid such a high price for. Memorize Romans 8:1: "There is now no condemnation for those who are in Christ Jesus." Remember that truth and teach it to your children as they grow.

Father, thank You for sending Your Son, Jesus, to die on the cross for my sins. Because of Jesus, my debt of sin has been paid and I am forgiven. Thank You, Father, that I am not condemned because of my sin. I choose today to forgive myself. Thank You for such a gift of grace. Amen.

Forgiven for everything

*Therefore, my friends, I want you to know that
through Jesus the forgiveness of sins is proclaimed to you.*
Acts 13:38

❧———————❧

Being forgiven is powerful. Through Jesus, all who accept Him as their Lord and Savior are forgiven of their sins. Think about that. All the sin that you have ever committed and will ever commit is wiped clean. Along with forgiveness, there is no more shame and no more guilt. This gift is almost too much to accept and many times we don't accept it, telling ourselves there is no way God could forgive what I have done. But the truth is Jesus forgives all of your sins.

He paid a high price to wash your sins away, and that price was His life sacrificed on a cross. All the sins of the world were placed on Him that day at Calvary. Consider the unbearable burden on Jesus – carrying all the sins of the world, all the guilt and all the shame. But He bore them out of love for all humankind. Don't let His death be in vain. Accept the wonderful gift of forgiveness today and forgive yourself. Jesus paid too high a price for you not to forgive yourself. You are free from sin, so live and rejoice in that freedom today!

•••————————————•••

*Father, thank You for sending Jesus to pay for my sin.
I accept Your forgiveness and I am choosing today
to forgive those who have hurt me. I am also choosing to
forgive myself. I am not going to walk around anymore bearing
my shame. You have already taken it away, so I refuse
to continue to drag it around with me. Thank You, God. Amen.*

Formula for contentment

Rejoice always, pray continually, give thanks in all circumstances; for this is God's will for you in Christ Jesus.
I Thessalonians 5:16-18

Be joyful for the large things in life: a bonus at the end of the year, an unexpected vacation with your husband, a new house, a new car, or a salary increase. Be joyful for the smaller things in life too: a working washing machine and dryer, indoor plumbing, or healthy children.

Pray continually. If you are a mom, you should be praying continually and asking your heavenly Father to give you what you need to train up your children. Ask God for wisdom as you guide your children through life. Ask God to give you the kind of love that He has for people. Pray and share your heart with God, crying out to Him when you need to tell someone your sorrows.

Give thanks in all circumstances. The key word in this part of the verse is "all." When bad things happen, give thanks. When good things happen, give thanks. During the bad times, thank God that even though the situation is not as you would like, He is sovereign and holy, and He will direct your path. Thank Him for never leaving or forsaking you, no matter how bad things get. Be thankful that He has overcome the world.

Father, I want to be a joyful person as I go about my day. God, remind me to seek You in prayer. As I sit in the carpool lane, as I wash dishes or as I fold laundry, draw my mind back to You in prayer. I want to give thanks in all circumstances. Amen.

Fresh outlook

He put a new song in my mouth,
a hymn of praise to our God.

Psalm 40:3

❧ ——— ❧

Are you tired? Tired of just being a mom, feeling like you need a new song in your heart? There may not be anything bad going on, but the wear and tear of life has worn you down and you are just tired. Do you need a fresh outlook? It's not that you want to trade in your life for another life; you just need a fresh breeze to blow through your soul. Pray to God and ask Him to put a new song in your heart.

While God may decide not to change your circumstances, He can powerfully change your perspective of those circumstances. Cry out to God and ask Him to perform such a miracle in your life. Ask Him to give you a fresh breeze, to be like a spring air that gives hope and a new excitement.

David asked for such a miracle and God came through for him. God will do the same thing for you. He will put a new song in your mouth so that you can return all your praise to Him. God understands the life of a mom and He wants you to look to Him to meet your needs – all of them. Reach out to Him and ask Him for a new song.

••• ——— ⁓⁓ ——— •••

Father, it's amazing that You already know
what I need before I know it. I love how You love me
and how You prepare a way for my life to be fresh,
even during these mundane days that I'm in right now.
God, give me a new song and a heart of praise for You. Amen.

Friends who encourage

And let us consider how we may spur
one another on toward love and good deeds.

Hebrews 10:24

The life of a mom can be lonely. We can get so bogged down in our daily routines that we forget to reach out to others to fill us up with love and friendship. Friendships are key in a mom's world. You need fellowship with other women, to talk about what your children are doing, to vent about how hard it is to be a mom and to be encouraged by another mom that you are doing a good job.

God knows that we need friends and Paul encourages us in Hebrews to seek out those friendships. We need to lift each other up in love and good deeds. Do you have a friend that is going through a particularly hard time this season with her children or marriage? Maybe you should make her a meal as a surprise or just go over to her house and have a cup of coffee and talk. There are so many ways we can encourage and love one another.

Your home is important, but don't forget about your friends. Make time to invest in them and yourself. We all need love and good deeds in our lives.

Father, thank You for my friends. Show me, Lord,
how to be a better friend to others. Please send me
a good friend, one that will encourage me and lift me up.
I want to have good friends and be a good friend. Amen.

Generational influence

I am reminded of your sincere faith,
which first lived in your grandmother Lois and in your
mother Eunice and, I am persuaded, now lives in you also.

2 Timothy 1:5

The influence of a mom is like no other. The legacy a mom leaves behind doesn't just affect her child, it affects how the child will eventually parent her own children. Therefore, as a mom, take notice of the kind of influence you have on your children. Are you passing along your bad habits, your quick temper and your sense of entitlement? Or are you passing along love and grace – reflecting Christ in your daily walk, showing your children how different your life is because of Jesus?

In this verse, Lois and Eunice had a life that exhibited God's love and faith. The way they loved their families was so noticeable to the outside world that Timothy wrote about them. You could have this kind of effect on your family. Keep in mind, the type of love and faith that Lois and Eunice exhibited only comes from God. So, don't try to do it in your own strength. If you do, you will be frustrated. Lean on God; ask Him to give you what you need to love your child. Read His Word on a daily basis and walk with Him. The first step, however, is to notice the type of legacy you are leaving behind.

Father, I want to leave a legacy of sincere faith and love. God, I would love my great grandchildren to know me for my strong faith in You and to know that I loved people because You loved me. Fill me with Your love, Your grace and Your faith, so that it overflows from me onto everyone I encounter. Amen.

Generous living

*Command them to do good, to be rich in good deeds,
and to be generous and willing to share.*

I Timothy 6:18

Teaching your child how to live a generous life can be difficult. In our human nature, we tend to be selfish. A child is no different. It's no co-incidence that one of the first words a child says is "mine."

Begin teaching your child generosity from an early age. One way to do this is to be generous. Being generous with your time, money and talents is something you will need to make yourself do. It won't come naturally.

Ask yourself a few questions:

∗ Do I think of others before myself?
∗ Do I put others' needs before mine?
∗ When I see someone struggling, do I reach out to help or do I just say, "I'll pray for you"?
∗ Is it hard for me to be generous with my money?

Start today thinking of others. Run through your list of friends and lift them up in prayer to your heavenly Father. Ask Him to open your eyes to those around you and their needs. Is there a need someone has that you could generously meet? It could be as simple as a smile.

*Father, I pray You will fill me with Your Holy Spirit
and Your love. God, You love people beyond measure
and I seek to have that kind of love in my heart for others.
I also want to teach my children how to live loving,
generous lives toward others. Teach me Your ways. Amen.*

Gentle shepherd

He gently leads those that have young.
Isaiah 40:11

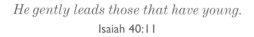

When you're a mom, you don't have a ton of time to get into deep Bible studies or lengthy prayer times. The good news is that we serve a loving God who understands exactly where we are. Just because you are busy taking care of your family doesn't mean you are too busy to stay connected to your heavenly Father. We need God during this season of our lives more than ever. Think about it ... when you get busy, you don't stop talking to your husband. You may have to be more intentional about scheduling a date night, but you try to keep that relationship going. It's the same with God.

Try these tips:

Talk to God throughout your day, not just at night when you are falling asleep. Invite Him into your daily routine – making lunches, driving the carpool, shopping, cleaning your house.

Throughout your day when you feel yourself becoming stressed, tell God about it; give Him all your burdens.

Focus on a short passage or just a few verses per day.

Father, what a relief to know that You will gently guide me because I have young children. I don't feel like anyone gently guides me anywhere, so it's such a comfort to know that You do. I want to seek You throughout my day. Gently remind me when I forget. And even when I forget, please know that I love You! Amen.

Get wisdom

Get wisdom, get understanding;
do not forget my words or turn away from them.

Proverbs 4:5

Moms want to be wise in how we parent our children, interpret situations and when we advise our children. Wisdom – true godly wisdom – will not just happen. It must be sought after passionately.

One way to gain wisdom is to ask God (see James 1:5). He promises if we ask for wisdom, He will give it and give it abundantly. Another way to gain wisdom is to seek wise counsel from someone older and wiser than you, someone who walks with the Lord and in whom the fruits of the Spirit are evident.

Whether that person is your mom, a dear friend or a pastor, just be sure to have people in your life that can offer sound counsel and godly wisdom. We also gain wisdom in reading God's Word, the Bible. God's wisdom is above man's wisdom; therefore, you will not find His wisdom in the world. You must seek it.

The final step in becoming wise is to act on what you learn. It's not enough to learn and then walk away and do what you want. If you seek wise counsel, read God's Word, and then put it all into practice, you will grow wise.

Father, thank You for creating a way for me to become wise.
Lord, I want to be a wise mom. I am asking You right now for
wisdom and I am asking that You send wise people into my life
to pour into me. I pray I will accept wisdom and then
practice what I learn … always leaning into You. Amen.

Give it all

He also saw a poor widow put in two very small copper coins.
Luke 21:2

The widow in the story gave all she had to God. Think about it. She was a widow and she didn't have the luxury of a husband to provide for her. She was completely alone. Yet, she put her fear aside and gave what she had to God. Two coins were not really going to help the church budget, but Jesus saw her gift and He knew what a huge sacrifice she was making. That small donation had the biggest impact on Jesus because He saw her heart.

Many times, we don't give our money to God because we feel we don't have a lot to offer. But God doesn't care about the amount. He actually doesn't need your money. God is more interested in your heart and your willingness to give. Push past your fear of not being able to give to God because you don't think you have money to give. Keep in mind, it's all His anyway. He's the one that has blessed you with the amount of money you have and He is able to meet all of your needs.

Father, thank You for the many blessings in my life, especially in my finances. God, I want to depend on You completely and, like the widow in the story in Luke, I want to give to You all that I have and believe You will provide for me. I am not there yet, Lord, but I want to be. Please grow my faith in You and show me how faithful You are. Amen.

Give them room

So then, each of us will give an account of ourselves to God.
Romans 14:12

Understanding this verse in Romans is critical for a mom. Our children must understand from a young age that they are accountable for their own actions. Yes, we moms have a huge job teaching them and guiding them in their younger years. But in the end, our children must stand alone before God.

Sometimes in order for our children to truly understand the significance of owning their actions, we must step back and give them space to grow. That's not an easy task, because after all, we need to "help" them. But sometimes we "help" so much that we end up creating children who are so dependent on us that they are hurt in the long run.

We don't want to see our children fail at anything; therefore, we try to protect them in everything they do. We forget that our children have a heavenly Father who loves and adores them and who is waiting patiently to pick them up when they fall, dust them off and guide them. The best thing we can do as moms is to give our children some space, tell them we're available when they mess up, and, most importantly, to always point them toward God.

Father, teach me how to set my children up for success.
I understand they will ultimately make their own decisions,
but while they are under my roof, give me the words
to teach them of Your love and devotion to them,
so they will choose to follow You. Amen.

Give up control

Look to the LORD and His strength; seek His face always.
1 Chronicles 16:11

As moms we struggle with our need to be in control. Not only do we try to control our worlds, we also try to control our children's worlds. It can be exhausting, and the reality is, none of us are in control of anything.

We tell ourselves that if we're in control, our world will be safe and secure. This false sense of security drives our need to manipulate and control outcomes. If we try to control our children – orchestrate who they can play with, which classroom they will be assigned to or which team they will be put on – then we feel they will be successful in life. But we are putting way too much pressure on ourselves and on our children when we try to manipulate everything.

God is in control. God is a God of the smallest of details to the grandest miracles. If your child is placed in a classroom for the year and you believe it is a horrible, big mistake, trust God. He allowed it to happen for a reason. Seek God's wisdom, strength and sovereignty. He will not leave you or your child, but will guide you through the school year.

Father, I pray that I will resist the urge to control,
but instead will look to You for Your guidance and wisdom.
Lord, as I start this day, I am seeking Your face. Every step I
take, go before me. When I want to control, gently whisper
in my ear that You've got the situation under control. Amen.

Give what you have

On coming to the house, they saw the Child
with His mother Mary, and they bowed down
and worshiped Him. Then they opened their treasures
and presented Him with gifts of gold, frankincense and myrrh.

Matthew 2:11

When the wise men saw Jesus, they instantly worshiped Him and offered their treasures to Him. Think about that for a minute ... Jesus was a baby, born to a woman of no real significance in life. The wise men were Magi, priests of high social standing. Yet the wise men recognized instantly that Jesus was different; He wasn't a normal baby. So, they worshiped Him, offering their gifts.

What gifts do you have to offer Jesus? Many moms seem to think they have nothing to give. That's not true. You have many treasures to offer Jesus. You can offer to feed His sheep (see John 21:17) – your children, your neighbors, anyone you meet. You can give the treasure of your time: serving others, volunteering in your church, stopping your busy schedule to sit down and read a book with your child.

Money is also a treasure you have to offer God. It's not that God needs your money – baby Jesus did not need gold, frankincense or myrrh. It is, however, symbolic. You are giving what you have been blessed with and you're not keeping it for yourself.

Remember, it's not what you give; it's the heart with which you give.

Father, thank You for sending Your only Son to be born,
to live and then to die for me. I want to give back to You –
anything and everything that I have. Because, like the wise men,
I am acknowledging Jesus is Lord of all. Amen.

Giving grace

The Word became flesh and made His dwelling among us.
We have seen His glory, the glory of the one and only Son,
who came from the Father, full of grace and truth.

John 1:14

It's so easy to blame others. We do it all the time, because then we don't have to examine ourselves. What if we stopped blaming others even when things went wrong? Instead of blaming others, we chose to give grace. We love when grace is given to us, especially when we are so undeserving.

Has there ever been a time in your life when you deserved to be punished, but for whatever reason, you were not? Do you remember what a great feeling that was? Maybe your debt was forgiven, or the teacher forgot you had detention, or the police officer just gave you a warning for speeding. That is what grace feels like – to get a free pass.

God's grace is so much greater. He loves us even when we're unlovable. He gives grace even when we don't notice or are unappreciative. God's grace has given us eternal life. Talk about the gift that keeps on giving; that's exactly what God's grace does. It keeps on giving. Today, choose to give grace. Stop yourself when you start to blame others and make a conscious effort to give grace instead of judgment.

Father, thank You for Your abundant grace.
We cannot completely comprehend Your endless love because we
are human, but I am so thankful that You love and accept me the
way You do. God, I want to have a loving heart like Yours and to
always give grace. Teach me; I am willing to learn. Amen.

Glory to God

So whether you eat or drink or whatever you do,
do it all for the glory of God.

1 Corinthians 10:31

I love that I don't have to be someone big and important to glorify God. I can bring glory to Him in my own home by rocking my baby to sleep. I can bring glory to Him by serving my children their dinner or going to the grocery store. How cool is that? I think it's amazing because the world we live in focuses on the rich and famous, two things I will never be. We are reminded in this verse that even the small things in life, like eating or drinking, are important to God and should be important to us too.

This verse reminds us that everything in life has purpose if we glorify God in the process. How do you glorify God while rocking your children to sleep? By being peaceful, patiently waiting for them to drift off, you glorify God. You can glorify Him by serving your family with a good attitude and loving spirit. You can glorify God at the grocery store by giving those around you grace when grace is not deserved. And you can have a smile on your face as you check out. It all matters!

Father, be with me throughout my day and remind me that
everything matters to You. Give me Your love, Your grace and
Your amazing mercy. Show me how to love others the way You
love them. Thank You that the small things matter to You, so I can
bring glory to You in my home even while doing laundry. Amen.

God alone

Wealth and honor come from You; You are the ruler of all things. In Your hands are strength and power.

1 Chronicles 29:12

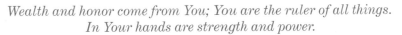

We love to blame other people when things don't go our way. Whether it's our jobs, marriages, children or social standing, we love to place the blame on other people when we fail. In blaming others, we give way too much power to people that don't deserve such power. If I'm upset that I didn't get a promotion at work and my co-worker got the promotion, I will place all my anger onto that person; I will become bitter and resentful. But if I realize God is actually the one in control, and all wealth and honor come from Him, I won't blame my co-worker for not getting the promotion.

God is in control of all things. If you're not getting what you want in life right now, try not to blame others, but instead ask God why. There is a reason. Maybe you're not ready for the promotion or God is protecting you from something in the future that you can't see now. Whatever the reason, God ultimately wants the best for you. Realize who is ultimately in charge and who is the ruler of all things.

Father, You are in control of all things.
You are sovereign and Lord of all. I need to remind myself
of that every day. I tend to believe the lie that I am in control,
but that's not true. You are the ruler of all things. My prayer
today is that I will etch that truth in my mind forever. Amen.

God is big

He sits enthroned above the circle of the earth,
and its people are like grasshoppers.
Isaiah 40:22

How big is your God? If you ever have the thought, God can't fix this problem, it's too big, think again. God is bigger than any problem, difficulty, sickness and circumstance. We get disillusioned when we put our faith in the outcomes of the situations. When the outcomes don't go the way we want, we think God let us down. But, in reality, our faith should not be in the outcome; but in God ... that He alone will get us through our circumstances.

The majesty of God is beyond comprehension. He sits above the earth watching over all of us and we are tiny in His shadow. Even though He is grand and majestic, He seeks a relationship with you. He wants to come into your world of motherhood. He is waiting for an invitation to encourage you, fill you and lift you up when you're weary. Invite Him in today.

Father, thank You that You are so majestic and holy. I pray that my view of You would be accurate and not distorted. God, I am guilty of not realizing Your true magnitude. Open my eyes today, so I may see Your glorious nature and deep love for me. Amen.

God is in control

If you go to the left, I'll go to the right;
if you go to the right, I'll go to the left.

Genesis 13:9

We desire to control every outcome. We try to orchestrate all of our plans, decisions and choices so that we will receive the benefits. In this story in Genesis, Abram did not care to control the situation or to manipulate on his behalf. His trust was in God. Abram selflessly allowed Lot to choose which land he wanted to have. In fact, Abram didn't even know what hung in the balance of this blind faith … he put his trust in God and God blessed him (with immeasurable land and descendants).

If we as moms would develop this type of mindset, we would be unstoppable. Our trust needs to be in our heavenly Father, not ourselves. We need to allow God to work and do His will, not try to manipulate and orchestrate what we think is best for us. God wants to bless us. We need to choose to trust in Him.

Father, thank You for this reminder in Abram's story to trust You,
especially when we have no idea what the outcome will be.
God, I know I try to control things and hold on so tightly to my
decisions and their outcomes. Help me realize that Your plan
ultimately brings me blessings and peace. Help me loosen my
grip and trust You with my life and my decisions. Amen.

God is love

And so we know and rely on the love God has for us. God is love.
Whoever lives in love lives in God, and God in them.

1 John 4:16

❧ ——○—— ❧

People search for love their whole lives. We search for acceptance and love in so many places: marriage, work, friends, children and society. There is one person who will always love us and that person is God. We need to rely on God's love. There is no other love like the love of our heavenly Father. He adores you.

Soak that thought in today as you go about your day, whether you're in a meeting, the carpool lane, the grocery store or on an airplane. Wherever you go and whoever you're with, remind yourself, "I am fully loved." Tell yourself repeatedly until you believe that God loves you like no other. He knows everything about you and He loves you. God knows all your secrets, even the ones you have never shared with your husband, yet He loves you.

It's important that you realize how much you are loved, because then you will be more likely to love others in return. Teach your children about God's deep love for them. Point out every little aspect about them that is wonderful and say, "God loves this about you and this about you; He loves all of you." What a gift you will be giving your children!

••• ———⟨⟩——— •••

Father, thank You for Your love. Thank You for always loving me
no matter what I have done and always giving me grace. God,
I want to love the way You love. Teach me Your ways. Amen.

God is my source

*It is God who arms me with strength
and keeps my way secure.*

2 Samuel 22:33

Every mom has a source in her life that gives her strength, purpose and drive. What is your source? You may have never thought about this question. Your source could be your church that dictates to you a certain way to live and think. It could be the influence of your friends and neighbors. Your source could be the media and what our culture thinks is worthy. Whether you realize it or not, you have a source in your life that you look to in order to determine your path.

God is the ultimate source. God is the only source that will make your way perfect, because He is God. Other sources will leave you alone, desperate for acceptance. God arms you with strength. He lifts you up and shows you the way. In God, your life will be secure and you will no longer be subject to the insecurity that comes with putting your faith in a fickle, always-changing world. Tether yourself to God; allow Him to show you the way to go.

*Father, You are my strength and my fortress. In You, Lord,
I will find my way. God, I pray that I would put all my trust
in You, because only You are trustworthy. Guide my life
and direct my course. I have complete faith in You. Amen.*

May

God is sovereign

Sovereign Lord, You have begun to show to Your servant Your greatness and Your strong hand. For what god is there in heaven or on earth who can do the deeds and mighty works You do?

Deuteronomy 3:24

As moms we can easily become overwhelmed with the huge task of parenting. In a world that feels like it is spinning out of control, our natural instinct is to try and control more. But God is in control and He has a plan. Our trust needs to be in Him, not in ourselves.

The fact that God is sovereign and Lord over all should give us comfort and peace. We don't have to be in control, because He is. We as moms don't have to know everything, because He knows. We don't have to look out for our best interests because He is looking out for us.

Take a step toward trusting your heavenly Father today and rest in His sovereignty. Learn to be okay with not being in control and to trust in the One who is in control.

Father, it is comforting to know You are sovereign and in control. I pray that I would learn to keep my eyes on You and not on my circumstances. Circumstances change, but You never change. Teach me how to trust in You always. Amen.

God of order

For God is not a God of disorder but of peace.
1 Corinthians 14:33

No matter what age your children are, chaos is never far behind – whether you have just brought your newborn home from the hospital and are struggling to get sleep cycles started, your toddler has learned the word "no" or "mine" and is no longer compliant with your every wish, your elementary-aged child has discovered that you are his personal taxicab driver, or your teenager is now bigger than you with attitude and ideas that push you to your breaking point.

As a mom I want peace, not chaos. Peace is found in God. Therefore, I must draw near to God (see James 4:8). You can draw near to God without having a deep Bible study every day. You can start each morning thanking God for that day, your family, your home and your health. Starting every day with the right mindset is so important and needs to be the first thing you do.

One quick step that will make a world of difference is to ask God to go before you. Ask Him to bless your life. Ask Him to give you wisdom as you parent your children and love your husband.

Father, I give You this day and all that it brings. Thank You for bringing peace into my crazy life. I so need that. I pray that as I go through my day, I will look to You for peace and contentment. Thank You for always loving me and taking care of me. Amen.

God will do it

The one who calls you is faithful, and He will do it.
I Thessalonians 5:24

A two-year-old is independent. Countless times a day toddlers can be heard saying, "I can do it!" Isn't that the way we are with our heavenly Father? To our Father, who is faithful and has promised us He will get us through this life, we say without any hesitation, "I will do it myself."

As Christians, we need to be 100 percent dependent on God for everything in our lives. Our goal should not be independence, but dependence. The closer we walk with Jesus, the easier it is to live that way. Our dependence on God is directly tied to our walk with Him. If we are not seeking after Him, reading His Word and praying without ceasing, we will end up depending on ourselves.

Maybe today you need to assess how independent you are as a Christian. God is a gentle God and will never force His way into your life. Jesus said, "Here I am! I stand at the door and knock. If anyone hears My voice and opens the door, I will come in and eat with that person, and they with Me" (Revelation 3:20). You must open the door.

Father, thank You for being faithful!
Thank You for being patient with me in spite of all
my independent ways. Your love is never failing and is always
full of grace and mercy. Strip me of my independence so I am
fully dependent on You for all things. Thank You for loving me
the way You do and for never giving up on me. Amen.

God's grace

Now Stephen, a man full of God's grace and power,
performed great wonders and signs among the people.

Acts 6:8

What would it look like to be a woman full of God's grace and power? What kind of a life would you have to live? You would have to live a life full of love, a life fully devoted to and focused on God. Your life would have to be full of compassion and mercy. You would have to be bold in your faith, not for the sake of being bold, but because you couldn't contain it. When people would look at your life, they would instantly see something different in you. Your love for others would set you apart.

In the everyday world of a mother, how can you show God's full love? Would you need to have love while you wash the dishes or take out the trash? It is all in your attitude. You can be full of love while washing dishes or taking out the trash. You can realize that no job is too small, that God is in the smallest of details as well as the bigger things in life. A mom needs to recognize the importance of her job and embrace it. Being the mother is the greatest gift a woman can have. We as moms get the privilege to train up the next generation. We are influencing our children and setting the course for the future.

Father, thank You for the privilege and gift of being a mother to my children. Help me to recognize that all the tasks of motherhood – from the mundane to the soul shaping – require Your full love. Thank You, God, for the grace, power and love You have given me. Help me daily to pour these gifts into my children. Amen.

God's timing

Then the LORD *said, "Rise and anoint him; this is the one."*
1 Samuel 16:12

⇒ —— ⇐

David was anointed king at age 17, but was not appointed king until he was 37. There was a 20-year gap between anointing and appointing. During those 20 years, God "grew" a king out of the dark times in the caves running from Saul. David learned to trust in God through the good and the bad, whether he could see God or not. There were many times during those 20 years when David thought his kingdom would never transpire because he was certain Saul would kill him.

Are you in the midst of your 20 years in-between your anointing and your appointing? When you read Proverbs 31:28 where it says, "Her children arise and call her blessed," do you think to yourself, When? If so, then you are in your "20-year gap."

We want to see the fruits of our labors and to see them quickly. The reality is that it takes 18 years to train up a child. The reality is that being a mom is hard, tedious work. It is not for the faint of heart. Don't be discouraged; God has anointed you! He will be with you during your 20-year gap just like he was with David.

•••———————•••

Father, thank You for staying with me in the "gap."
There are times when I feel like I will never reach the other side.
At times, I believe my children don't appreciate me and what I
sacrifice for them every day. But, God, I know that You appreciate
me. You see everything that I do, and You are enough! Amen.

God's way

As for God, His way is perfect.
2 Samuel 22:31

We strive to live perfect lives, to have perfect families and to have perfect children. But all of our striving is in vain. No matter how much we reach for perfection, it is always just a little further than our grasp. God, however, is the exact opposite. He is within our grasp if we will reach for Him and His ways are perfect.

It is silly when you think about it. We hunger for something we cannot have – perfection. Yet we reject perfection in God, who is always available to us. God knows all, sees all and is all. Begin to include Him in your life … every aspect, big and small. Ask Him to direct your path concerning your life, from deciding which preschool to pick for your child to what type of family vacation is the best to take this year. God's way is perfect and He is a God of details. Start including Him into your everyday, normal, imperfect life.

Father, thank You that You are all-knowing and sovereign over all. Lord, I depend on You in every aspect of my life. Forgive me when I strive to be the perfect mom and not depend on You. I want to be so dependent on You that it comes as naturally to me as breathing. Thank You for directing my path and for Your never-ending patience. Amen.

God's will

*Going a little farther, He fell with His face to the ground
and prayed, "My Father, if it is possible, may this cup
be taken from Me. Yet not as I will, but as You will."*

Matthew 26:39

⤜ ——— ⤛

We plan, organize, scheme and manipulate so "life" will go the way we want. How many times do we pray asking God for His will in our lives, but then when things don't turn out the way we wanted, we say, "God didn't hear me," or "This cannot be His will"? God's will will be done; we cannot stop it. Our prayer should be, "God, this is what I want, but I want Your will over what I want. Give me the grace to accept Your will in my life." After accepting God's will, ask Him to give you contentment and to reveal His wisdom.

We can always pray and ask God for what we want, but more than our asking, our hearts should be bent toward God's way. Jesus modeled this so beautifully for us. He did not want to die on the cross or go through the brutal beating that was about to take place. He asked God to remove it from Him, but in the end submitted His will to God. This character trait is learned and does not come naturally, but the benefits are countless when you start living your life this way.

••⤍ ———⤎⤌✣⤍⤏——— ⤌••

*Father, I want to be like Jesus and accept Your will
over my will. God, teach me. I am naturally selfish
and naturally want things to go my way. Teach me
to walk after Your Spirit and not after my fleshly ways. Amen.*

God's wisdom

For the foolishness of God is wiser than human wisdom,
and the weakness of God is stronger than human strength.

1 Corinthians 1:25

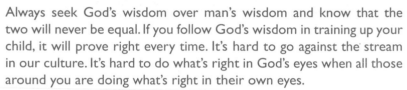

Always seek God's wisdom over man's wisdom and know that the two will never be equal. If you follow God's wisdom in training up your child, it will prove right every time. It's hard to go against the stream in our culture. It's hard to do what's right in God's eyes when all those around you are doing what's right in their own eyes.

As a mom, I can rationalize going along with the crowd and convince myself that holding to my convictions doesn't really matter. But I need to pray and ask God for His wisdom and how my decision will affect my child in the long run.

Trust your decisions in how you parent your child and don't give in to what the culture says is "okay." You may feel alone, but it's better to stand alone than to follow the crowd and regret the outcome. The world pushes our children to grow up faster and faster. Faster is not always better. Keep in mind that God has entrusted you with your child and He will direct you if you ask Him.

Father, give me wisdom as I parent my children.
Help me to discern the wisest choices. I don't want to be
overprotective, but I don't want to be permissive either.
Teach me the delicate balance as my children grow.
Help me to keep my eyes on You and not on the world. Amen.

God's workmanship

For we are God's handiwork, created in Christ Jesus
to do good works, which God prepared in advance for us to do.

Ephesians 2:10

❧ ——— ❧

I love a good purse and I'll admit it, I especially like designer purses. There's something about the handiwork of a designer purse. So much effort goes into every detail, from the leather to the stitching to the style. One of the best perks of carrying a designer purse is that people "know" your purse. They understand the investment you've made and the quality behind the name. You don't have to brag about your purse or show it off. The name speaks for itself.

We as Christians also come with a name. God has stamped His almighty name on us, and unlike a purse, we actually have a choice whether we show the qualities of our Maker. God created us to do good works, to love other people as we love ourselves.

Do people look at you and instantly know you are a Christian because of your actions and how you love and serve others? Or are you just like everyone else, taking care of yourself and not worrying about anyone else? When people look at your life, they should be able to "see" Jesus in you.

•••———————•••

Father, You are my Creator. You have prepared me to put others first, to love unconditionally, to serve and walk humbly before men. God, I want to represent You well and for people to know You are the source of my love. I want to glorify You in all I do. Amen.

Good listener

Then Samuel said, "Speak, for Your servant is listening."
1 Samuel 3:10

Train yourself to hear God's voice regardless of where you are in your life. God is a God who communicates with His people and He wants to communicate with you, but it requires you to listen. In the story of Samuel, God called out to Samuel three times before he realized it was God calling him and not Eli calling him. But once Samuel "knew" it was God speaking, Samuel said to God, "I am listening." Are you listening? Have you trained your ear to hear God's voice?

Throughout the Old and the New Testaments, God "talks" to His people. He wants to talk to you, but you have to train yourself to hear His voice. Jesus said, "His sheep follow him because they know his voice" (John 10:4). In order to distinguish God's voice from others, you must spend time with Him. You must learn who He is and what He is all about. Think about when you take your child to the playground and there are lots of children playing. When it's time to go, you call out to your child and your child "knows" your voice and obeys. Do you know your Master's voice? It's not too late to learn to recognize it.

Father, thank You for wanting to speak to me, either through Your Word, through others or directly. You are amazing! I want to hear Your voice. I want to know when it's You speaking to me. Teach me Lord; I am willing and able to learn. Give me an Eli in my life that will show me when it's You speaking to me. Amen.

Grace and love

*One who loves a pure heart and who speaks
with grace will have the king for a friend.*

Proverbs 22:11

—◦—

Love and grace seem to be leaving our society, but they are what set us apart from the masses. Because love is rarely given, when you do see an act of kindness, it makes a big impression. Teach your children how to love others and how to give grace.

In order to teach these qualities, you need to be living them out in your life. When the waiter messes up your order at a restaurant, do you give him grace or do you complain and talk to the manager? When your child comes to you with a problem and confesses his wrongdoings, do you listen in love or do you immediately start correcting and scolding? When your child's teacher makes a mistake, do you give her the benefit of the doubt or do you jump to your own conclusions?

Grace and love are hard to practice and if we aren't thinking about them, our old habits will take over. As you go about your day, think about how you can show love and give grace to someone outside of your family. Who knows? It may catch on. Before you know it, we'll be living in a more loving society.

•••——∙◦∙——•••

*Father, in my quest to get everything done
throughout my day, I tend to have a short fuse with people.
I tell myself that these people are messing up my day, when in
reality I'm not extending love and grace. I want to be a loving
person, one that always gives grace. I realize I can only do
that through You. Help me to love people today. Amen.*

Great gain

But godliness with contentment is great gain.
I Timothy 6:6

We strive to get ahead in life. Sometimes our efforts pay off and other times we come up short. The Bible teaches us that contentment is found through pursuing God. When you do, you will be given great gain.

We cannot find contentment without God. We as Christians must be diligent in seeking God, asking Him to fill us with His Holy Spirit. We must submit our wills to Him and allow the fruits of the Holy Spirit to pour out of our lives – love, joy, peace, patience, kindness, goodness, faithfulness, gentleness and self control (see Galatians 5:22-23). If we abide in Christ and all of these fruits flow out of us, we will be content; we will have peace and "great gain."

Father, I want to know You, and I want to be a good mom.
I want to be content with my life – with my possessions and with
my family. God, create in me a pure heart. I submit my life to
You. Fill me with Your Holy Spirit; fill me with Your love. Amen.

Great project

I am carrying on a great project and cannot go down.
Nehemiah 6:3

❧ ——— ❧

Being a mom is a never-ending job. Most of the time, it is a thankless job, a mindless job, a job that no one else really wants to do. But, it's an important job! Moms have the greatest influence on our society and how it functions. Think about it: a mother influences the next generation more than she influences anyone. Maybe that's why Satan attacks moms and plants ideas in their minds that their job is mindless and pointless. Satan wants moms to think there has to be more in life and they are capable of doing more.

You are capable of doing more, but don't allow Satan, for one second, to make you believe the lie that your work is not important. Your dedication has the potential to change generations to come.

Nehemiah was not tempted to come down from the project of rebuilding the wall around Jerusalem, even though he had great opposition. He declared, "I am carrying on a great project and cannot go down." We, as moms, need to be just as single-minded. Our great projects are our families. Stay true to what is important and don't go down!

•••———————————••••

Father, Keep my eyes focused on You! At times, being a mom is a mundane job. Sometimes, I do feel that life is passing me by, but I know that's not true. God, open up my eyes and show me the significance of my role. Help me to be disciplined and not wander off to fulfill my needs, because my children need me to stay focused. And I need you in order to finish well. Amen.

Grudges and letting go

Bear with each other and forgive one another
if any of you has a grievance against someone.
Forgive as the Lord forgave you.

Colossians 3:13

To "bear with each other" is hard at times. Moms have to deal with a lot of people and juggle a lot of emotions. Not only does she need to keep peace within her own family, with different personalities and maturity levels, she also has to "bear with" her husband, in-laws, extended family, teachers, coaches, children's friends, etc.

In this verse, Paul teaches us that we are to forgive grievances we have against people. I must forgive the child that deliberately hurt my child by calling her names at school and excluding her from the group. I must forgive the coach that continues to overlook my son and never gives him a chance to play in the game. I'm to forgive and "bear with" family members that don't seem to notice that they continually offend me.

In order to follow Christ and be devoted to Him, forgiveness is a must. God forgave us; therefore, He calls us to forgive others. Remember, forgiveness is a choice. Even if you don't "feel" like it, you can choose to forgive. Make the choice today to forgive those people in your life against whom you have been holding grudges.

Father, thank You for forgiving me. Thank You
for sending Your Son, Jesus, to die on the cross for my sins.
I don't deserve such forgiveness and love. I'm choosing today
to obey You, believe You and to follow You. Please help me
to forgive those who have wronged my family or me. Amen.

Guardian for life

... for He guards the course of the just
and protects the way of His faithful ones.

Proverbs 2:8

It is comforting to know that God is our Protector and He will guide us in this journey of life. So many times we look to our husbands to fill this role and when they don't come through the way we would like (or think they should) we get frustrated and angry. Only God can guard and protect us at all times. Only God can take the bad circumstances, gently walk us through them and get us safely to the other side.

We as women need to lean into God more and trust in Him more. Are we being faithful to God in our daily lives? Do we fall into the category of what this verse is talking about? Are we God's faithful ones? If we are, then there is a promise attached to this verse: He will protect us. That doesn't mean nothing bad will ever happen to us, but we are promised that God will be with us through those times.

Stop looking to your husband to always guide you and protect you from harm; start looking to God. Your husband cannot predict the future, but God knows the future. Your husband cannot shield you from harm, but God can.

Father, I want to be known as a faithful child of God.
Teach me how to do that. I want Your protection
and Your guidance. I realize that only in You
can I find a true sense of security. I'm asking You today
to guide my life and to protect me. Thank You! Amen.

Guilt free

Cast all your anxiety on Him because He cares for you.
I Peter 5:7

It seems as though the minute you become a mom, you begin feeling guilty for everything concerning motherhood. A new mom feels guilty for wanting to sleep and not get up for the midnight and 3:00 a.m. feedings. She feels guilty when she takes her child to get new shoes and realizes his feet grew two sizes and he's been wearing shoes that are too small. A mom feels guilty when her child wants the latest and greatest item and she can't afford to buy it for him. Moms carry guilt around like balls and chains, dragging them everywhere we go.

Good news! You don't have to feel guilty for everything. In order to push past these overwhelming feelings of guilt, ask yourself one question: Have I committed a sin? If the answer is no, then push the guilt out of your mind. Most of the time we feel guilty because we feel like we "should" have known his feet were growing. In reality, we've done nothing wrong and have not committed a "sin."

You can't be all things to your children, but God can. We should do our best, but then leave the rest to the Lord.

Father, thank You that in You I can find freedom. I don't have to be burdened with guilt. I can live a life of freedom in Christ and I know that this is what You truly want for me. God, I pray that when I begin to feel guilty for things that I shouldn't, I would release the guilt and give those feelings to You. Amen.

Happiness comes from God

Jesus answered, "Everyone who drinks this water will be thirsty again, but whoever drinks the water I give them will never thirst. Indeed, the water I give them will become in them a spring of water welling up to eternal life."

John 4:13-14

We are all needy. We look around us to find people or things to fill our needs. But these things will never completely fill the void inside of us because God did not create them to fill us; only He can do that.

In order for us to find true happiness, we need to acknowledge a few things:

We are needy people. Even though we try to fill the void in our lives with material things or relationships, they will never fill that void.

We need God. We should ask Him to meet us where we are and to fill us with His living water.

After you declare your empty state to God, ask Him to fill your void. Ask Him to quench your thirst to be valued, listened to and acknowledged by your loved ones. God may use your husband to fill a need in your life, but realize that God is the ultimate giver, not your husband. Adopting this perspective will take so much pressure off of your loved ones. Instead of expecting them to fill the void in your life, turn to God and ask Him to do it for you.

Father, I acknowledge today that I am a needy person. I ask that You meet me where I am and fill my every need. My tendency is to look to my husband or my children to meet my needs, but I realize I shouldn't do that. I must look to You. Help me reprogram my mind to look to You for my happiness. Amen.

He will fill the void

You make known to me the path of life; You will fill me with joy
in Your presence, with eternal pleasures at Your right hand.

Psalm 16:11

We get our needs met every day in different ways. We search for security, significance and satisfaction in different things – money, success, a job or marriage – but only God can truly fill all of our needs. We will always come away feeling incomplete if we try to fill our needs with anything other than God.

In today's world there will always be people who accomplish more than us, earn more money than us and stand more out than us. Are we supposed to then just live this life and never find true peace? No.

God will guide us and teach us His way. With God's way, we can find peace, joy and contentment. As you search for security, ask God to make you feel secure. Only He can bring you true security. When you are searching for satisfaction, ask God. He will give you a deep sense of purpose in just loving your children. As you search for significance, look to God. You are significant in God's eyes whether you "do" anything or not. You are significant because you are His child and He loves you dearly.

Father, I look to You to guide my life.
I continue to make a mess of things.
I continue to go down paths that leave me
empty inside and feeling insecure. I acknowledge
that my way isn't working and I'm turning to You for wisdom
and guidance. Lead me and show me Your way. Amen.

Hear me!

*Hear me, L*ORD*, and answer me,*
for I am poor and needy.

Psalm 86:1

If there is ever a time we need our Lord it's during motherhood. Even if everything goes well, we need God. Just when a mom figures out one stage of her child's life, the child grows and moves into a different stage of life.

Take your many questions to the Lord. The questions don't stop after the toddler years; having teenagers can be even more overwhelming. Ask God what is going on with your teenager and the best way to relate to her during this season of her life. Does she need an extra measure of love and grace, or does she need stricter rules? God knows. He knows how to handle every season and He knows exactly what your child needs and when she needs it.

Ask God to listen to your prayers and give you what you need. He has the answers concerning your children. Pay attention, though, when He answers. Be open to what He says. Sometimes we hear Him, but we don't want to listen, because we don't like what He says. Remember, God knows your children better than you do. He can look straight into their hearts and know the best course of action.

Father, thank You for listening to me when I am in need.
I pray that I would always seek You, especially concerning
my children. God, there are so many times I have no idea
how to parent and I'm so thankful that I can come to You,
knowing that You will direct me. My prayer today is that
I will open my heart to Your Word and Your way. Amen.

Heart of the matter

*The heart is deceitful above all things and beyond cure.
Who can understand it?*

Jeremiah 17:9

Our emotions can rage war within us on a daily basis if we allow them to control us. With one negative comment from someone or a smirk on a family member's face, our emotions can tell us people are angry with us, or cold-hearted, or even that they don't like us. But we don't know what people are thinking and we shouldn't allow our emotions to rule us. Emotions are deceitful, they aren't truthful.

When we believe the lie that our emotions represent truth, we can bring down a friendship, or we can build walls to protect ourselves. But walls keep us isolated. In a mom's world, isolation is not a good thing. Instead of building walls, try to renew your mind and tell yourself the truth: emotions are deceitful. Give your offender the benefit of the doubt. Try to believe the best about that person and remind yourself that no one really knows the heart of another person. Only God does.

Next time someone offends you, try to control your emotions. Instead of letting your emotions run wild, give your hurt to the Lord. Ask Him to take your negative emotions and replace them with His love and compassion. You will gain a new perspective on people.

*Father, only You know a person's heart. Therefore,
I will look to You to be my guide. I don't want to live a life with
walls built all around me, not allowing anyone close. I want to
push past my emotions and learn how to extend grace and mercy
to everyone I meet. I can only do this through You. Amen.*

Help not required

And He is not served by human hands,
as if He needed anything. Rather,
He Himself gives everyone life
and breath and everything else.

Acts 17:25

In our daily lives, how many times do we tell ourselves, I *need* to serve; I *need* to make this meal for a friend, or I *need* to work harder at my quiet times with God? What's interesting is that God doesn't need us to do anything. He loves us just the way we are, whether we're serving, loving or spending time with Him. He accepts us completely just the way we are. He doesn't need our help. He's not like us, needing people's help all the time. He has it all covered.

God loves it when you spend time with Him. He loves it when you pour out your heart and share your dreams. The more time you spend with God, the more you will realize that you can't "do" anything for Him, but you can accept His love for you. When you believe how much He loves you, you will want to return that love to Him and to others. You won't be able to help yourself. Get into the habit of spending your days with Him and you will find yourself loving others, serving others and wanting more time with God. Loving and serving will come naturally.

Father, it's amazing that Your love is unconditional. My love can be so conditional at times and I confess that is why I can't completely understand Your love for me. Fill me with Your Holy Spirit and Your love, and guide me in Your ways. My heart is Yours; my life is Yours. Do with it what You will. Amen.

Hide and seek

Nothing in all creation is hidden from God's sight.
Everything is uncovered and laid bare before
the eyes of Him to whom we must give account.

Hebrews 4:13

Children love to play hide and seek. Sometimes we do this in our adult lives too when we have secrets or when we're not proud of our actions. It's easy to hide our pasts, our lies and our actions from our families and friends. We'll even hide from God. We convince ourselves that it doesn't matter and we think God will never know. Satan also whispers in our ears that we "should" hide from God, because God will probably be very unhappy with us and punish us for our sins.

The truth is that nothing is ever hidden from God. He knows all. The beautiful thing about God is that He already knows and He loves us anyway. By hiding from God, we are separating ourselves from the One who will bring healing and love back into a life that is wounded and hurting. God knows and God loves. Your sin has already been paid for through Christ. Don't play hide and seek with God. Confess your sin, own up to it and be restored to a loving Almighty God. Tell Him today what He already knows. Confess your sins before Him and receive His overflowing love and forgiveness.

Father, it blows my mind that You know all things and
nothing is hidden from Your sight. It also blows my mind
that You love me despite my wicked ways. Your love goes
beyond my wildest dreams. God, give me the courage to
not hide from You, but to always be willing to share what
I have done so I may be reunited with You. Amen.

Hit pause

Yes, my soul, find rest in God;
my hope comes from Him.
Psalm 62:5

We are busy as moms. We are constantly working, serving, organizing, planning and thinking. Sometimes we need to slow down and just rest in God. When you do slow down, you may be tempted to think you are being lazy. But you need to hit pause.

What does that look like for you as a mom? Sitting quietly before the Lord? Taking a walk to observe something in nature that you normally take for granted and have never took the time to notice? Sitting down with your children when they come home from school and just listening to them talk about their day? Sitting and listening to your husband, just the two of you?

These simple things seem odd, almost childlike, but hitting the pause button can be life-giving. Try it today. Just pause and see what happens. You just might be surprised by the result.

Father, I want to find rest in You. Teach me how to slow down;
it's so hard for me to do. I feel like my life is speeding by,
faster and faster each day. I don't want to look back on
these years and realize that I was so busy that I forgot
about the most important thing in my life – You. Amen.

Hospitality counts

Do not forget to show hospitality to strangers, for by so doing
some people have shown hospitality to angels without knowing it.

Hebrews 13:2

When you go about your day, do you pay attention to strangers? Do you offer them a smile or do you brush past them in a hurry to get to your destination? Most of us are in our own little worlds, never having time to think about what other people are doing around us. We rarely think we could offer hospitality to a stranger.

You don't have to look hard to find a stranger whom you can show hospitality to. He or she could even be someone you are in contact with every day, but you've never looked past the person who is standing in front of you.

For instance, the bus driver that takes your children to school every day, your mailman, the receptionist at your pediatrician's office, the beggar at your grocery store – all of these people are essentially strangers who you could offer a hospitable smile or a word of encouragement to. Who knows, by showing hospitality to strangers, you might just be showing hospitality to angels. That's amazing!

Father, I think I need to slow down and "notice"
the invisible people in my life. Every person that I meet
throughout my day has a life and a story. I know I can't talk to
every person in my world, but I can start with one stranger today.
Open my eyes Lord and allow me to view people the way You see
them – not as invisible, but as children of God. Amen.

How much is enough?

"The leech has two daughters. 'Give! Give!' they cry.
There are three things that are never satisfied,
four that never say, 'Enough!'"

Proverbs 30:15

◆——◇——◆

To be brutally honest, you can never give your children enough. Children will always want more: more time, more money, more attention, more sacrifice on your part, more material things. Children are constantly asking us to give more. Therefore, you need to give what you can give and resist the temptation to feel guilty for not giving more.

We feel guilty when we can't give our children what they want. Ask God to give you the strength to say to your child, "I can't give you what you want." If we give our children everything and never say no, they will never see the need for God in their lives. Plus, it sets them up for unrealistic expectations.

Do yourself and your children a favor; learn to say no without feeling guilty. God will provide for you and your children what you truly need.

•••————◦◦◦◦◦————•••

Father, I do want to give my children everything they want,
but I can't. I don't have unlimited time, money or energy.
God, give me the strength to say no and to not feel guilty about it.
I also pray for my children – please help them to develop the
maturity they need to accept my "no." Amen.

Husbands and submission

*Wives, submit yourselves to your
own husbands as you do to the Lord.*
Ephesians 5:22

Let's be clear about one thing: no one likes to submit and it doesn't come naturally to anyone. Submission is a choice. God asks wives to submit to their husbands, not because the husbands are better or greater than the wives, but because there can only be one person in charge. And God has chosen that person to be the husband. Therefore, as a wife, I have a choice to make in my marriage. Am I going to obey God and submit to my husband, or am I going to rebel?

If you choose to submit, it doesn't mean you never express your thoughts and feelings to your husband about situations. Communication is a key component in a happy, successful marriage. You absolutely should tell your husband your ideas, dreams, goals, and opinions. But, in the end, your husband has the final word. Take heart ladies. This also means that your husbands are ultimately the ones accountable for the outcomes of their decisions. That takes a big weight off of our shoulders. So, in a way, God is protecting us.

In our submission we are actually choosing to submit to God, to obey Him.

*Father, I don't like to submit, especially when I think
I'm right. But, Lord, I need to obey You and not question
Your wisdom. I pray that I will communicate to my husband
the things I need to and yet still submit when I need to.
Give me strength to do what You command me to do. Amen.*

I'm known

"Before I formed you in the womb I knew you."
Jeremiah 1:5

Think about that verse for just a second. Before you were ever conceived, ever formed in your mother's womb, God knew you. He knows everything about you, from your deepest secrets that you won't even whisper to a friend, to your current struggles. God knows the exact time you were going to be born and the day you will die. Nothing in your life is outside of His grasp or knowledge. God has you in the palm of His hand and He's not going to let go, no matter how great or hopeless your life appears to be.

What an amazing gift to be loved so greatly by your heavenly Father! So many of us walk around with distorted views of God. We believe He's distant, uncaring and waiting to punish us at every turn. We're wrong. God is as close to you as your breath. He is loving and kind, and doesn't want to punish you. He wants to rescue you from your sins.

What an amazing God we love and serve. Today, stop and take notice that your heavenly Father adores you!

---

*Father, thank You for Your sovereignty and Your deep love for me.
I want to wake up every day and think of You first. How
wonderful that You know me and I don't have to say a word.
I don't have to perform or even act a certain way. You already
know me and love me completely! Thank You, God. Amen.*

I'm right

In the same way, you who are younger,
submit yourselves to your elders. All of you,
clothe yourselves with humility toward one another, because,
"God opposes the proud but shows favor to the humble."

I Peter 5:5

How many times in situations with your children, your husband or your friends have you fought till the bitter end because you knew you were "right"? Sometimes, in our eagerness to win and be right, we make a left turn and it all becomes very wrong. Think about that for a second. In your need to be heard, if you lose sight of the person with whom you are arguing and become proud and mean-spirited, then you are wrong. Be careful not to cross that line.

Humbling yourself means you can give your point of view, but then leave it and walk away. Give the person you are arguing with some time to think about your point. While they're thinking, ask God to open their eyes to your point of view and to help you to also see their point of view, taking away your desire to "win." We all get into these situations. But the wisest people will learn to drop it and move forward. Is it worth risking the relationship just so you can say you were right?

Father, I am a prideful person. I usually want to be right and I will fight to the end, which I now realize is very wrong. God, teach me how to be humble. It's so foreign to me. It almost feels like I'm being weak. Give me the courage to be humble and walk away if I am damaging a relationship with a loved one. Amen.

Idols in your life

"You shall have no other gods before Me."
Exodus 20:3

In today's world, our idols consist of materialism, health, our looks, being loved, job security and sometimes even our children. An idol is anything you place ahead of your heavenly Father. We have many idols today; they are just not carved figures. They're much more subtle and harder to recognize.

We have the idol of keeping up with everyone. We have the idol of climbing up the corporate ladder to secure the best job to provide for our families and fuel our egos. We struggle with the idol of wanting the "perfect marriage," and when we don't feel like our marriages are what they should be, we give up, seeking new relationships.

We also have the idol of our children. We won't be satisfied until we believe we've given them every opportunity to experience the "best" life possible, regardless of the cost. We place our children above everyone, including our husbands and even God. Think about it: idols are very much alive and well. Make no mistake, God is a jealous God and He will not tolerate other gods in your life. Maybe today is a great day to start assessing who is number one in your life.

*Father, forgive me. I do have idols in my life
and I didn't even realize it. Open my eyes and show me
the idols I've allowed to creep into my life and take over.
Give me the strength I need to tear down my idols.
I want You to be number one in my life. Amen.*

Imitator of God

Follow God's example, therefore, as dearly loved children and walk in the way of love, just as Christ loved us and gave Himself up for us as a fragrant offering and sacrifice to God.

Ephesians 5:1-2

Imitation has been said to be the highest form of flattery. To imitate someone or something means to copy it exactly. In Ephesians, Paul tells us to be imitators of God. We are to copy God's behavior exactly, living a life of love and sacrifice. Christ loved us so much that He sacrificed His life for us on the cross.

God loved us so much that He gave His ONLY Son to die on the cross for our sins (see John 3:16). I would never sacrifice one of my children for another person. NEVER. But God did. He loves us that much. We are to exhibit that kind of love to others. We are to lay down our lives for them.

In a mom's world, we do live out that kind of love for our children. Every day we have opportunities to express sacrificial love to our children. Make the most of your time with your children and ask God to show you areas where you can be an imitator of Him.

Father, thank You for loving me enough to send Your only Son to die for my sins. Thank You for sacrificing so much for me. I want to be an imitator of You and love others the way You love me. Give me that love Father; give me Your love. Amen.

Immeasurably more

*Now to Him who is able to do immeasurably
more than all we ask or imagine, according
to His power that is at work within us.*

Ephesians 3:20

As a mom, how many times a day do you feel ill-equipped to do your job? How many times have you thought to yourself, *What do I do in this situation?* You want to be a great mom, but do you think you are? Most moms would answer no. We tell ourselves we'll start anew tomorrow. We love our children, we care for them and protect them, but most days we feel inadequate.

There is good news for moms everywhere! Jesus' power is working within us. Through Him we are able to do immeasurably more than we can even imagine. When we feel like we don't have another ounce of energy to continue, Jesus has that energy. When we feel our patience is at an end, if we call on Jesus, He will come through for us and give us patience.

When we are weak, He is strong. Moms, you can't do this job on your own. You need the power of Jesus working through you – always. When you rely on Him, He will provide everything you need. Today, when you get to the end of your rope, call out to Him and ask Him to give you immeasurably more.

*Father, thank You for always being with me.
I can't raise these children by myself. I used to think I could,
but I am realizing, more and more, that I can't. Thank You for
knowing this before I ever did and for preparing a way for me …
that through Your Son, Jesus, I can accomplish more than
I ever dreamed of accomplishing. I love You. Amen.*

June

Impossible situations

Nothing is impossible with God.
Luke 1:37 (NLT)

❦————————❦

Nothing is impossible with God, even when it comes to our children. So many times, I am involved in an "impossible" situation with one of my children. These impossible situations include potty training, sleeping through the night, breaking my child of the habit of lying, teaching my child how to develop a loving spirit, talking to my teenager in a calm voice and setting up boundaries. While these situations seem impossible to me, it's comforting to know that with God nothing is impossible.

God sees the way, knows the way and wants to walk me through each step. I just need to have faith in Him and believe that He is the God of the impossible.

What is the impossible situation you are faced with today? Ask God to meet you where you are and to give you what you need to accomplish the impossible.

•••————————••••

Father, thank You for being the God of the impossible.
My prayer is that I will keep my eyes on You
and not on the impossible situation at hand. God,
teach me how to have faith that moves mountains. Amen.

In due time

*Humble yourselves, therefore, under God's mighty hand,
that He may lift you up in due time.*

I Peter 5:6

As a mom, do you ever feel like life is passing you by? Like there's a big world out there, but you are stuck in your four walls surrounded by children, laundry, cleaning, etc. Do you feel there is nothing exciting going on in your world?

Take heart! God has not forgotten you. He will take care of you and lift you up in due time. The problem for most moms is the phrase "due time." Moms think, I don't want to wait for God's due time. But that's where humbling ourselves comes in.

If you humble yourself by putting your children first – serving them, nurturing them and teaching them – then God will lift you up in due time. It will be worth the wait. We only get one chance and a limited amount of time to raise our children. If you look to the Lord to get you through these hard days, He will bring you to the other side. Who knows how He will lift you up in due time. Only God knows. It's His promise and He will fulfill it.

*Father, give me patience to wait on You
and Your "due time." Open my eyes to the importance of my job.
Fill me with Your love, Your joy and Your contentment.
I humble myself before You today. Amen.*

In God I trust

In you, Lord my God, I put my trust.
Psalm 25:1

In our culture, it's so easy to put our trust in things other than God. We focus our attention on finances, marriage, job security, family and even our church. But God wants us to put all of our trust in Him. He is the one we can trust 100 percent all the time. The economy will fall, marriages go through difficult seasons, jobs can be lost and our families can let us down. Even the church is not perfect. Putting our trust in these things sets us up for disappointment.

But even through the hard times – financial ruin, divorce, sickness or even death – God is still faithful. Focus on God and ask Him to meet you where you are and to give you what you need. Don't be surprised when He does, even when the circumstances remain the same. So many of us think if our circumstances change then God was for us and if they don't, He wasn't. God is for you regardless of your circumstances. Trust Him.

Father, help me to live my life fully trusting in You.
I want to have a deep faith grounded in You and not in my
circumstances. You are always faithful and You are always good.
Thank You for being my rock. Amen.

Include everyone

But when you give a banquet, invite the poor, the crippled, the lame, the blind, and you will be blessed. Although they cannot repay you, you will be repaid at the resurrection of the righteous.
Luke 14:13-14

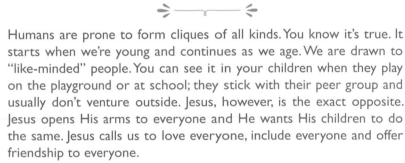

Humans are prone to form cliques of all kinds. You know it's true. It starts when we're young and continues as we age. We are drawn to "like-minded" people. You can see it in your children when they play on the playground or at school; they stick with their peer group and usually don't venture outside. Jesus, however, is the exact opposite. Jesus opens His arms to everyone and He wants His children to do the same. Jesus calls us to love everyone, include everyone and offer friendship to everyone.

Teach your children how to accept and love everyone unconditionally. Teach your children to be on the lookout for those who are excluded from the group and to welcome them. Some children are born with tender hearts and this act of kindness will come naturally to them. For others this might be difficult. They may never "see" these types of scenarios or want to extend love to outsiders. You as a mom can make your children more aware of these situations and encourage them to show love. As followers of Christ we need to love and accept everyone. Make sure you are modeling this in your life.

Father, give me a loving heart that loves unconditionally and never rejects anyone. Teach me how to model a loving heart for my children and plant in them a desire to live a life of love. I want to "see" everyone as the same and not put them into categories, but I know I need Your love to do that. Amen.

Interceding for others

I urge you, first of all, to pray for all people.
Ask God to help them; intercede on their behalf,
and give thanks for them.

1 Timothy 2:1 (NLT)

We live in a broken world. There is so much sorrow around us. When you listen to the news, talk to your teenagers about what is going on in their world or even listen to your neighbors talk about their struggles, it feels overwhelming at times. We listen and feel helpless because we realize there is nothing we can "do" to fix these situations. One thing we can do, however, is pray.

When you see people hurting or they share their hearts with you, you can lift them up in prayer. Sometimes people are suffering so much they can't pray for themselves. Maybe your friend, child or husband has lost hope and cannot pray to God for help because he or she feels helpless or far from God. You can step in and pray for them – intercede with your heavenly Father.

Jesus prayed for us (John 17), and we can pray for others. Don't just say to yourself, "I feel bad about what's going on in that person's life," instead, pray for them. Your prayers could make a huge difference. Their circumstances may not change, but your prayers could provide the exact measure of hope and peace they need to persevere.

Father, thank You for listening to my prayers.
I do have a person in my life that needs prayer. I am lifting them
up to you right now. You know what they need. You know exactly
where they are in their life. I'm asking You to meet their needs
and carry them through this difficult time. Amen.

Interests of others

Not looking to your own interests,
but each of you to the interests of others.
Philippians 2:4

Taking care of our families and us is as natural as breathing. We don't need anyone to tell us to look out for our needs. We do that instinctively. But who has time to pay attention to the interests of others? We get so busy that we don't have time to look up and notice that there is a whole world outside of the four walls of our homes.

When you are at the grocery store and someone is rude to you in the parking lot or checkout line, instead of getting mad, take a step back and say a silent prayer for that person. Maybe that person just got fired or needs to rush back home to take care of a sick child. Maybe that person is going through a divorce and is angry and hurt.

Keep this in mind – hurting people hurt people. If someone is lashing out at you, there is a reason, and it's usually because they are hurting. So pray for that person. God knows exactly what's going and He alone can bring comfort and peace into a troubled life. Lift that person up in prayer.

Father, I am so prone to only look out for my family and myself.
Make me more aware of other people in my life, people that I don't
ever notice. Help me to "see" people and situations the way You
see them. I don't want to be selfish. I want to try to understand
people the way You understand me. Amen.

Invisible mom

Jesus said, "Truly I tell you, this poor widow has put more into the treasury than all the others. They all gave out of their wealth; but she, out of her poverty, put in everything ..."

Mark 12:43-44

The story of the widow's offering in the book of Mark is an important lesson for moms. The widow put in everything she had to give and Jesus noticed. How beautiful is that picture? Jesus noticed the smallest offering, because it was given with the biggest heart.

As a mom what we give every day to our family often goes unnoticed; it is almost like we are invisible. Who in our family notices how we fold laundry, dust the bookshelves, clean out dirty lunch boxes or even stock the pantry with food each week. It can be discouraging, because we work so hard and no one seems to be paying attention.

God pays attention to every bit of work we do and He sees that we are giving everything we have. God sees how we comfort our children when they are hurt, hold them when they are sick and provide a clean, loving home for everyone to come home to. Take heart, your heavenly Father sees what you do and He will reward you for it.

Father, help me to remember that You notice me and all of the work that I do. I can get so frustrated with my family and feel taken advantage of very easily. Help me to keep my eyes on You and to do my work whether I am being noticed or not. Thank You for noticing. Amen.

Isolated and alone

I lie awake; I have become like a bird alone on a roof.
Psalm 102:7

As a mom, do you ever feel alone? Do you feel like you are trapped in your world of work, laundry, cooking, cleaning, breaking up fights between siblings, carpool driving and more? Most of the time, you feel alone in this all-encompassing job of being a mom. Sure, there are other moms out there doing exactly what you are doing, but each mom is on her own path, trying to figure it all out.

But you are not alone. God is with you in your isolation, and He is your support and strength. He sees all the hard work you do. He sees the love you show your children when no one else is paying attention or noticing. God notices. God cares. Cry out to Him throughout your day. Ask Him to fill you with His love and mercy for your children.

Ask Him to give you creative ways to keep your four walls from becoming your prison, and to help you view your four walls as a wonderful, creative workspace where you go every day to mold and shape the next generation. Ask God to meet you in those lonely days and to fill your life with His joy.

Father, I embrace today and all that it will bring.
I know that You "get me" and my circumstances,
and I am so grateful that I am not alone. You know exactly
where I am today – all my feelings, fears and weaknesses.
Give me what I need to do this very important job. Fill the long
day ahead with Your joy, Your zeal for life and Your love. Amen.

It's a process

*Be patient with each other, making allowance
for each other's faults because of your love.*
Ephesians 4:2 (NLT)

Our children come into this world as blank slates. It is our job as moms to teach them, love them and guide them into adulthood.

There is one key concept we need to always remember: children are learning as they grow. We need to be patient and recognize it is a process. Over time, hopefully, our children will say please and thank you more times than not. Over time our children will learn to not interrupt when we're talking. Over time they will learn to stop arguing with their siblings and get along. But it takes time, love, guidance and teaching.

We know we must be patient with our children, but patience runs thin when you are correcting your child for the umpteenth time in one morning. Realize that patience is a fruit of the Spirit and not something that you can "will" into yourself (see Galatians 5:22-23). The only way you can have true patience is to walk with Christ and lean on Him – that's when His fruit will start to show in you. You can pray for patience, but unless you are abiding with Christ, you will not receive it. Jesus is the source of all patience.

*Father, I must exhibit patience and self-control with my children.
Those qualities are fruits of the Spirit. In order for me to have
such fruit, I need to be walking with and abiding in You.
That is my prayer today … that I would walk closely
with You and You would fill me with Your Spirit. Amen.*

It's easy for God

*"Ah, Sovereign LORD, you have made the heavens
and the earth by your great power and outstretched arm.
Nothing is too hard for you."*

Jeremiah 32:17

When children are learning a new skill, like tying their shoes, the task seems so hard — almost impossible. As the mom you model to your child how to tie their shoe. You share with them the little rhyme about going over and under and they think it looks so easy. Then the child tries it and the shoelaces end up in a knotted ball, and your child walks away frustrated with shoelaces flapping on the ground. As you give your pep talk, coaxing them to come back and try it again, your child usually says, "It's so easy for you, but I can't do it!"

Isn't it the same with God and us? God is our heavenly Father, our Dad. He lovingly walks alongside of us, His children, showing us His way. Yet we complain to Him, "I can't! It's easy for You, but too hard for me." The good news for all of us is that God's power is in us through His Son, Jesus. Therefore, nothing is too hard for us, because in Christ we can do all things (see Philippians 4:13).

God is sovereign. He is Lord of all. He is all-powerful. In His majestic love for us, He gives us a way to tap into all of His power — through Jesus. So, nothing is too difficult for us.

Father, I can't fully comprehend Your amazing love. But I know, even in my limited knowledge, that You love me. I know this because You gave Your Son, Jesus, as payment for my sins. What a gift Jesus is to all humankind. Through Him we have Your power. Thank You for making the impossible in my life possible! Amen.

Jesus paid it all

"He Himself bore our sins" in His body on the cross,
so that we might die to sins and live for righteousness;
"by His wounds you have been healed."

I Peter 2:24

Because Jesus died on the cross for my sins, I can live a life of right-eousness. Because Jesus bore my sins on the cross, I can have a relationship with God. Because Jesus paid the price for my sins, I have been healed. So many times, we brush over these words and the high cost of what Jesus did on Calvary. As painful as it is, we need to think about it. We need to understand the huge price Jesus paid so that we could have a relationship with Almighty God. Without Jesus' shed blood, we would still be separated from God. He is a holy God and we would not be able to have fellowship with Him without God's sacrifice of His Son, Jesus. We have a Redeemer and His name is Jesus.

It's important as a mom that you think on such things and teach them to your children. Children are eager to learn and there is nothing more important to teach them than the fact that God sent His only Son to die for our sins so that we could have a relationship with Him! Christ is the bridge to God. Without Christ we all fall short of the glory of God (see Romans 3:23).

Father, thank You for this day. Thank You for Your Son,
who died for my sins. Without Jesus, I wouldn't be
able to have a relationship with You. Without Jesus,
I would still be full of sin. Thank You that I can now live
a righteous life and be holy in Your sight. Amen.

Joy-filled life

*"I have come that they may have life,
and have it to the full."*

John 10:10

It's amazing that through Jesus we can live a joyful life no matter what our circumstances. When we get caught up in our daily routines, joy can escape. How can there be joy in laundry, cooking, cleaning, changing diapers, homework and errands, and then the next day having to start it all over again? Take heart. There can be joy in abundance through Jesus.

Joy can be found in the small things as well as in the big things of life. The key to finding joy, even in the midst of the small and mundane, is to realize that all those jobs we are doing, we are doing for God's glory. You are taking care of Jesus' sheep by doing the laundry, cooking, cleaning and other house work. You are being the hands and feet of Christ by loving His children and always pointing them to Him. Through your love and dedication, God will fill you with joy.

*Father, fill my life with Your joy! Make my days full of You and Your love. Open my eyes, Lord, so I will see the importance of my role as a mom. When the world deemphasizes my role, help me to deafen my ears and to open my mind to You. God, thank You for seeing and understanding me as a woman and a mother.
I love You and am grateful for the joy You bring me! Amen.*

Joyful days

I will give thanks to you, Lord, with all my heart;
I will tell of all your wonderful deeds. I will be glad and rejoice
in you; I will sing the praises of your name, O Most High.

Psalm 9:1-2

Finding joy in the "ordinary" is a hard thing to do at times. It is easy to be joyful when great things are happening in your family, when you or your husband gets a raise, when your child excels in sports or school. But finding joy in everyday things like doing your tenth load of laundry, going to the grocery store or driving the kids to school – those ordinary moments – can be very difficult. You can find joy in those moments when you realize that joy comes from the Lord.

Today, as you go about doing your tasks, be joyful! Praise God throughout your day and glorify Him in the ordinary things. We serve the Creator of the Universe, a holy and righteous God, Lord over all, One who is worthy of our praise. Thank God for even the smallest things today. It will change how you see the world.

Father, thank You for this day. Thank You for my children
and my family. God, You have blessed me beyond measure.
You have flooded my life with Your blessings, even in
the small ways. Help me to open my eyes to the wonders of
Your world. Give me Your joy today and every day! Amen.

Joyful family

Worship the LORD with gladness;
come before Him with joyful songs.
Psalm 100:2

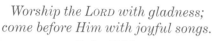

A family evolves over time and usually develops a name for itself. When you think of certain families, you put them into categories: "They love sports," or "That family is always going on vacations," or "They are homebodies," or "That family loves doing projects together." How would someone describe your family? Would they describe your family as fun? If you are Christians, fun, joyful and happy should be part of the way people describe you and your family. Are you joyful?

All Christians should be joyful because we worship an amazing God! He has filled us with His joy and we need to be exuding joy always. Be the family that opens their doors to the children around the block, creating a place that's safe and welcoming. Be the home in the neighborhood where the mom welcomes other children by making hot chocolate in the winter and passing out popsicles in the summer.

If you tell yourself you don't have time for such nonsense, then you are the one that needs it more than anyone. What's nonsensical about having fun and giving love? Who knows, your family may be the only sign of Jesus your neighbor's child will ever see.

Father, I need to lighten up! Open my eyes so that I will
no longer be so downcast, worrying about what tomorrow will
bring. Help me to just savor today. I need to enjoy my children
and their friends. Give me joy! I pray that when people look
at me and my family they will see You. Amen.

Labor of love

Therefore, my dear brothers and sisters, stand firm. Let nothing move you. Always give yourselves fully to the work of the Lord, because you know that your labor in the Lord is not in vain.

1 Corinthians 15:58

The work of a mom is never done. Think about it: cooking, cleaning, carpooling, helping with homework, shopping, doing yard work, disciplining, counseling, teaching manners, and so much more. Moms can often feel overwhelmed and under appreciated. Take heart! Your work is not in vain and it is extremely valuable. Whether your family gives you praise or not, whether the world sees your worth or not, God sees everything you do and He knows that what you are doing is valuable and good. Your job is the hardest work you will ever do, but it also has eternal value.

Moms, you are training up the next generation. You are shaping and molding little minds – encouraging them, teaching them, and instilling morals and values that will last a lifetime. You are teaching your children to be responsible, to value another human being, to love and take care of those less fortunate, and to be kind and gentle. The world may devalue your work, but don't listen to them. Feel good about yourself today as you do your mom duties and know that your labor is not in vain.

Thank You, Lord, for blessing me with my children and for giving me the huge responsibility of being a mom. God, I pray that I will not be discouraged, but would embrace each season and see the true blessing that it is. Give me wisdom to know how to parent in a godly way and give me a passion to do my job well. Amen.

Lack of faith

"The Lord has kept me from having children. Go,
sleep with my slave; perhaps I can build a family through her."

Genesis 16:2

Sometimes we take matters into our own hands because we are fearful that what we want will never be accomplished. Moms jump in to "help" our children so they won't be hurt or we manipulate our husbands to agree to buy a larger house because we convince ourselves we need it.

We do these things because we lack faith. We don't truly believe God will protect our children, so we must protect them. We don't believe God will bless us financially, so we rush ahead and buy things on credit. We lack faith that God will provide.

Sarai was getting old and still had not given birth to a child, so she took matters into her own hands and allowed Abram to sleep with her maidservant. Of course, that decision set off all kinds of emotions and bitterness towards Hagar and her son. Sarai did not have faith that God would provide, so she orchestrated it herself. God's way is always better than our way, even if we can't see what He is doing.

Father, give me the ability to wait on You. I do have a tendency
to rush ahead and mess things up. I could save myself so much
heartache if I would have faith in You. Grow my faith in You.
When I start to take matters into my own hands,
please whisper in my ear to wait. Amen.

Lead a life worth following

Follow my example, as I follow the example of Christ.
1 Corinthians 11:1

❧ — ❧

The best way to teach children, or anyone for that matter, is through the way you live your own life. If you want your children to love well, then you need to love well. If you want your children to have generous hearts and be compassionate toward others, then you need to be serving others and loving them even during the rough times. If you want your children to be honest, then you need to be practicing honesty in every aspect of your life. If you want your child to be walking with the Lord on a daily basis, then you need to be walking with the Lord and learning from Him each day. I shouldn't be asking my children to do anything that I'm not already doing myself.

God needs to be a priority in my life if I want Him to be a priority in my children's lives. Don't make the mistake of believing that your children are not paying attention; they are. They are noticing how you treat others in the grocery store, the mall or in traffic. They are taking notes. Is your life worth taking notes on? That's a tough question, but one that needs to be asked regularly.

•••————❦————•••

Father, is my life worth following? Can my children
see You in my everyday life or do I only show You
on Sundays at church? God, I want my life to be a reflection of
You. Search my heart and bring to the surface the areas that I
need to confess, make right or even purge in my life. Amen.

Lead by example

*"So in everything, do to others
what you would have them do to you."*

Matthew 7:12

Your children are always watching you to see if you are consistent, fair, loving and if you really care about them. The best way to teach your children is to lead by example. Ask God to fill you with His loving Spirit so that the traits you want to teach your children will flow out of you.

Practical ways to lead your children are:

* Give your husband grace when he arrives home late from work
* Show compassion to your parents or in-laws when they call to just "talk"
* Make a meal for a friend going through a tough spot
* Give to your local church or charity and give with a generous heart

You may be thinking, how do these areas relate to my child? The answer is, when you model love in all forms of your life, it will naturally spill over into your child's world.

Father, pour into me so I can in turn pour into my family. I want to walk with You and depend on You so that Your loving ways will flow through me. I cannot give what I do not have, and I know that I need You in order to love my children the way You love me – unconditionally. Thank You for giving love freely. Amen.

Legacy of faith

*I am reminded of your sincere faith, which first lived in your
grandmother Lois and in your mother Eunice and,
I am persuaded, now lives in you also.*

2 Timothy 1:5

What type of legacy will you leave behind? I want my legacy to be one like Paul is talking about in the verse above. He was talking about a third generational legacy, so strong that it was noticed in all three generations. That is powerful! Notice that it all started with Lois, a mom and grandmother. Her legacy consisted of sincere faith in her Lord, Jesus Christ.

Faith in God cannot be denied. If your faith is grounded and secure in Jesus, then nothing in life will sway you. Storms will come and may knock you over, but they will not knock you out.

Does your life reflect Jesus? Can your children see His love, patience, gentleness, kindness and forgiving spirit in you? If they can, you are leaving a legacy of sincere faith for your children to learn and grow from that will be passed on to the next generation. Start today to reflect Christ in all that you do.

---

*Father, I want to leave a rich legacy to my children
and grandchildren. I want to be like Lois.
I want my life to reflect You, Jesus, so that when people
look at me, they don't see me, but they see You. Amen.*

Less is better

He must become greater; I must become less.
John 3:30

As we grow in our Christian walk with God, we come to a place where we realize there can only be one master. We must decide who will be master in our lives: God or us. Just like you cannot have two head chefs in a kitchen, you cannot have two masters in your life. If you decide you want God to be the master over your life, then you must become less.

What does that look like in everyday terms? God's will must trump your will. You still have a will, but you must decide that you want God's way more than you want your own way. This will be different for all of us. For some it will mean giving up our right to be heard and instead being quiet for a change. For others it will mean opening our mouths and speaking up more. God will show you and direct you, but you must make your decision first.

Jesus even prayed this type of prayer in the garden of Gethsemane when He prayed, "Yet not as I will, but as You will" (see Matthew 26:39). If Jesus submitted, we can too. There can only be one master.

Father, I want You to be Lord in my life, and I realize that means I need to back down. I want Your way and Your will over my own. Give me the courage and strength to live this principle out in my life. I lay my life down for You. Amen.

Let freedom reign

*"Then you will know the truth,
and the truth will set you free."*

John 8:32

Freedom is a wonderful thing. There are all types of freedom: freedom from poverty, freedom from oppression and freedom from dictatorship. There is also freedom from the lies we believe. We as women lie to ourselves all the time. The lies can sound something like this:

* I must perform to be loved or accepted.
* What I do defines who I am.
* My husband should be my soul mate and complete me.
* The truth is, those thoughts are not true in God's Word. Those beliefs do not line up with what Scripture says. The truth is:
* I don't need to perform in order to be loved; God loves me regardless of my performance (see John 3:16).
* My worth comes from my identity in Christ, not what I do (see 2 Corinthians 5:17).
* My husband doesn't have to be my perfect soul mate; God will meet all my needs (see Philippians 4:19).

God's Word is truth. Read the Bible and learn what God has to say about you and for you. His truth will set you free!

Father, thank You that Your Word is truth and that Your truth brings freedom. Lord, I pray that I will seek You today with all my heart. When I start to believe the lies, I pray that Your Holy Spirit would reveal to me that I am believing lies against myself. God, replace those lies with Your truth. Thank You for showing me the way to freedom. Amen.

Let God fix things

Do not take revenge, my dear friends,
but leave room for God's wrath, for it is written:
"It is mine to avenge; I will repay," says the Lord.

Romans 12:19

Moms are fixers. We fix broken toys, we mend torn shirts, we remove stains from clothes and we nurse our sick children back to health. Sometimes, however, we can't fix things. Sometimes our best efforts seem to just make the situation worse. What is a mom to do? We can have empathy and listen to our children's broken hearts, but acknowledge, "Mom can't fix this for you, but God can." Many times, we need to point our children to God and teach them to take their hurts and anger to God and leave it in His very capable hands.

To point your child to God is to acknowledge that you are human, but you love and serve an Almighty God who is not human – a God who is powerful, holy and sovereign. God wants to hear your children's hurts, to take on their burdens and to be their Advocate. The gift you will be giving your child is immeasurable. You may not be able to always fix things; you may not even physically be around to help your children. So point them to God, who will always be there to guide and direct them.

Father, thank You for always loving my children and me.
I pray that my children will learn to go to You for help,
guidance and to pour their hearts out to You.
You are faithful and You love my children even more than I do.
Give me the courage not to have to be the fixer in
my children's lives, but to teach them to go to You. Amen.

Let it go

Forget the former things; do not dwell on the past.
See, I am doing a new thing!

Isaiah 43:18-19

Whether you're always reliving your glory years or you can't get past something terrible you did in your youth, focusing on the past is never a good idea. Our pasts have the potential to haunt us like a horror movie. We can get thoughts stuck in our minds and they can play over and over again, not allowing us to rest. But that is no way to live our lives! What does dwelling on past events do for us today? By constantly thinking of past wrongs, you become paralyzed and unable to move forward.

God has made you a new creation: the old is gone and He has breathed a new life into you – Jesus' life (see 2 Corinthians 5:17). We should start every day with thanksgiving, allowing Christ to live through us in everything we do. God does not focus on our pasts, so why should we? If God has forgiven my sins, then I should be able to forgive myself. God will use my past to minister to others, but He will not use my past to make me feel guilty. God is a God of forgiveness. He is a God of redemption, not a God of making us pay our debts. Thank God today that He is a God of the future and not the past.

Father, thank You that when You look at me,
You do not see my past, but rather You see Jesus.
I tend to hold onto my past – even the pasts of other people in my life. I realize that is wrong. I need to move forward and accept Your full forgiveness and love. Please help me to do this. Amen.

Life is not fair

*Don't extort money and don't accuse people falsely –
be content with your pay.*

Luke 3:14

We compare our salaries with that of other people all the time. But comparing is destructive. In comparing we become dissatisfied and envious of what others have. Listen to what Jesus is telling you in this verse: be content with what you make. Comparing steals your joy and sows the seeds of jealousy. Resist and run away from the comparison trap; you will always lose if you don't.

We tell ourselves, "Life is not fair," and in reality, life is not fair. There will always be people who make more money than you do. Train yourself to get in the mindset of: That's not my story; this is my story. Thank God that I have a story. It is so much easier to look around and want someone else's story instead of being happy with our own.

We all believe if we just had a little more money we would be happy, but in reality, some of the most miserable people are the ones with the most money. You cannot buy happiness. The key to being happy is choosing joy regardless of your circumstances. Once you embrace the story God has given you, you can then share it with others to encourage them.

*Father, I don't want to compare, because I lose either way.
I either come away feeling superior or I feel less than I should.
Both thoughts are wrong and are not how You see me.
Help me to keep my eyes focused on You alone and to be
happy with the story You've given me. Amen.*

Life of peace

Discipline your children, and they will give you peace;
they will bring you the delights you desire.

Proverbs 29:17

———◇———

More than anything else, I want to be at peace in my parenting, to know I am doing a good job. The Bible teaches that I will find this peace through discipline and my children will bring delight to my soul. What an answer to my prayers!

Many times, God's way of thinking is the exact opposite of what we think and discipline is one area that holds true. In our way of thinking, if we love our child, we will sometimes let certain things go. But God is very clear in the Bible and He tells us over and over again that we must discipline our children and that discipline will actually bring peace. Even though we might not understand God's thinking, we need to trust Him.

We need to work hard at the beginning, pushing past our hesitation to discipline. Disciplining is hard, but don't grow weary, it will pay off in the long run.

•••———◦◇◦———•••

Father, I want peace in my parenting and for my children
to be delights to me. Give me the courage to correct my
children when they are making unwise choices. When I get
tired of disciplining them on the same thing over and over again,
give me endurance. Bring to my mind the right ways to
discipline and make me dependent on You in all of this. Amen.

Life of prayer

Do not be anxious about anything,
but in every situation, by prayer and petition,
with thanksgiving, present your requests to God.

Philippians 4:6

Our children are gifts from God; no one would argue that point. All moms would agree that they would do anything for their children. However, one thing that we oftentimes forget to do is to pray for them on a daily basis. Our children are under attack in so many ways in today's society, whether through the influences of social media, the Internet or the destruction of the family, our children face a cruel, scary world at times. The best gift we can give them is to bathe them in prayer.

Every day, we as moms should be lifting our children up in prayer to their heavenly Father. We need to be thanking God for the blessings they bring to our lives and asking Him to protect them and guide them. God knows what their futures hold, therefore, we should be asking Him to prepare our hearts and our children for the future. Pray for your children's friendships, for their time at school and for their future spouses. Don't ever underestimate prayer and its power.

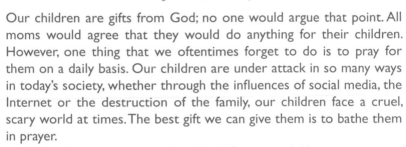

Father, I commit my life to You and to praying earnestly
for my children. Please protect them as they go about
their day and keep them safe. Only You can take the pain
of this world and make it good. Thank You for loving me
and loving my children in such a tremendous way. Amen.

Life of pure joy

Consider it pure joy, my brothers and sisters,
whenever you face trials of many kinds,
because you know that the testing
of your faith produces perseverance.

James 1:2-3

God does not promise us a life with no problems. In fact, He tells us we will have trials. He does, however, promise us that in our trials He will not leave us. Every day we make a choice, whether to find joy in life or to wallow in our circumstances. Trials come in all different forms and many times we experience trials in motherhood. It is easy to fall prey to self-pity when experiencing difficult times with your child, but try to find joy in the hard days.

One way to fight discontentment is to be joyful. If you look at your life through God's eyes, there is much to be thankful for in life. We can be thankful for our children. Thank God that He has a plan for both you and your child. He will use the trials to strengthen both of you, if you let Him. Draw near to Him in the dark days and ask for wisdom. You may not like the circumstances you're in, but you can choose to focus on the positive. Find joy in the knowledge that God will not leave you, that He loves you and that He will provide for you.

Father, show me how to choose joy. I want to learn how to look
past this world and its circumstances, to see life as You see it.
I cannot do that on my own; I need You to teach me.
As I go throughout my day, gently remind me of areas
in my life where I can choose to be content. Amen.

Life-giver

She brings him good, not harm, all the days of her life.
Proverbs 31:12

This verse is powerful. Just sit and think on it for a minute. "She brings him good, not harm." Those are life-changing words. Solomon is talking about a husband-wife relationship. Are your words toward your husband uplifting and encouraging? Does your husband feel safe when he is around you? Does he know you are for him, not against him?

At times we can put our mommy hats on and end up treating our husbands as if they are our children; we boss them around, scold them and even correct them. But they are not our children. No, our husbands are our friends, companions, lovers, providers and should be the closest people in our lives.

As you go about your day, notice the words coming out of your mouth, specifically toward your husband. Do your words weaken your husband or make him a better man? It's hard to examine yourself, but you need to do it. We think we can say anything to our spouses, but we shouldn't. Self-control is a fruit of the Spirit and sometimes we need to exhibit self-control with our words.

Father, this verse is eye-opening for me. I love my husband, but I have to admit that sometimes I do treat him like he's another one of my children. That is wrong and I want to change my behavior, but I need Your help. You alone know what my husband needs from me. Teach me. I am a willing student. Amen.

Light of the world

"You are the light of the world."
Matthew 5:14

If you are a child of God, you have the light of Jesus in you. Whether you are a working mom, a stay-at-home mom or somewhere in-between, your light needs to be shining for God.

How can you be a light to the world? You can shine your light when you are riding public transportation into work every morning. You can smile at your neighbors and ask how they are doing when you get your mail. Ask the local grocer how their day is going. Shining light is not hard to do, but you have to start thinking of others.

When you go into a dark room, what do you do? You turn on a light so you can see where you are. The world is a dark place and sometimes you are the only version of Christ people will see. Ask yourself: Are people better off after spending time with me or are they the same? People should be better off after spending time with you; they should be encouraged, blessed and loved. Spread your light; don't hide it.

*Father, even on the days when I don't feel like I am a light,
I am. My prayer today is that You would shine through me
at all times. Whether it is when I am changing my baby's diaper,
talking with my husband, sitting in traffic, carpooling my
children or making dinner, shine through me. Amen.*

Love everyone

"The LORD does not look at the things people look at.
People look at the outward appearance,
but the LORD looks at the heart."

1 Samuel 16:7

It's easy to love people who are like us – people who believe the same things we believe, people who act the way we act. But it's difficult when they're nothing like us. As moms we are no different. If our child brings home a friend who is similar to our family we embrace that child and are happy that a friendship is being formed. However, if our child brings home a friend who does not dress appropriately, talk appropriately or has different kinds of thoughts and morals, we tend to be afraid of the influence that child will have on our child. So we push the "alien" child away and don't welcome them into our home. What does God have to say about this? God calls us to love, not push people away.

We can be clear that certain language is not permitted in our home, certain partying is not allowed, but we can say it in love and offer a better alternative. People want to be loved and they seek it everywhere. Sometimes God uses normal, everyday people like us to show His love to the world. Look past the exterior and realize that every person is searching for love. Simply reflect Christ by loving those people.

Father, why do I only look at the outside of a person?
I know this is wrong and I desperately want to change.
Give me Your eyes to see people the way You do and Your heart to
love and accept them as they are. Help me to love everyone that
enters my home and to treat them with love and respect. Amen.

July

Love means everything

Let love and faithfulness never leave you;
bind them around your neck,
write them on the tablet of your heart.

Proverbs 3:3

Paul tells us in 1 Corinthians 13 that without love, all our accomplishments and accolades mean nothing. Solomon, the wisest man who ever lived, tells us never to let love and faithfulness leave us. Jesus said that loving our neighbor is the second most important commandment (see Matthew 22:39). Obviously, love is a big deal to God.

To love people sounds so incredibly easy … until life happens. Even loving others in just normal, everyday life – not catastrophic events, but regular driving-in-traffic, checking-out-at-the-store, dealing-with-people-in-your-workplace, coordinating-with-other-moms-on-a-project kind of life – can be very difficult. It is difficult because people are broken and hurting. They may hurt you because they're hurting. To love someone who lashes out at us for no reason is hard, and our normal natural response is to strike back.

When we react in love toward people, they often do not understand. Remember that the love of Jesus can heal any hurt. It may not happen instantly, but the Holy Spirit just may prick their hearts. It's not our job to bring healing. It's our job to love.

Father, You tell me not to remove love or faithfulness from my life; I know I need both. I need to remain faithful to You so that I am able to love. I cannot love hateful people on my own; I need You in my life to empower me. Love and faithfulness work hand-in-hand. God, help me to always keep both in my life. Amen.

Love that gives hope

*Because of the LORD's great love we are not consumed,
for His compassions never fail. They are new every morning;
great is Your faithfulness.*

Lamentations 3:22-23

Every morning God gives us a new perspective. With the dawn of each new day, hope comes. The birds welcome each day with their singing and the sun brings light to the dark sky. No matter how dark or long our nights are, the morning brings a new promise.

Moms need hope every day. Whether you are the mom of a toddler or the mom of a teenager, we are all weary and need hope.

Take hope, because God has great love for us and we do not need to be consumed by the pressures of this world. God will always be faithful, even when we're not faithful.

Cling to this promise in Scripture. Start fresh today with your children. Greet them with a good morning kiss and tell them that you love them. Accept God's love and faithfulness. Allow it to be like a blanket on a cold night, embracing you with its warmth.

Father, thank You for Your love and compassion. I don't deserve it, but I accept Your love. Father, give me hope for today. I am weary and tired. I do not feel like I have the energy to welcome a new day, but I cling to Your faithfulness. Fill me with Your Spirit. Give me what I need today when I need it. Amen.

Love without boundaries

*Neither height nor depth, nor anything else in all creation,
will be able to separate us from the love of God
that is in Christ Jesus our Lord.*

Romans 8:39

God's love for us is unconditional. Nothing we do will ever separate us from His great love. We often believe that we have messed up to such a great extent that there is no way of getting back in His good graces. That is our human mind talking and it is a lie. God's love for us does not have boundaries. Nothing and no one can separate us from His love, not even us.

As a mom, it's imperative that we believe those words and teach them to our children. We all mess up and we all sin, but God still loves us. Most people don't realize that when God is looking at them, He does not see sin; He sees His perfect, righteous Son, Jesus. Jesus paid the price for our sins. Our debt has been covered.

The next time the enemy whispers in your ear that you are not good enough, worthy enough or that your past is too great to forgive, shout at the top of your voice, "Get behind me, Satan! God loves me! Neither height nor depth, nor anything else in all creation will be able to separate me from the love of God!"

*Father, thank You for Your love! I am undeserving,
but I am thankful! Thank You for loving me just the way
I am and that I don't have to work to gain Your love. Amen.*

Loving example

*Fathers, do not exasperate your children; instead,
bring them up in the training and instruction of the Lord.*

Ephesians 6:4

Parents should be the safest people children can turn to for help. If you want a close relationship with your child, then you must create a safe environment in which they live. It is a high calling to be a parent; don't abuse that privilege by aggravating or exasperating your children.

Keep in mind that children are learning and growing in their knowledge of life. Don't tease them or make fun of their errors. Children are very sensitive and if their parents are the ones poking fun at them, even if it's in love, it will make them shut down. Always love them and be gentle, building them up as they learn.

Remember, you are the first representation of Christ they will see in their lives. God doesn't make fun of us when we make mistakes. He is patient with us, very kind in all His ways. God is our example, and we are our child's example.

*Father, fill me with Your loving Spirit so I will not frustrate
or aggravate my children. Give me a deep love for my children
so that I will instill Your love in them. I pray that in
everything I do, I will point my children to You. Amen.*

Loving your child

Look to the LORD and His strength; seek His face always.
1 Chronicles 16:11

Raising children can be an exhausting task. Children can make the calmest person scream. As a mom, it is best to remain calm with your children, but the only way to do that is through Christ.

Realize that you can't do this job on your own, but Christ can. You can't be patient on your own, but Christ can. You can't love unconditionally on your own, but Christ can. You can't be just in all your decisions, but Christ can.

As moms, we need to seek Christ first and then parent second. If you try to parent in your own strength, you will only get so far. Ask God for His strength, His love and His wisdom. Ask God daily to do it all through you. Once you get into the habit of seeking Him first, His love will begin to shine through you, and your children will benefit from it.

Father, thank You for giving me these children.
I confess that I get so busy in my "mom duties"
that many days I forget about You. I am sorry. Starting today,
I want to change. I want to put You first, even before my children.
I want to start today by thanking You for all of the blessings
in my life and give You all the glory. Amen.

Make the most of your day

*Sow your seed in the morning, and at evening let your hands
not be idle, for you do not know which will succeed,
whether this or that, or whether both will do equally well.*

Ecclesiastes 11:6

An idle mind will usually lead to destructive patterns – you might
become full of self-pity, become depressed or even become a recluse
because you tell yourself, "What's the point in going out?"

How do you stay busy? Think of projects you can do around your
house: Paint a room, organize a closet or plan the next birthday party.
If your house is already completely organized and taken care of, then
venture outside your home and find ways you can help people in your
church, neighborhood or the local school.

Maybe you are an empty nester: You find yourself with so much
extra time that all you can do is focus on whether your children are
going to visit you or not. Get involved in a local charity; volunteer your
time and energy to help. Do what you can to make the most of each
day.

*Father, I confess that I have an idle mind at the moment.
I am thankful for my children, but they are not always enough
for me. I find myself feeling sorry for myself and wanting more.
God, give me wisdom to know in what ways I can utilize my
mind to be productive and not give in to idleness. Amen.*

Make time for yourself

I lie down and sleep; I wake again,
because the LORD sustains me.

Psalm 3:5

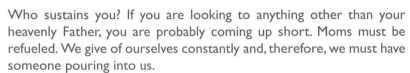

Who sustains you? If you are looking to anything other than your heavenly Father, you are probably coming up short. Moms must be refueled. We give of ourselves constantly and, therefore, we must have someone pouring into us.

Jesus says that He is living water, and if we go to Him, those waters will flow out of us (see John 7:38). Instead of walking around like depleted and parched, empty vessels, we could be revived and restored with waters flowing out of us. In order to live like that, we must go to our heavenly Father.

God knows you are empty. Allow Him to sustain you today. Ask Him to fill you up with His living waters. You may not be going through a crisis right now; it may just be life. Life is busy, life is messy and life with children can suck the life right out of you. So, look to God to fill you back up.

He wants to fill you up with His Son, Jesus. You are His child and He wants to take care of you, just like you want to take care of your children and meet their needs. All you have to do is ask.

Father, thank You for loving me so well.
God, I am asking today for You to meet me where I am.
Father, I need rest, refueling and to be filled with Your
living water. Please fill me. Please revive me. Amen.

Making it fair

The LORD works righteousness
and justice for all the oppressed.
Psalm 103:6

Life is not fair. We as adults know and understand this concept. But when it comes to our children, we want to make life equal … going against all odds to create a just world. As much as we try, however, we cannot make life fair.

We shelter, we protect and still our child comes to realize the cold, hard truth that in this life things are not always equal. Instead of trying to make life fair, we should teach our children from a young age that God's timing is not our timing.

Ultimately, we should be teaching our children to see past a life that is fair. Our goal should be to realize that no matter the circumstance, we are to look to our heavenly Father and put all our trust in Him. If that is the message we teach our children, then they will be better equipped to deal with life, no matter the circumstances. What a gift to give your child!

Father, give me eyes to look past my circumstances
and to see this world through Your eyes. When I struggle
to make life fair, remind me that this life is not perfect,
but that You are my protector and shield. Through You,
justice will come. Thank You for always loving me and
protecting me, regardless of what is going on in my life. Amen.

Manna from heaven

Thin flakes like frost on the ground appeared. Moses said to them, "It is the bread the LORD has given you to eat. 'Everyone is to gather as much as they need.'" … Then Moses said to them, "No one is to keep any of it until morning."

Exodus 16:14-16, 19

When the Israelites were wandering in the desert for 40 years, God gave them manna to eat, but He only provided what they needed for each day. The Israelites could not store extra food because if they did, the manna would begin to smell and attract maggots (see Exodus 16:20). It's interesting that God only gave them what they needed one day at a time.

As moms, we worry and fret over our children and their futures – whether we will send them to the right school, whether they will have the right friends in their teenage years or whether they will be safe when they learn to drive. But God wants us to be in the here and now with our children. There is enough to focus on for this day. God will provide what you need, when you need it.

Start your morning by thanking God for His provision for your life today. Submit your requests to Him and accept what He gives you. God knows what you need even before you ask for it (see Matthew 6:8). He knows what your children need as well. Keep in step with God and don't run ahead.

God, my tendency is to run ahead of You and to look to the future. Please help me to stay in step with You and to stay in the moment with my children. I don't need to worry about what the future will bring concerning them because You will take care of them. Thank You for Your provision. Amen.

Martha, Martha

*"Martha, Martha," the Lord answered, "you are worried
and upset about many things, but few things are needed –
or indeed only one. Mary has chosen what is better,
and it will not be taken away from her."*

Luke 10:41-42

We are busy as moms, constantly working, serving, organizing, planning and thinking. Sometimes we need to slow down and let the busy world keep going. Sometimes we need to hit pause. This is hard to do. When you do slow down or pause, you may think you're being lazy. However, sometimes you need to take a break.

Sometimes you need to just sit quietly before the Lord. Walk outside and observe something in nature that you never noticed before, like ants building their homes. Maybe you could sit down with your children when they come home from school and just listen to what they have to say about their day. At night, when your children go to bed, climb into bed with them and ask them about their day. Don't interrupt them or make a teaching moment out of what they are telling you. Just listen. Or you could listen to your husband or take a walk around the block and hold hands.

These simple exercises can seem so bizarre to us, almost childlike, but hitting the pause button can be lifegiving. Try it today. Just pause and see what happens. You just might be surprised by the results.

*Father, give me courage today to pause. In the midst of the silence
and awkwardness, meet me where I am and show me something
that is uniquely You. Whether You reveal to me where my child's
heart is, the beauty in nature or just that I need to sit down,
whatever it is, Lord, meet me when I am quiet and still. Amen.*

Master of all

*And He marked out their appointed times in history
and the boundaries of their lands. God did this so
that they would seek Him and perhaps reach out for Him
and find Him, though He is not far from any one of us.*

Acts 17:26-27

We plan and scheme where we want to live, what we want to do and which paths our lives will take, never considering that God already has it all figured out. God is in control of our lives, whether we realize it or not. God is loving, good and wants the best for us.

Many times we don't "see" His goodness, because life takes a twist or a turn that we didn't see coming. What do we do in these times? Do we blame God for not taking care of us, and get angry? We should trust God. He has it all under control.

God is the Creator of the universe. Even when life throws us curve-balls, God will work it out in His time. We just need to trust Him, even through the bad times. We need to reach out to Him and allow Him to work in and through our lives. We do not need to trust in our circumstances, our wealth or our dreams, because they can fail us. God, however, will never fail us. He is for us!

*Father, thank You for loving me and for orchestrating my life.
There are times when I question Your wisdom. Help me to push
past my fears and fully trust You. Lord, You alone are sovereign.
You alone are worthy of trust. Help me to remember how You
have been faithful throughout the ages and that You will
be faithful until the end of time. Amen.*

Master of your life

Devotion to God is, in fact, a way for people to be very rich, but only if it makes them satisfied with what they have.

I Timothy 6:6 (ERV)

❧ ——— ❧

To be satisfied with what you have is a gift from God. The way to satisfaction is to be dedicated to God in all that you do. But what does that mean? It means to keep Him first, to share your life with Him – your dreams, desires and thoughts. Invite Him into every aspect of your life. Share with God "your plan" for your life, but keep your mind open to His plan. Practically speaking, you may want a bigger house and that is your dream. Tell God about your dream, but ask Him to go before you and if your desire is not what's best for you, to change your heart. Hold loosely to your dream and trust God.

What a gift that God teaches us how to be rich despite our circumstances. In order to be satisfied, our trust must be solely in God. We must die to ourselves and realize that God is our all. There can only be one master (see Matthew 6:24). You must decide who is the master in your life – you or God. When you give your life completely to Him and surrender your plan, satisfaction usually follows.

•••———❧❧❧———•••

Father, I invite You into my normal, everyday life. I want to walk with You and share my whole day with You – the good and the bad. I ask You to give me satisfaction in all that I do today. God, You know my heart; You know my dreams. Either change my desires or give me patience to wait on Your timing. Amen.

Me first

*An unfriendly person pursues selfish ends
and against all sound judgment starts quarrels.*

Proverbs 18:1

Teaching our children not to be selfish is difficult. Adults are selfish by nature and children are no different. But even though it's hard, you must press on and teach your children to think of others and to love generously. These are a few easy ways to implement this lesson in "real" life:

For one week, the firstborn always goes last: last to get in the car, last to fix their plate at dinner, last to walk through the door. After the week is up, let the second-born child take a turn. Then go down through the whole family.

Take your child to the store and have them pick out a toy. After purchasing the toy, ask them to whom they would like to give the toy.

As your children play together and argue over a prized toy, sit down with them and come up with a game plan to share, giving everyone a turn. If no one can agree, take the toy and put it away.

Unselfish behavior has to be learned, because it doesn't come naturally. We must teach our children to live a life of "you first."

*Father, I struggle with selfishness in my own life,
so why am I so surprised when my children act selfishly?
God, give me patience as I teach them how to put others first.
Give me the love that I need to not become aggravated
with my children when they are selfish. Help me
to remember that I can be just as selfish. Amen.*

Memorize Scripture

My son, if you accept my words
and store up my commands within you ...

Proverbs 2:1

It's not enough to take our children to church once a week to instill God's principles in their lives. We must get into God's Word and "store up" His commands in our hearts.

The Bible is powerful and helpful. God has given us His Word to teach us, guide us, encourage us, and to show us His character and love for us. We need to spend time with God on a regular basis in order to learn His ways and to instill His truths in our children.

Taking your child to church is not enough, just as you watching a tennis match doesn't make you a good tennis player. In order to be a tennis player, you must get on the court and play tennis. The same truth applies with God. If you want to know God, you must get into His Word. Make the most of what little time you have with your children and instill God's Word in their lives from a young age.

Father, thank You for Your Word. Thank You for
giving me a Book to read that shows me who You are and
is filled with instructions on how to live. Give me insight, Father,
on how to teach Your Word to my children. Help me to
make the stories interesting and enjoyable. Give me wisdom in
creating a love for Your Scripture in my child's heart. Amen.

Miracles in everyday life

*Taking the five loaves and the two fish and looking up to heaven,
He gave thanks and broke them. Then He gave them to the disciples to distribute to the people. They all ate and were satisfied.*

Luke 9:16-17

Jesus needed a miracle to feed the 5,000. All He had was five loaves
of bread and two fish. Isn't it interesting what Jesus did? He took what
he had and gave thanks. Jesus didn't ask for more; He humbly thanked
God for what had been provided and had faith that God would perform the miracle.

Many times we need a miracle in our lives and we focus so hard on
that miracle that we forget to thank God for what we already have. We
pray and pray for God to change our circumstances and to get us out
of the mess we are in, never stopping to thank Him for our blessings
and how He might show up to perform another miracle.

The next time you find yourself doubting your ability as a mom
and you ask God to give you something you don't have, stop and thank
Him for what you *do* have. For instance, if your child is not obeying you
and pushing all your buttons, and your husband will not be home for
three more hours, stop and thank God that He is the source of your
love and grace.

*Father, getting through each day can be a miracle in and of itself.
I need to remember to give thanks even when it looks like an
impossible task. Nothing is impossible with You, God. Amen.*

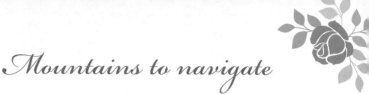

Mountains to navigate

He makes my feet like the feet of a deer;
He causes me to stand on the heights.

2 Samuel 22:34

Mountainous terrain is a challenge to navigate … but not so for a deer. A deer can climb and leap around the mountain like they are walking on a grassy field, all because of their hooves.

How amazing then that God uses the example of a deer in 2 Samuel! God knows that sometimes in our lives there will be rocky patches where we physically, mentally or emotionally cannot walk. He knows it will be too hard or too painful. So, in His infinite love, He makes our feet like a deer, so we can go where we never went before. With God as our provider, we are able to stand on the heights; we are able to walk on the rugged terrain like it is a grassy meadow beneath our feet. Only through God can this miracle happen.

Are you allowing God to enable you? Your heavenly Father wants to provide for you in ways you cannot even imagine. He doesn't promise to take you out of your circumstances, but He promises to enable you to walk in the midst of your circumstances. All you have to do is let Him.

Father, Your power is beyond comprehension.
Thank You for loving me, even when I push You away.
Thank You for equipping me with what I need when I need it.
God, I want to be like a deer – to walk on the rocky mountain
and be surefooted. I want to experience the heights.
Take me there, Lord. I will allow You to work in my life. Amen.

"My burden is light"

"Take My yoke upon you and learn from Me, for I am gentle and humble in heart, and you will find rest for your souls. For My yoke is easy and My burden is light."

Matthew 11:29-30

This verse seems too good to be true, especially in a mom's world. The weight of our children alone weighs us down with the full responsibility of being a mom. Jesus tells us to take up His yoke and to learn from Him. To take up a yoke with another person is to allow that person to share our load. We don't have to carry the full load of being a mom on our shoulders; Jesus is telling us that He will help bear the load.

Jesus tells us in this verse to "learn" from Him. If we do so, our burden will be lighter. What can we learn from Jesus? Jesus always spent time with God. We need to learn to do the same, even if it is just for 10 minutes during our day in prayer.

You may need to have your alone time in the car driving to work or in the carpool line in the afternoon, but make sure you take advantage of any quiet time you may have. Jesus also took His burdens to God. He trusted in God in all situations and we need to learn how to do the same.

Father, I want to include You in every step of my journey of motherhood and to allow You to bear my burdens each step of the way. Thank You that I can share my highs and lows of motherhood with You, and for Your promise to take my burdens and to make them light. I give You all the glory and praise! Amen.

My defender

The LORD is my light and my salvation – whom shall I fear?
The LORD is the stronghold of my life –
of whom shall I be afraid?

Psalm 27:1

As moms, we want to protect our children – always. We want to protect them from harm, whether from another person or from themselves. Our children learn to depend on us for protection, which can be good and bad. It's good that they learn to trust us and that they know we are safe havens for them, but we can't always protect them.

We can, however, teach them that God is always there for them. With Him by their side, they have nothing to fear in life. What a powerful thought: Our children will grow up and realize that they don't have to go through this world alone; they have a Savior who will defend them.

Your child can learn to trust and depend on God. Your child can learn to talk to God as a companion, not only in times of need, but throughout the day. With God on your child's side, there is nothing to fear. Teach your child how to cry out to God in the night when they're scared. Model to your child what depending on God looks like and talk about how to incorporate Him into everyday activities. God will protect us; we can live victorious lives and not be afraid.

Father, You are my salvation and my defender.
With You by my side, I don't have to be afraid.
I pray that I will be able to teach this truth to my children
and that they will grow in their faith in You. God,
please meet them where they are, like You do with me. Amen.

My heart will not fear

Though an army besiege me,
my heart will not fear;
though war break out against me,
even then I will be confident.

Psalm 27:3

Fear can grip a mom like nothing else. But if you are a Christian, you do not need to fear. God has you in His hand. It doesn't matter what your battle is at this point in your life, God will go before you and give you the victory! Lift up your eyes today. Take your eyes off your circumstances and look to God. Once you change your perspective, you will begin to see His power and glory, and you will gain confidence. Your confidence will not be in yourself, but in God.

Sometimes we feel as if we are being attacked from all sides – problems with our children, sickness, death, finances, loss of work – but God's promises are true. He will be there for us and will walk with us through the storms.

Look up to God. Lift your eyes to Him and cry out to Him, asking Him to carry you through the tough days. Your circumstances may not change, but God will see you through them. Believe God and trust in Him. He will help you.

Father, I know that I live in a broken world
and life can be so hard and painful at times.
Thank You, Lord, that You see past this world, the pain,
and the hurt, and that You battle for me! You will carry me
through to the other side. I need You and I will not fear. Amen.

My helper

Keep your lives free from the love of money and be content with what you have, because God has said, "Never will I leave you; never will I forsake you." So we say with confidence, "The Lord is my helper; I will not be afraid. What can mere mortals do to me?"

Hebrews 13:5-6

It's so easy to compare. Have you ever noticed that you were happy with the way things were until you compared your life to someone else's? Maybe you found out your coworker made more money than you, and once you knew the difference, you were not content. You began to feel used, overworked and underpaid. Your tone changed toward your coworkers and your attitude began to spiral downward.

To be free, you must change your mindset and realize that the Lord is your helper. If God is in control, He will provide for you before you even realize you need anything.

Trusting God is the way to contentment and happiness. God is worthy of your trust. If you take steps toward trusting Him, He will be faithful. Ask Him to give you courage to trust Him for everything.

Father, thank You for being my helper,
for providing for me and for never leaving me.
Keep my eyes focused on You alone and when I am
tempted to compare what I have with others, provide a way
out of that temptation. I choose to trust in You, Lord. Amen.

My rock

Praise be to the LORD my Rock, who trains my hands for war, my fingers for battle. He is my loving God and my fortress, my stronghold and my deliverer, my shield, in whom I take refuge.

Psalm 144:1-2

A war is being waged within our families today. We battle against our children growing up too fast. We battle against the current culture that is influencing them. We battle against the values and morals in our country. We even find ourselves battling against disciplining our children the way God teaches us in the Bible.

Do not fear. God has won the battle and He will be your deliverer, your shield in whom you can take refuge. God will teach you and train you in His way. The best thing you can do as a mom is to commit to following God. Too many times we fret about what our culture is teaching our children, wasting time worrying about what we cannot control. Instead, keep your eyes focused on God. Learn His ways by studying His Word.

Be committed in prayer each day and share your concerns and worries about your children with God. Ask Him for wisdom (see James 1:5).

Father, I pray that I will not be fearful in raising my children in a world that is raging war against them. Lord, I pray that I will keep my eyes on You as I parent. Give me boldness and strength to follow You and not to give in to the pressure of what the world teaches. Thank You for being my refuge. Amen.

My shepherd

The LORD is my shepherd, I shall not want.
Psalm 23:1 (RSV)

Sheep are simple creatures and they follow very well. A sheep will either follow another sheep or will follow the shepherd, but have no doubt, they follow. So many times in Scripture, Jesus is referred to as our Shepherd, meaning that we need to follow Him. However, it takes a conscious effort to do that.

Whom do you follow? As you go about your day, do you find yourself following the crowd? Are you following what people are doing on social media? Do you follow your church or your friends? Only Jesus can make the promise that if you follow Him, you "shall not want." That's a big promise, a God-sized promise, and one that Jesus is very capable of fulfilling. Choose today to follow the one and only true Shepherd. Go to Him to get your needs met. Go to Christ to:

* Restore your soul (v. 3).
* Fear no evil (v. 4).
* Receive comfort (v. 4).
* Have your cup overflow (v. 5).
* Have goodness and mercy follow you all the days of your life (v. 6).

Father, thank You for being my Shepherd, always there to show me the way. My prayer, as I go about my day, is that You would come to my mind and that I would make the decision to follow You. So many times I follow without thinking about "what" or "who" I am following. But today I want to change the course of my day and follow only You. Amen.

My shield

The LORD is my rock, my fortress and my deliverer;
my God is my rock, in whom I take refuge, my shield
and the horn of my salvation, my stronghold.

Psalm 18:2

How refreshing it is to know that the Lord is our strength. In a world where we can feel that everyone is out to get us, that evil is lurking around every corner or that we can't trust anyone, we can have hope in the fact that the Lord is our rock and our fortress. If you believe that God is your shield and salvation, then you will go about your day in a very different way.

Instead of striving to protect yourself and your family, you will realize that God has your family's best interests at heart. God will be the One to protect, shield and deliver you. That pressure will no longer be on you. If you can believe this, then you will be able to put your energy towards loving others instead of worrying about yourself.

Think about the difference it will make when you realize that God has it all covered. You will be free to love, show compassion and let your guard down concerning others. When you reach out your hands, open to what God has in store for you, you will be ready to receive the blessings that He has for you.

Father, thank You for always being my rock.
I need You more than words can say. I give You this day
and all that it brings. I ask You to continually remind me
of Your strength. When I become defensive and close myself
off to others, gently remind me that I am safe with You. Amen.

My strength

LORD, be gracious to us; we long for You. Be our strength every morning, our salvation in time of distress.

Isaiah 33:2

Days for moms are often long and hard. Sometimes you hear your child wake up and walk down the hall and you just want to roll over in bed, pull the covers over your head and say, "Go away." But you never get that luxury. Before you know it, your child has crawled into bed with you, begging you to get up and persuading you to begin your day of service to them. And you do it.

We pray that these long hard days will pass quickly and our children will grow more independent and self-sufficient … and they do. In the older years it is no longer a plea to make breakfast or get out of bed at 6:00 am – it's bigger issues.

We are now discussing sex, college choices, the influences of friends and making wise decisions. Once again our days are long and hard – waiting up until midnight for our teenagers. God is our strength every morning and every night. He is gracious to us, understands where we are and is available to us. Don't travel this journey of motherhood by yourself. God is your companion.

Father, every morning I want You by my side to guide me, build me up and to give me strength. I cannot do this job of motherhood on my own. I am lost on my own, wandering about. I need You. Thank You for always being there for me and for loving me the way You do. Amen.

My way

What causes fights and quarrels among you?
You covet but you cannot get what you want, so you quarrel and
fight. You do not have because you do not ask God. When you ask,
you do not receive, because you ask with wrong motives.

James 4:1-3

The song *My Way* by Frank Sinatra could be the theme song for most of us. We push, we fight, we struggle to do things and have things "our way." But in God's economy, it's the opposite. The last shall be first and the first shall be last (see Luke 13:30). This way of thinking is foreign to us as humans. We must begin to renew our minds with God's ways by submitting our wills to Him.

Each day, pray that you will choose God's will over your own. If you are struggling to "win" the argument with your husband, ask God to give you the courage and strength to submit. If you are battling over grades with your child, ask God to give you a measure of grace and love for your child in this area. Take a step back and try a different approach. Regarding "your" time, are you being selfish right now? Are you thinking only about what you need and not others? Ask God to give you His spirit of selflessness.

As you go about your day today, ask yourself: Am I pushing for my way at this moment? Ask God to give you discernment.

Father, I need Your help in this area of my life. I do want my way.
I want to be right, to be heard, to be valued. But all I seem to be is
frustrated. I want to change, but I don't know how. Please teach
me. Open my eyes when I am being selfish, stubborn or unkind.
Show me how to love the way You love. Amen.

Nagging wife

A quarrelsome wife is like the
constant dripping of a leaky roof.
Proverbs 19:13

No one wants to be the wife that nags, but we are all guilty of it at times. It takes determination and constant submission to God to steer clear of this trap. We want our husbands to clean the house, to watch the children, to be the spiritual leader, to provide financially, to go the extra mile in the marriage. When these things don't happen, we start to fight or nag, like a constantly dripping faucet. A dripping faucet is not effective; it's annoying.

What do we do with our complaints? Do we just forget about them? Push them under the rug and hope that our husband will wake from his slumber one day and correct his ways? We must start taking our complaints, our needs and our desires to God. Lay your burdens at His feet and ask Him to meet your needs.

Allow God to meet you where you are and to take that burden off of your husband. God did not create your husband to be your everything. That's God's job. Sometimes God uses your husband to meet your needs, but that's a bonus! Only God can meet all of your needs and satisfy you completely.

Father, thank You for my husband. I confess today
that I do look to my husband to meet my needs
and when he falls short, I get angry with him.
I pray that I will stop looking to my husband
to meet my needs and start looking to You.
You are the one I need to look to for help. Amen.

Narrow gate

Never be lacking in zeal,
but keep your spiritual fervor,
serving the Lord.

Romans 12:11

What is a mom's job? If you want a simple answer, it's to love and nurture her children. Sure there are a lot of other ways to define it, but in its simplest form, we are to love and nurture our children. So often, however, this simple part of being a mom is missing because the "world" crowds it out. Instead, it makes room for complex, crazy schedules, giving our children everything their heart's desire and protecting them from harm.

Moms, do you need to take a step back and focus on your real role? Once again, the world will throw a lot of things your way to get your attention and take it off of the ONE thing God has called you to do – to love and nurture your children. Narrowing your focus takes effort and discipline, but it is worth it in the end. Think back to your childhood. What is the better memory, endless driving to ball practices or family dinners around the table? The challenge for today is to narrow your focus.

Father, I feel like I have a million things pulling me
in a million directions. I admit I do this to myself, convinced
I "must" put my child in this activity or the school across town.
But, in actuality, those things are not "musts".
God, give me strength to focus and to push against culture
and to get back to the simple way of life. Amen.

Never-changing Jesus

Jesus Christ is the same yesterday and today and forever.
Hebrews 13:8

It is an incredible blessing that Jesus is always the same. He never changes. We live in a world where everything seems to change all the time. Nothing seems to stay the same. Isn't it a relief that we love and serve a Savior who is always the same?

Think about it: Christ never changes. Just stop for one second and try to take in the magnitude of that statement – Christ NEVER changes. He is our anchor, our North Star, our compass. When we feel tossed and thrown about, we can reach out to Christ and He will bring us back to His center. Christ never changes, so what He talked about 2,000 years ago still works. His Word is consistent, just like Him. What an amazing gift this is for our lives.

Because Christ is the same, He brings order to our lives in a world where order is a rare commodity. Christ brings peace to our lives where we feel disharmony. Christ brings love, even when we feel hate. Christ never changes! We can count on Him 100 percent. People change, governments change, finances change and even we change, but God is constant. Rest in that thought for the rest of the day.

Father, thank You for being the same. I can depend on You and know that what You say is true and doesn't change with the times. Your constant love, grace and mercy are what I need in my life every day. Thank You! Remind me as I go about my day and chase after things that are not constant, that You are the only One that never changes. Amen.

Never-ending love

Hope does not put us to shame,
because God's love has been poured into
our hearts through the Holy Spirit,
who has been given to us.

Romans 5:5

Some days love pours out like a faucet onto our families and other days we look at the clock flashing 9:00 am and we think, I will never make it through this day with this child. Don't be discouraged; Jesus gave us the gift of the Holy Spirit. The Holy Spirit is full of love, grace and patience.

God loves us so much that He sent His Son. When Jesus ascended into heaven, God's love for us did not stop; He sent us the Holy Spirit. Through the Holy Spirit, we have God's love in us, which is all the love we will ever need. So, on those days when you feel that you will not be able to love your child unconditionally, lean into the Holy Spirit and ask Him to fill you with His love. Be honest! Tell God, "I'm ready to throw in the towel for this rebellious child of mine, but I know I need to love them, train them, and rise above. God I can't do that without You, without Your Holy Spirit loving my child through me." God will meet you where you are.

Father, thank You for the gift of the Holy Spirit.
I admit I don't always understand how the Trinity works,
but I know it does! I know You gave the Holy Spirit to us to
comfort us, to guide us and to fill us with what we need when
we need it. Thank You for this amazing gift! Amen.

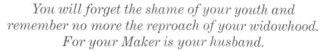

New creation

*You will forget the shame of your youth and
remember no more the reproach of your widowhood.
For your Maker is your husband.*

Isaiah 54:4-5

Our pasts can sometimes emerge in our role as moms. As we teach our children and train them up to be adults, we can see where they will make mistakes because we remember exactly where we made our mistakes. Sometimes remembering our pasts can haunt our presents and negatively affect our futures.

This verse in Isaiah gives us hope. God is a redeeming God, one that will restore our broken pasts and replace the ashes with beauty (see Isaiah 61:3). God has perfectly placed you and your child together for a reason. You are able to speak truth into your child's life like no other person. Use your influence wisely. Allow God to heal you from your past so that you will be able to effectively parent your child.

God is offering restoration and healing; take Him up on His offer. Always remember, you are a new creation in Christ (see 2 Corinthians 5:17).

*Father, I cannot begin to comprehend how You are able
to heal my painful past and restore me to a place of beauty,
but I trust in You. Thank You, Lord, for such an amazing gift.
I pray that I will be able to forgive myself and be the kind
of mom to my children that You called me to be. Amen.*

New sheriff in town

"Honor your father and your mother, so that you may live long in the land the LORD your God is giving you."

Exodus 20:12

Did you know that God has given you, the mom, authority over your children? He wants you to discipline them, teach them and guide them. And He wants your children to honor you. Therefore, we as moms need to take our authority seriously. We don't need to abuse it, but we also don't need to give the reins of our family over to our children. Neither a toddler nor a teenager should be calling the shots in your family. You must teach your child that God has given you this authority and you answer to Him.

If your home is one where the children have been in charge, you may need to have a meeting and announce that there is a new sheriff in town — and that sheriff is you! Show them the verses in the Bible where God instructs children to honor and obey their parents (see Ephesians 6:1). Explain your new strategy so they will be on the same page. Then be consistent and loving while carrying out your new plan.

Father, I have been slack in this area of my life, allowing my children to run all over me. I have been inconsistent because, to be honest, it is so much work trying to get them to obey. God, I want to change, but I need You to give me strength and endurance. Please help me. Amen.

August

New song

Sing to Him a new song; play skillfully, and shout for joy.
Psalm 33:3

⇜ ⇝

Each of us has a song that plays in our hearts. Different songs at different times in our lives. Sometimes our songs are joyful, while other seasons bring bitter songs or grieving songs. Is it time to change the song that is playing in your heart?

We hold onto past hurts because we believe if we move on, if we forgive, then those people will get away with the crimes they committed against us. But the only person you are hurting is yourself. The person you hold a grudge against actually has power over you. By not forgiving and moving forward, you are allowing him or her to have power in your life. Take away that power and sing a new song.

Maybe you are not able to change the song playing in your heart, but God can. Ask Him today to change your song from bitterness, unforgiveness, hurt, anger or self-pity to a new song – a song of joy, a joy that only He can give. God would love nothing more than to change your song to a joyful one.

⚜

Father, I have been bitter for so long. I'm tired of it.
I need a new song. I've tried so many times
to move past my hurt and pain, and every time
I end up right back in my anger. Fill me with Your joy
and give me a new song in my heart. Amen.

New way of thinking

Submit yourselves, then, to God. Resist the devil,
and he will flee from you. Come near to God
and He will come near to you. Humble yourselves
before the Lord, and He will lift you up.

James 4:7-8, 10

How amazing that we can submit ourselves to God and He will come near to us. Think about it. This is the God of the universe, the Creator of all things and He chooses to come near to you!

In our efforts to live out this verse, we should begin asking ourselves this question: Am I submitting myself to God right now? Asking that one simple question can change the course of our actions. For instance, I may not push for my way with my husband quite so much after submitting my pride to God and allowing Him to work through me. Or I may not get angry when driving to work when someone cuts me off on the highway.

Living out this verse will also impact how you parent your children. Submitting to God and humbling yourself before Him will create a life that is more consistent and full of love.

Father, I want to submit to You in all areas of my life.
I acknowledge that Your way is always better. God,
when I want to manipulate, take over or even give up,
gently remind me to submit to You. I know that when I give up
control, You will lift me up and draw me near to You. Amen.

No favorites

He made no distinction between us and them,
for He purified their hearts by faith.

Acts 15:9

In God's mind, we are all the same. He doesn't play favorites. We tend to think God will love us more than other people if we do good deeds or obey Him, but He loves us all the same. In this Scripture, Paul tells the Jews that God loves the Gentiles as much as He loves the Jews.

We tend to believe that if we go to church, obey God's laws and do good works, then we will gain a higher standing in His sight. It doesn't. God loves us regardless of what we "do" for Him. Actually, we can't "do" anything for God. He loves us because we are His creation.

As you go about your day today, if you find yourself thinking you are better than another person or less than another person, remember you are neither. You are the same as the other person. If you apply this type of thinking to your life every day, then you will stop comparing yourself to others and just start accepting and loving people for who they are. Isn't it wonderful that the God we serve doesn't distinguish between us, but loves us all the same?

Father, thank You for Your love and grace that You so freely give.
I pray that I would put aside my comparing and judgmental
ways, and just love freely like You do. Fill me with Your Holy
Spirit, who is full of compassion and grace. I pray that I will
exhibit all of the fruits of the Holy Spirit each day. Amen.

No fear

And you, son of man, do not be afraid …
Ezekiel 2:6

Fear is a powerful emotion. Fear can twist your mind into believing things that are not true. We as moms can become fearful of so many things: sickness, evil in our world, safety of our children, social media, the Internet, education, nutrition and even our children's future. But God doesn't want us to be fearful. When we are, we aren't trusting Him. If we allow fear to take over and control our lives, then we take our eyes off of God and put them onto our circumstances. God is bigger than anything we will ever encounter and He will direct us in the way we should go.

God commands us throughout the Bible to not be afraid. When we feel fear coming over us, we must remind ourselves that we need not fear – God is with us. Our trust is in a sovereign God, a God who created the entire universe. Our trust is in the One who is very capable of handling our fear. Choose trust over fear. Trust in God will empower you; fear over your circumstances will make you weak and vulnerable to Satan's attacks.

Father, thank You that I don't need to fear even when our world seems to be spinning out of control. Thank You that You are bigger than this world and You have already overcome it. Help me to keep my eyes focused on You. Thank You for Your love and direction in my life and in the lives of my children. Amen.

No grudges

"Go now and leave your life of sin."
John 8:11

The beautiful thing about Jesus is His ability to forgive. Forgiveness is a choice and Jesus always chooses to forgive. The woman referenced in this verse was caught in adultery yet Jesus forgave her.

Is there someone in your life you need to forgive? More importantly, do you need to not hold their wrong behavior over their head? As moms we tend to hold our children's misbehaviors over their heads and constantly recall their bad choices.

Are you holding past mistakes over your husband's head, waiting for him to redeem himself before you will move on? Whatever your expectations are for redemption, it will never be enough. He can never make things right again. You can start the restoration process by forgiving him and by not holding it against him anymore.

Grudges tear families apart. Forgiveness is the first step toward restoration. It is hard to forgive, and you may feel you will never be able to forgive some wrongs. But remember, Christ is in you and He absolutely can forgive, so ask Him to do it for you. Ask Christ to love that person for you, until your emotions can catch up.

Father, I admit I hold grudges against people even though I know it is wrong. Sometimes I just can't help myself. The offenses against me are too great. God, I know You can forgive anything and anyone. You forgave me. Please give me Your forgiving heart and help me to move on. Amen.

No judging zone

*"Stop judging by mere appearances,
but instead judge correctly."*

John 7:24

Do you feel judged as a mom? Do you feel people think you're not doing a good job? Often we feel harshly judged because we measure judgment according to how we judge others. If you are a critical person by nature, then you, by default, will believe that people are critical of you. When we judge others, it's really our own insecurities lashing out at us.

Jesus tells us to stop judging. He is the only true Judge. Jesus looks at the heart of a person and He alone can see true motives or someone's sincerity. If you find yourself criticizing others in your heart, ask for forgiveness.

As you go about your day, be aware of your words and actions. Then ask yourself: Are my words judgmental or kind? Jesus never lowered His standards, but He always showed grace and love.

*Father, please help me to stop looking at others trying
to find fault in what they do. Open my eyes to love those
around me. Help me to celebrate them and what they are doing,
even if it's not the way I would do it. God, take away my
critical nature and replace it with Your love. Amen.*

No remembrances

Their sins and lawless acts I will remember no more.

Hebrews 10:17

The power behind this verse is mind-blowing. If I am a Christian, God doesn't remember my sin and my lawless acts. What? Our human brains can hardly comprehend this thought. We can't comprehend that thought because we hold on to grudges and even remember hurts from twenty years ago. But God is not like us; He loves unconditionally. When He looks at you, He doesn't see your sin, He sees His perfect Son, Jesus. What a beautiful truth.

When Jesus died on the cross, He paid for all your sins. Therefore, there is no reason for Him to remember your sins, because that debt has been paid. What would be the point? Christ paid too great a price for you to keep remembering your sins. The next time your past haunts you and you think you will never be good enough, remember: God doesn't remember your past, He only sees your beautiful future with Him. Embrace that future and walk with Him.

Honestly, when I read this verse I think to myself,
that it is too good to be true. But God, I know it's true.
I know Your love is unconditional and because You loved me
so much, You sent Jesus to pay for my sins. You sent Your
perfect Son to pay for my imperfect life. Thank You! I love You
and am forever thankful that You are my Lord and Savior. Amen.

No turning back

Flee for your lives! Don't look back,
and don't stop anywhere in the plain ...
But Lot's wife looked back, and she became a pillar of salt.
Genesis 19:17, 26

Throughout the Bible, God gives us clear direction and wisdom. He tries to protect us, but sometimes we don't heed His warnings. Lot and his family were fleeing Sodom and Gomorrah because God was destroying these evil cities. The angel warned Lot's family to flee and not to look back. But, like so many of us, Lot's wife couldn't resist the temptation to look back. She chose to take matters into her own hands, not trusting what the angel had said. Unfortunately, her decision to look back one last time became her last.

God is a holy God. He is a loving God, but a righteous God. His Word will ring true every single time. The question is: Do we trust Him? Do we really believe His Word? Don't be like Lot's wife and test God. Believe Him and trust that He wants good for you, not harm (see Jeremiah 29:11). Trust in God today, that He is a loving father, protecting you from harm.

You are a loving Father, who only wants the best for me –
to protect and guide me. I want to live life Your way.
I have tried it my way and my way doesn't work! Open my eyes
to Your will. Teach me. I am willing to learn. Amen.

Noble wife

A wife of noble character who can find?
She is worth far more than rubies. Her husband has full
confidence in her and lacks nothing of value.

Proverbs 31:10-11

After our children are born, life can get out of control. We are filled with so many responsibilities that we sometimes forget the first person in our families – our husbands. Have you ever thought to yourself, He can take care of himself?

Your husband can take care of himself, but he needs you to take care of him, nurture him, love him and to build him up. It's hard, especially with all the demands your children put on you. But remember that your husband will, hopefully, stay with you in the house a lot longer than your children.

How do you take care of him? Keep communication open and free. Even if you are tired from the days' activities, don't forget to ask your husband about his day and tell him about yours. Share your dreams and listen to his. Fight fiercely for your marriage. If you don't, someone else might. Build your husband up with your words. Be his biggest cheerleader. Men need the respect of the women they love. If you are struggling in this area, share your concerns with God. Ask Him to fill your heart with a renewed love for your husband.

Father, thank You for my husband. I admit I have allowed him to slip from number one to about number four in my life. God, give me the courage to confess that to my husband and teach me how to rekindle our love. I realize my husband needs to come first. Give me energy when I have none and make my efforts count. Amen.

Not alone

But I have raised you up for this very purpose,
that I might show you My power and that My name
might be proclaimed in all the earth.

Exodus 9:16

God chose Moses to deliver His people out of slavery. Moses didn't feel equipped for the job that had been assigned to him, but he trusted in God. Not only did God want to free the Israelites, He also wanted to show the whole world that He was Lord. That powerful and mighty God still lives today and He has not changed.

God wants His power to be proclaimed and what better way for His power to be seen than in the life of a mom. Being a mom is hard. So many times I have been brought to the end of myself, realizing that I did not have what it took to do the job well or even finish the job. I am gently reminded in this verse that I may not have the power and strength, but God does. He has given me my children for this very purpose – to train them, teach them and love them.

God will give me what I need when I need it.

Father, as I go about this day, I pray I will be aware of Your
presence, obey Your commands and serve You in all that I do.
I ask You to give me what I lack. Fill me with Your Holy Spirit,
Your joy, Your patience and Your unconditional love. Thank You
for wanting a relationship with me and for pursuing me. Amen.

Obedience is the key

To obey is better than sacrifice,
and to heed is better than the fat of rams.

I Samuel 15:22

There is nothing better than an obedient child. When a child obeys their mother, they display respect for her. In order to obey, a child must choose to submit their will to their mom's will. Obedience reveals to a mom that her child agrees that she is the boss and that they will comply with her decisions. In order for most children to obey, they have to feel safe and to know in their hearts that their moms want the best for them. Therefore, obeying is not a sacrifice, but a win-win situation for everyone.

Obedience is one of the major qualities God looks for in His children as well. A heart that is obedient to the Lord is a heart that is yielded to God. In order for any of us to yield our hearts to God, we must submit our wills to God's will and our way of doing things to His way of doing things. This submission takes respect for God, to believe that He is completely sovereign and trustworthy.

Obeying God is simple. First, you must trust Him; then you obey Him.

Father, thank You for this day and thank You for Your love.
I want to trust You with all my heart and to submit my will
to Yours. I know You are faithful, but sometimes I doubt
because I can't see You face-to-face. Give me faith that
goes beyond sight. Help me to trust You. Amen.

One brick at a time

Love is patient, love is kind …
1 Corinthians 13:4

Marriage is like building a house. After the foundation has been set and the framing, plumbing, electricity and walls are completed, you must build the brick wall. The brick wall is the key to building a great-looking house that is strong, and protected from the outside elements. In this metaphor, the bricks are our words and how we communicate to our spouses.

We often work hard at laying our foundations and the actual building of our houses, but we don't pay attention to the words we speak to our husbands every day. We think, I should be honest and be able to say what I want to my husband. That's true, but we should always measure our words and the effects those words might have. Just because you are married and have a close relationship doesn't mean you can say whatever you want without consequences.

Think about it this way … with every kind, loving and compassionate word that comes out of your mouth, you are laying a brick on the frame of your marriage. Likewise, with every unkind, sarcastic, cutting word you say, you are removing a brick from your house.

Father, please give me Your love for husband.
I can't love unconditionally, but I know You can.
I submit my life to You! I want to love the way You love.
Help me to build my house well, one brick at a time. Amen.

One day

He will wipe every tear from their eyes.
There will be no more death or mourning or crying or pain,
for the old order of things has passed away.

Revelation 21:4

❧ —————◦————— ❧

We try so desperately to make this world perfect, but it's not. We want there to never be wars, death, cancer, broken families or any kind of pain. Unfortunately, that is not the world we live in. One day, that world will come. One day, God will wipe away our tears away. He will walk with us and live among us. He will take away all pain.

Until that day comes, focus on God during the hard days. Cry out to Him for wisdom and discernment on how to navigate this world. Ask God to give you what you need each day until He returns.

Children also desire life to always be fair, with no pain and no hard times. Remind your children, as well, that one day what they dream for will come true. Until then, we wait patiently and look to God to get us through our days.

•••————◦◦•◦◦————•••

Father, thank You that one day You will live among us
and there will be no pain. I anxiously wait for that day.
Until then, I want to live my life to the fullest and to bring glory
to You in all that I do. Help me to live my life full of grace
and love in the present, but always looking forward to
my future with You in a perfect world. Amen.

Our guide

But when He, the Spirit of truth, comes, He will guide you into all the truth. He will not speak on His own; He will speak only what He hears, and He will tell you what is yet to come.

John 16:13

We have a Helper and a Guide, and His name is the Holy Spirit. When Jesus left this earth to return to heaven, He did not leave us alone. He left a Comforter (see John 14:26), whose main job is to teach us all things.

We strive to live life in our own strength, but God never intended it to be that way. God knows it's too hard to live the Christian life on our own. So, in His loving way, He gave us the Holy Spirit. The Holy Spirit will teach us, guide us, reveal to us and bring Christ's words to our minds.

The Holy Spirit is always directing us to Jesus, who is the way, the truth and the life (see John 14:6). Instead of relying on your own strength, rely on the gift that God gave you – the Holy Spirit.

Father, I like to think I can do life by myself, but I'm realizing I can't. Teach me to rely on the Holy Spirit. Show me how to submit my will to Yours. I want to learn. You are the potter, and I am the clay. Take my life and do with it what You will. Amen.

Overcoming the world

Who is it that overcomes the world?
Only the one who believes that Jesus is the Son of God.

I John 5:5

As a mom, do you look around and think to yourself, Everyone seems to have it all together, so I must get it together? Do you put on your game face for others so they will see you as a strong, independent mom who knows all the answers to parenting, but in the meantime you are praying that no one will see that you are struggling? Guess what? No one has all the answers except God. And in Him, you don't have to be tough or independent.

God actually likes it when you realize your weakness, because then He shines through. In God's strength is where you will find your victory. No mom is perfect. No mom has all the answers. Therefore, reach out to God, cry out to Him, and tell Him you need His direction and guidance.

What an amazing gift God has given us moms. He is our strength, our support and through Him we will find strength. We don't have to have all the answers. What a blessing! Sit for a minute and think that through. You are a perfect mom just the way you are. The only thing you need is God.

Father, You are too good to me! You take my insecurity,
my weakness and my inability to parent well, and You give me
grace, love and wisdom. In You I have everything I will ever need
to be the parent I want to be. Thank You! I am blown away by
Your goodness and unconditional love for me. Amen.

Owned by God

You are not your own; you were bought at a price.
1 Corinthians 6:20

So many times, we get caught up in our rights. We demand the right to be heard, the right to be right, the right to our way, the right to be respected. The list goes on and on. But the Bible teaches us that if we are Christians, we don't have rights. We are not our own any longer; we belong to Jesus. We have been bought and paid for by Jesus and His shed blood on the cross.

Our human natures resist this total surrender. We argue, "I must stand up for myself; I can't lose my voice." But in God's economy, it's better to lose your voice and gain His voice. It's better to submit my will to His will. Only then will I find true happiness and experience joy to the fullest. We are not giving up our rights. We're just exchanging them for God's plan for our lives.

You will never go wrong following God's way. His way is always better.

Father, I need to remember that I was bought at a price.
I need to remember that it is no longer I who live, but You
who lives in me. Jesus, as I go about my day today, gently remind
me that I was bought at a price, that You want the best for me –
better than I could ever accomplish on my own. Amen.

Pain now equals peace later

No discipline seems pleasant at the time, but painful.
Later on, however, it produces a harvest of righteousness
and peace for those who have been trained by it.

Hebrews 12:11

As hard as discipline is to put into practice and as painful as it can be both for the mom and the child, the end goal must be kept in mind. If the end goal is to raise a child who is well adjusted, loving and has a healthy outlook on life, then discipline is not only needed, it is required.

This verse in Hebrews tells us that even though discipline is painful, it brings a harvest of righteousness and peace. Do you want to give your children the gifts of righteousness and peace? I would imagine every mom's answer would be yes.

Choose to push past the pain of discipline and think of your end goal.

Father, give me the strength to discipline my children even though it's hard. Give me discernment to see the ramifications of my children's actions. Lord, I love my children so much that I do not want to skip over this important part of being a parent. Amen.

Patience is key

*A hot-tempered person stirs up conflict,
but the one who is patient calms a quarrel.*

Proverbs 15:18

It's so easy to be hot-tempered in today's society. Life goes at such a fast pace that it's easy to get angry when the drive-thru line is taking ten minutes longer than it should. Where does losing my temper get me? I only stir up dissension when I allow my temper to get the best of me.

This verse also applies to my family life. How many times have I had a hot temper concerning my husband or my children? Every single time I allow my temper to rule my emotions, I cause dissension in my marriage and in my relationship with my children.

Patience is the key to calm quarrels. Patience is also a fruit of the Spirit, which means I cannot manufacture it on my own. I must abide with God and allow His Holy Spirit to work through me. Then the fruit of patience will be obvious in my life. See how that works? It's not by me willing myself to be patient with my children; it's by my dependence on God.

*Father, my prayer is to be aware of my temper and to be patient.
I acknowledge that I cannot produce patience on my own,
but I need the Holy Spirit to bear it in my life. I submit
my life to You; mold me into who You want me to be.
Keep me ever mindful of whether I am bringing dissension
into my home or making it a peaceful place to live. Amen.*

Peace and security

*He strengthens the bars of your gates
and blesses your people within you. He grants peace
to your borders and satisfies you with the finest of wheat.*

Psalm 147:13-14

God brings security to our lives. When we set boundaries, our relationships become stronger, because we understand where we stop and others begin. In Psalms, we are given a promise from God that He will bring us strength and He will bring peace to our borders.

Think about that for a minute: you have a God that protects you from your enemies. You have a God that is looking out for you, watching for those that want to harm you, and His goal is to bring you provision and peace. We scheme and plan all of our lives striving to get ahead, but God is taking care of us. We need to trust in Him. Christians should be the most joyful group of people because we have a Protector.

Accept God's provision and protection in your life, allowing His peace to flow out of you.

*Father, thank You for bringing Your strength into my world
and for giving me peace where I have set my boundaries.
I pray that I will be mindful of Your presence throughout
my day today and that I will offer my praise up to You. Amen.*

Peace with God

But Joseph said to them, "Don't be afraid …
You intended to harm me, but God intended if for good …"
Genesis 50:19-20

God is a God of peace even during uncertain times and circumstances. Sometimes we can feel that God has fallen asleep on the job, that He is not aware, nor does He care, what is happening in our lives. That way of thinking is false. God does care! He cares intensely for each of us. Through the hard times, God is there. He has not forgotten about us. What is meant to harm or destroy us, God will use for good. We must trust Him.

Begin to pray that you will be able to see God during the dark times. Ask Him to show Himself to you. God is a loving Father who wants you to trust Him. He is always working on your behalf, because you are His child. Think about how much you parent out of love for your children, always desiring the best for them, yet your children don't understand why or think you're unfair. It's the same with God, yet He has a distinct advantage; He knows your future and He intends it for good.

Father, give me childlike faith. Help me to always see
Your love for me and to not doubt You. Wrap Your arms
around me when my days are dark and whisper in my ear that
You love me and will carry me through the hard times. Amen.

Peaceful days

In peace I will lie down and sleep,
for You alone, Lᴏʀᴅ, make me dwell in safety.

Psalm 4:8

There is nothing better in a mom's world than a child who sleeps through the night. We pray for this gift, especially when our children are babies. But even as our babies grow into young teenagers, we keep praying for peaceful days and nights for them.

We can't control our children; we can't make them do anything. So, where do we find peace during the tumultuous times? We can look to the Lord. God is with us even during the hardest of days and the longest of nights. He can bring peace into your life if you allow Him to.

Since you can't control your children, focus on what you can control – yourself. Ask God to bring the peace that goes beyond understanding (see Philippians 4:7) into your life today. Give Him your burdens in exchange for His peace.

Father, thank You that in You, I can have peace.
Thank You that even when my world is turned upside down,
You will give me peace and allow me to feel safe and secure.
In my own flesh, I don't know how to acquire such peace,
but You can give me that peace, so I look to You today
to fill my life and soul with Your peace. Amen.

People of wisdom

Walk with the wise and become wise,
for a companion of fools suffers harm.
Proverbs 13:20

Wisdom is found in God. James tells us to ask God for wisdom and He will give it to us abundantly (see James 1:5). Ask God for wisdom and, in the meantime, surround yourself with wise people. There is no greater asset to have than moms that are a few steps ahead of you … moms that have already been through the potty-training days, the first days of school, the first sleepovers, the first dates, the first days of high school and college. It is prudent to surround yourself with wise people to guide you through this journey of motherhood.

In order to benefit from wise people, you need to humble yourself and realize that you don't know everything. There is no shame in that. The shame comes when you don't ask and then operate out of ignorance.

Ask your mom, grandmother, small group leader or your children's Sunday school teacher. These women are usually willing to help you and if they don't have the answers, they will help you find someone who does.

Father, thank You for giving wisdom to all who ask.
I am asking now for the wisdom to know how to parent effectively.
God, until I get there, bring someone into my life who will share
her life experiences and who will always point me to You. Amen.

Perfect peace

You will keep in perfect peace those whose minds are steadfast, because they trust in You.

Isaiah 26:3

⤐———⤏

Peace in a mom's life can seem like an impossible dream. What does peace even look like when there is constant noise, talking, questions being asked, and bodies jumping, hitting and tugging on you? Usually a mom can't even go to the bathroom by herself without a knock on the door asking when she will be finished. Moms dream about peaceful days, when the house will be quiet and she can read a book in peace or when children are not arguing. We long for peace, but sometimes in order to find peace, we need to change our perspective.

Whether your children are toddlers or teenagers, life is usually not calm. God, however, can bring peace into any situation. God can quiet a storm with His mere presence. Ask Him to change your perspective during this season and to meet your need for peace. He might not send you away to a quiet place; He might keep you right where you are and instead give you a peaceful spirit in the middle of your chaos. Only God can do that, so we must look to Him. He promises us perfect peace. Ask Him for that today …

••———————••

Father, just the thought of gaining peace in the midst of my hectic days makes me want to do whatever I need to do in order to get it. God, if all I have to do is set my mind on You, then I will do that. In You, I will find my peace. Thank You, Lord, for promising me peace and for meeting me where I am. Amen.

Perfect shepherd

He tends His flock like a shepherd:
He gathers the lambs in His arms and carries them close
to His heart; He gently leads those that have young.

Isaiah 40:11

God understands that our days are consumed with taking care of our children. The busyness of a toddler's life alone makes a mom's life full. Take heart. God "gently" leads those that have young.

We need to change our expectations and focus on one verse per week. Allow that verse to soak into your soul. Write it out and place it somewhere in your home where you will see it often and read it often. Allow the Holy Spirit to teach you the meaning of that verse and how it applies to your life.

Then, instead of having long prayers, have conversations with God throughout your day. Invite Christ into every aspect of your life and talk to Him about your day. Tell God when you are discouraged, aggravated, frustrated and deflated because you don't know how to parent your child. God is interested in all of those details and He wants to carry those burdens for you. The last part of changing your expectations is to quit trying to be a super mom and to start "resting" in the Lord.

Father, thank You that You understand my life. I don't even understand the whole scope of it at times, but I am so thankful that You do, and that You promise to take care of me and gently lead me. I need You! God, show me how I can spend time with You. Help me to adjust to this new pace of life. Amen.

Perfectly capable

His divine power has given us everything we need
for a godly life through our knowledge of Him
who called us by His own glory and goodness.

2 Peter 1:3

So many times we feel like we come up short as mothers, becoming impatient when our children don't listen or do what we ask. We end up asking ourselves whether we are even qualified to be a mother. It pushes most of us to a place of insecurity and doubt.

There is good news though! God has already given you everything you need to be the perfect mom for your children. You already have patience, love and self-control tucked deep inside of you by God. The key is to stay connected to God and to seek Him for wisdom and discernment. So many times we forget this truth and we try to do it all in our own strength. We cannot parent effectively in our own strength. It's too much! We need to grow in our relationship with God and ask Him for His power and love. Only then will we see fruit in our parenting.

Lord, thank You that You give me everything I need to be a
wonderful mom. Because of You, I don't have to worry about how
to be a good mother. I already am. Thank You, Lord, for providing
for me even before I knew I needed it. Remind me to depend on
You and not to try to parent in my own strength. Amen.

Perfectly made

I praise You because I am fearfully and wonderfully made;
Your works are wonderful, I know that full well.

Psalm 139:14

We are all created and made exactly the way God wanted us to be here on this earth. You may look around and think to yourself, Why didn't God give me blue eyes, or long blonde hair, or make me a bit taller or shorter. But in God's wisdom and His perfection, He made you just the way you are and there is a reason behind His creation.

When my children were young, they would compare themselves to their siblings, always wanting what the other had. I had to teach them that they were created the way they were for a reason and God does not make mistakes. My youngest daughter wore glasses as young as 15 months. As she grew up, she hated her glasses, because she didn't feel pretty in them. Sometimes people made fun of her. Because she wore glasses, she started to see the world from a different perspective and developed a tender heart for people who were different.

As a mom, teach your children this verse in Psalms that God created them in a very special way and we are all precious to Him. Celebrate your uniqueness and teach your children to embrace their own distinct DNA.

Father, thank You for creating me.
Thank You that You don't make mistakes.
When I have days when I feel ugly or not good enough,
please remind me of this truth. I need to be grateful
and celebrate the ME that You created. Amen.

Perseverance builds character

So do not throw away your confidence;
it will be richly rewarded. You need to persevere
so that when you have done the will of God,
you will receive what He has promised.

Hebrews 10:35-36

Teaching your child perseverance is never an easy task. Children have a tendency to try something and if it is hard or doesn't go well, they want to give up. But perseverance is a character trait that will benefit them their whole life, so it is important that you teach your child how to persevere.

When your child wants to give up, wants to not work hard to advance to the next level, try to encourage them to stick it out. As a parent you can teach them how hard work can pay off and reap many benefits and rewards. Be sure to share with them that you understand it is hard. Share with your child a time when you wanted to give up, but you chose to work hard and persevere.

When your child does finish the job or sport or music training, praise them for it. Take that opportunity to celebrate and reflect on what they have accomplished. When they think back to how they finished the job, they'll be more confident for the next one. Continue to grow their confidence by going through this exercise repeatedly.

Father, as I persevere in my job as a mom, I pray that I will teach this lesson to my child. Please give me endurance. When I want to give up, show me the benefits of hanging in there. Thank You for Your patience with me. I couldn't do this job without You. Amen.

Perspective of wisdom

Do not be wise in your own eyes;
fear the Lord and shun evil.

Proverbs 3:7

We are not to consider ourselves wise. Instead, we should look to God and know He is wise. As humans, pride easily sets in and we can begin to believe that we are better than we are — a trap that leads to heartache. Focus your mind on God and His wisdom. When you ask Him for wisdom (see James 1:5), He will give it to you, but always acknowledge where it comes from.

As you go about your journey as a mom, try to steer clear of the thought that you have it all together. Humble yourself before your heavenly Father and ask Him how to parent your child, what your child needs from you, and what is the most effective way to teach them. God has all the answers, not you.

God created each child and knit your son or daughter together in your womb (see Psalm 139:13). Why not ask the Creator? He is eager to show you the way.

Father, thank You for being wise and for allowing me to come to
You each day and ask for Your wisdom. Teach me how to be
the kind of parent You want me to be. I want to train up
my children in the way they should go, so they will be healthy
and loving adults. Please teach me how. Amen.

Pity party

*I am worn out from my groaning. All night long I flood
my bed with weeping and drench my couch with tears.
My eyes grow weak with sorrow; they fail because of all my foes.*

Psalm 6:6-7

Moms witness pity parties every week. When our children don't get their way, they pitch little fits of rage and then they begin to feel sorry for themselves. Teenagers are the worst, because they believe that the whole world is against them.

Actually, we as moms can also put on good pity parties. You know it's true. Your husband gets a trip to another country – all expenses paid, stays at a five-star hotel, eats steak dinners, etc. We begin our pity party: "I'm stuck at home with the children, again eating hot dogs, and mac and cheese." We complain that the never-ending job of a mom is way harder than we ever realized and it's not fair.

Many times, good and hard run on parallel lines. We say to ourselves, "This is so hard!" but then we get to experience this deep love for our children and we say, "This is so good." Being a parent is so rewarding because you work hard at it and then you get to see your children grow into mature, responsible, loving adults. There is nothing better. Try to remember to resist the pity party and to focus on the reward of motherhood!

*Father, help me to stop feeling sorry for myself. I believe it's okay
to cry out to You and share my feelings of exhaustion and emptiness, but I don't want to stay there. Show me the "good" things
about being a mom and help me stay focused on those things.
With Your help I can do this very hard job of being a mom. Amen.*

Plans that go God's way

Many are the plans in a person's heart,
but it is the LORD's purpose that prevails.

Proverbs 19:21

We make plans all day long. We plan our meals; we plan the order in which we will run our errands; we plan our vacations; we plan our next project around the house. Moms plan and plan and plan all day long. Sometimes our plans don't go the way we intended. When this happens, do you ever think that God might have had a hand in the change? At first we think, This is terrible, but later realize we would have never gotten where we are without that change? God is in all of our plans and His plan is always better than ours.

The next time you find your plans taking an unexpected left turn, say to God, "Okay, what do You have for me?" Instead of fighting with Him or trying to convince Him that He made a mistake or He was sleeping on the job, ask Him what purpose lies with the unexpected left turn. You might be surprised and realize that His plan is way better than yours. It's better to allow God to have His way than to fight to accomplish your plans.

Father, thank You that Your plan is always better. My prayer
today is that I will live a life always expecting the "left turns"
and not be surprised by them. I pray that I will be open to Your
will and stop fighting You. Teach me how to be open minded with
my life. I have decided to follow You in all things. Amen.

Pleasing God

*And without faith it is impossible to please God,
because anyone who comes to Him must believe that He exists
and that He rewards those who earnestly seek Him.*

Hebrews 11:6

So many times I wonder how to please God. The answer is simple: I can please God by having faith and believing He is who He says He is. If I have faith, then I believe 100 percent in God's word and His promises. I will take His wisdom to heart and trust Him.

As a mom, I understand this, because I want my children to have faith in me. I want them to believe with all their hearts that I love them, want the best for them and would go to the ends of the earth for them. But depending on the circumstances in my children's lives, they may not feel that I want the best for them. A child could interpret my protection as negative and, therefore, believe that I am harming them, not helping them.

The idea is the same with God. Am I going to put my faith in my circumstances and believe that when things are good, God is good? Or am I going to put my faith in God and believe that regardless of my circumstances God is good and He will work all things together for good? Circumstances will change, but God and His love for me will never change.

*Father, grow my faith in You to where I don't change
depending on my circumstances, but I remain true in my faith
in You. I want to please You, Father. I want to seek You with all
my heart and trust You for all my needs. Thank You for Your
patience with me and for Your unending love. Amen.*

September

Power of God's Word

For the word of God is living and active. Sharper than any double-edged sword, it penetrates even to dividing soul and spirit, joints and marrow; it judges the thoughts and attitudes of the heart.

Hebrews 4:12

Many of us only think of the Bible on Sundays or during Christmas when we hear the story of the birth of Jesus. Some people refer to the Bible as a Book of interesting stories that chronicle the history of the Jewish nation and the birth, life, death and resurrection of Jesus. But the Bible is so much more. God's Word is alive.

In the life of a mom, the Bible can be the difference between living your life full of joy and freedom, and being bound up with guilt and fear. Through the Bible you are able to learn who God is, what His character looks like, what He values and treasures, and what He detests. In God's Word you learn what it looks like to walk with Christ and how walking with Him gives you power. In God's Word you learn how much your heavenly Father loves you and how good He is.

If your Bible has been sitting on your bedside table gathering dust, try dusting it off and start putting into practice some of the great wisdom shared in those pages. Ask God to give you an understanding of what you are reading and to make the Scriptures come alive as you read them.

Father, thank You for Your Word. Thank You for not leaving us here on this earth without a way to connect with You. Through Scripture we are able to learn more about You and how You operate. God, I pray that You would give me a hunger for Your Word and an understanding of what I read. I want Your Word to transform my life and how I live every day. Amen.

Powerful words

"... speaking to one another with psalms, hymns, and songs from the Spirit. Sing and make music from your heart to the Lord, always giving thanks to God the Father for everything."

Ephesians 5:19-20

Think about how many words you speak each day to your children. Think of all the opportunities to speak encouraging, uplifting words ... words that give life. Ask yourself:

* Are my words harsh or gentle?
* Are my words loving or angry?
* Are my words sarcastic?
* Are my words uplifting?
* Are my words glorifying God?

God calls us to speak to each other with gentle, loving, kind words. We should always be mindful of what our words are toward others, especially our children. We should guard our tongues and be ever aware if we are breaking someone down or building them up with our words.

Today, as you go about your day, be aware of your speech. At the end of the day, ask yourself: Did my child see Jesus through my words today? Start each day anew. Remember, a mom's words are very powerful indeed.

I pray that I would be very mindful of my words today, Lord. If I get frustrated and angry with my children, remind me that I need to hold my tongue and not lash out. Replace my anger with Your love and grace. You give me an endless amount of grace throughout my day. Please help me to extend the same grace to those around me. Amen.

Prayer is powerful

So Peter was kept in prison,
but the church was earnestly praying to God for him.

Acts 12:5

Prayer is essential for parents regarding their children. We as moms need to be praying earnestly every day for our children. The pressures and temptations that our children face today are greater than at any other time. They are constantly being tempted, seduced and brainwashed, and we need to be on our knees, lifting them up in prayer each day.

Peter was in prison in chains, but the church did not give up on him. God heard the prayers of the church and rescued Peter. As a mom you have the opportunity to lift your children up to your heavenly Father. Ask God to protect them, to keep them safe from harm. When praying for your children, ask God to reveal to you specifically what your child needs from you.

Pray for a great friend for your son or daughter, for godly mentors and for teachers that will invest in their lives. Ask God for wisdom as you parent your children.

Father, thank You for the blessing of my children.
I lift my children up to You and ask that You cover them
with Your love and protection. Lord, You know exactly
what they need and I pray that You will meet them where they are.
I ask in the name of Jesus that You would reveal Yourself to my
children and show them Your deep love for them. Amen.

Prayer life

*"My prayer is not that You take them out of the world
but that You protect them from the evil one."*
John 17:15

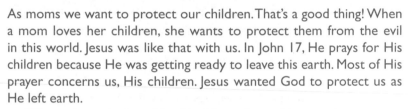

As moms we want to protect our children. That's a good thing! When a mom loves her children, she wants to protect them from the evil in this world. Jesus was like that with us. In John 17, He prays for His children because He was getting ready to leave this earth. Most of His prayer concerns us, His children. Jesus wanted God to protect us as He left earth.

We need to take Jesus' lead and learn from this verse how to pray for our children. We can only protect our children to a certain extent. We can't lock them in the house and keep them from experiencing life, but we can pray earnestly and regularly for them. Jesus prayed that we would be protected from the evil one. Ask God to protect your children from Satan and his schemes. Ask God to give you wisdom and discernment as you parent your children. He knows what the future holds.

There is peace that comes from prayer. Reach out today and begin a prayer campaign for your family.

Father, thank You that Jesus prayed for me. He knew exactly what I needed and He knew You would provide it. I lift my family up to You in prayer, and ask for Your guidance and protection. I can't be with my children all the time, but You can. I give them to You and I place my trust in You. Amen.

Prayer of Hannah

Then Hannah prayed and said: "My heart rejoices in the LORD; in the LORD my horn is lifted high. My mouth boasts over my enemies, for I delight in Your deliverance."

1 Samuel 2:1

Hannah was so grateful to God for the birth of her son. She had experienced great sorrow in being barren for her entire life and then God answered her prayer by giving her a son, named Samuel. She is thanking and praising God in this verse because she knows her deliverer was God.

God, the Creator of all things, blesses us with children and we need to give all praise and glory to Him. How many times as a mom do I take my children for granted? A mother that is barren and finally conceives or adopts never takes her child for granted, because she realizes how precious that little life is.

Give your child a sweet hug today and thank God for the miracle of life.

Father, thank You for the blessing of my children. I don't want to take even one day for granted concerning my children. Each day is a gift from You. My prayer is that I will treasure these days and be a great steward of the gift You have given me. Amen.

Preparing for battle

Therefore, put on the armor of God,
so that when the day of evil comes, you may be able to stand
your ground, and after you have done everything, to stand.

Ephesians 6:13

We are in a spiritual battle every day; we have an enemy who is dedicated to destroying our peace and joy. But take heart! Jesus has overcome the world. In this verse, God gives us the recipe to victory. We need to memorize this recipe and teach it to our children. We need to be teaching our children that there will be trouble in life, but we are not left alone to fight. God is with us and in Him we will have victory.

We should be putting on the armor of God daily. The armor includes:

* The belt of truth
* The breastplate of righteousness
* Feet fit with readiness that comes from the gospel of peace
* The shield of faith
* The helmet of salvation
* The sword of the Spirit, which is the Word of God.

Is the war raging and you feel defeated, isolated and alone? Or are you claiming victory, ready for battle, ready to rely on God? Our victory lies in using the armor God has given us.

Father, give me strength to call on You throughout my day. I pray that I will realize I can't fight this fight alone. I pray that I will wake up every day and my first thought will be, God, fill me with Your Spirit; take this day and do with it as You will. Amen.

Pressures of life

People were overwhelmed with amazement.
"He has done everything well," they said.
"He even makes the deaf hear and the mute speak."

Mark 7:37

Life can be overwhelming at times and moms can feel like they are constantly under pressure. We feel pressure to raise perfect children, create the perfect home and look perfect wherever we go – to be perfect! It doesn't work though, does it? The reason it doesn't work is because we're not perfect creatures. But be encouraged, Christ is in us and we are in Him, and He is perfect.

You need to give yourself a break and admit once and for all that you can't do it all. You need to remove that pressure. You can allow Jesus Christ to live through you. Jesus will fill you with His Spirit and you will be able to accomplish more than you will ever be able to do on your own. The beauty of Christ doing it through you is that you will have peace.

What this looks like in everyday terms is walking with Jesus daily. Lay your burdens at His feet. Keep your eyes focused solely on Him. Ask Him to remove the constant pressure to be perfect. Ask Him what He wants you to accomplish each day – His "list" might look very different from yours.

Father, thank You that I can live my life in You and that I don't have to perform or be perfect in order for You to love me. God, show me how to walk closely with You and show me the most important things to pursue in my life. Help me keep my eyes on You and take this life one day at a time. Amen.

Promise from God

"Then you will call on Me and come and pray to Me, and I will listen to you. You will seek Me and find Me when you seek Me with all your heart. I will be found by you," declares the LORD.

Jeremiah 29:12-14

Do you ever feel like God is nowhere to be found? You pray and pray, but you feel like your prayers only reach the ceiling and then fall flat on the floor. God understands these feelings and He has given us all a comforting answer. In Jeremiah, God gives us the promise that if we seek Him with all of our hearts, we will find Him.

The key to the verse is seeking God with all of your heart. Is there anything in your heart that is blocking your path to God? It could be wanting your way over God's way, your stubborn will, a grudge you are holding against someone or unforgiveness.

Any of these traits could be an obstacle that hinders you from seeking God with all your heart. He is ready and willing to be found, but you can't play games with Him. Remove any roadblocks and be honest with God – He is waiting.

Father, thank You that even though You are a holy God, You are still willing to have a relationship with me. I pray that You would reveal to me anything blocking my path to You. If there is, give me the strength to deal with it so that I may seek You with all of my heart. I want to be heard by You and to walk with You. Amen.

Proud father no matter what

*"So he got up and went to his father. But while he was still
a long way off, his father saw him and was filled
with compassion for him; he ran to his son,
threw his arms around him and kissed him."*

Luke 15:20

We are proud of our children; we just can't help it! From the moment they are born, we are filled with love and pride. We try not to be one of "those" parents, constantly bragging about our children, but deep down we want to shout from the rooftops, "I love my children and they are awesome!"

Our heavenly Father feels the same way about us. He loves us so much that He moves heaven and earth to have a relationship with us. Even when we mess up, He is still there for us, running toward us with open arms. How comforting! How powerful! Think about it: if we fully believed that God would always be on our side, no matter what we did, it would change the way we think, act and live.

The story of the Prodigal Son is a beautiful picture of God's love for us. Embrace the grace that God so generously gives to you. Soak in His love and teach your children from a young age that God loves them beyond measure!

*Father, thank You for Your love. Thank You for Your grace
and mercy that You give so abundantly. I pray that I will truly
believe and embrace the depths of Your love for me. Father,
guide me in teaching Your great love to my children. I want
them to know beyond a doubt Your infinite love for them. Amen.*

Putting your family first

*He must manage his own family well and see
that his children obey him, and he must do so in a manner
worthy of full respect. (If anyone does not know how to manage
his own family, how can he take care of God's church?)*

I Timothy 3:4-5

We talk a lot about the need to put others first and to not be selfish, to give and be generous. A balance is needed though. Sometimes your family needs you to put them first. Sometimes it's hard to know when and sometimes you don't see it until it's too late. As the mom you are the barometer for your family. You need to gauge when you need to rally the troops to serve and give, and when you need to circle inward and focus on your own family.

When to dial back and focus on your family:

* When your children are young, you operate on empty most days. This is not the time to be serving others.
* When your children are teenagers times can be very trying, but they don't have to be. Stay engaged with your teenagers. In order to do that, you may need to dial back your extracurricular activities.

As the above Scripture says, you have to focus on your own family before going out to help others and to do God's work. Ask God to help you keep that balance.

*Father, keeping my life in balance is hard and I need You
to show me how to maintain that balance. I shouldn't just
focus on my family and forget about the world around me,
and I shouldn't only focus on others and forget about my family.
God, guide me and give me wisdom. Amen.*

Real guilt or false guilt?

Therefore, there is now no condemnation
for those who are in Christ Jesus.

Romans 8:1

❖

Feeling guilty seems like it's part of the job description of a mom. If our child falls and scrapes his knee, we feel guilty that we were not watching him well enough. If we put our child in daycare and she gets sick, we beat ourselves up because we are working outside the home.

At some point, however, we have to break this cycle of guilt. Feeling responsible for everything that happens to your child is not healthy. One question you can ask yourself is: Is this real guilt or false guilt? Real guilt comes from committing a sin, having done something morally wrong (e.g. lying, stealing, slander, adultery). False guilt is when we have not committed a sin, but we "feel" bad (not buying your child the toy, not going outside to play). These are not sins you have committed, but somehow they still make us feel guilty.

Guilt, whether false or real, has no place in our lives. The verse in Romans boldly states that there is no place for condemnation or false guilt. It's time to abolish this cycle of self-condemnation and live free.

❖

Father, I desperately want to be a good mom.
I realize that sometimes being a good mom means
I need to say no. But, Lord, the guilt comes in a
massive wave when I say no. Help me to say no when
I need to say no and please take away my guilt. Amen.

Reaping and sowing

A man reaps what he sows.
Galatians 6:7

If you are sowing a life that never slows down, you will reap shallow relationships with your children. If you are spending time with your children, you will reap the benefit of knowing each child. As a mom, the sooner you realize you can't do it all, the sooner you will relax and release the huge burden so many moms carry.

Begin to develop the mindset of sowing and reaping. If you are sowing a nonstop pace, don't be surprised when your children grow up and don't have time for you. You reap what you sow. If you don't teach the value of slowing down and resting, then your children will not grow up realizing that rest is an important part of life.

We get so busy that we forget there are consequences to our actions. Take some time today to ask God to show you the areas of your life in which you need to slow down. Listen to Him and take heart; today is a good day to start a new healthy habit of slowing down.

Father, open my eyes to what You see in my life and give me the courage to act on what You reveal to me. I want to sow good things for my family. I want to reap a beautiful harvest. I can only do that with Your direction and strength. Amen.

Renewed spirit

Create in me a pure heart,
O God, and renew a steadfast spirit within me.
Psalm 51:10

During our journey of motherhood, it's easy to become disillusioned and downtrodden, thinking there's no hope for the younger generation in today's society. We can allow fear to creep in and control our minds. When we allow those thoughts to take over, we are operating out of fear and not faith in our Almighty God.

When you find your heart becoming cynical, pray this prayer in Psalms. Ask God to create in you "a pure heart", a heart that believes the best of people and loves everyone.

Ask God to renew your spirit and to keep it focused on Him, not the world. You can't change the world; it's an evil place. But Jesus has overcome the world. In Jesus, you will find peace and the courage to keep moving forward.

Father, my heart is not pure, but full of fear and disbelief.
Please create in me a pure heart. I look around
and only see evil in this world, and fear for my children.
I know that's not how I need to live my life. Renew a steadfast
spirit within me, one that will look to You and believe in You.
Fill me with Your Holy Spirit and Your love for everyone. Amen.

Rescue mission

So I have come down to rescue them from the hand of the Egyptians and to bring them up out of that land into a good and spacious land, a land flowing with milk and honey.

Exodus 3:8

Do you need God to rescue you? Is your life reeling out of control and you feel as though you're spiraling downward? God loves to rescue His children. He loves to bring you out of your "desert land," whether it be marital problems, troubled children, financial debt or sickness. God hears your cry and He will go before you this day.

This world is full of trouble and we are not exempt from its pain and suffering, but Jesus promises us that He has overcome the world and He will get us through it. No matter what your circumstances are right now, God is greater. He will bring you out of your sparse and dry land, and take you to a good place – a place of milk and honey. Trust in Him.

The Israelites had a difficult journey and they questioned God's provision, but God was faithful. He was faithful then and He is faithful now. Trust Him today.

Father, thank You for Your faithfulness.
Thank You for being a God who rescues. Thank You
that You want good things for me and that You will
deliver me from this season. Help me to stay focused on You
and to see You even in the midst of pain and suffering. Amen.

Respect in marriage

However, each one of you also must love his wife as he loves himself, and the wife must respect her husband.

Ephesians 5:33

One of the main difficulties in marriage lies in the fact that you have two people living together, each trying to get his or her own way. In order for a marriage to work, both parties have to submit to one another in love. They need to give each other respect. Giving love comes naturally to women, just as giving respect comes naturally to men. But God calls us to do the opposite of what comes naturally. God calls a man to love his wife as he loves himself and a woman to respect her husband.

Respect honors the person and does not insult him or cut him down with sarcasm. Unfortunately, when women feel empty and unloved, they tend to lash out with their words. Hurtful words damage a man's self-worth. A wife should always be aware of the words that come out of her mouth. Women tend to spew hurtful words without thinking about the harm they might be causing.

Today, be aware of your words and show your husband respect, whether he deserves it or not. By doing so, you will be honoring God and your marriage.

Father, give me kind and loving words toward my husband. I find myself lashing out at him without even thinking about what I'm saying. I know this is wrong. Forgive me. Remind me throughout my day to be respectful and honoring toward my husband. Amen.

Respecting God

*"A son honors his father, and a slave his master.
If I am a father, where is the honor due me? If I am a master,
where is the respect due me?" says the LORD Almighty.*

Malachi 1:6

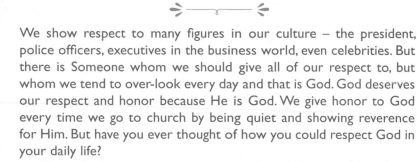

We show respect to many figures in our culture – the president, police officers, executives in the business world, even celebrities. But there is Someone whom we should give all of our respect to, but whom we tend to over-look every day and that is God. God deserves our respect and honor because He is God. We give honor to God every time we go to church by being quiet and showing reverence for Him. But have you ever thought of how you could respect God in your daily life?

Giving God your respect means to acknowledge who He is. He is the Creator of all things! He is sovereign, Lord of all. He is holy. He is the Alpha and the Omega, the beginning and the end. He is mighty, powerful, all-knowing, loving, merciful, just and full of grace.

As you go about your day today, keep in mind who created the world. Don't overlook the magnificence of God in nature, in the human body and even in each breath you take. God deserves all honor and respect all of the time.

*Father, I want to be mindful of Your presence
and commit my day to You. I don't want You to be an
afterthought at the end of my day. In the morning when I wake up,
I want to give You the praise and glory for another day. Thank
You for Your love and grace. You are mighty and amazing! Amen.*

Rest for the weary

Let a little water be brought,
and then you may all wash your feet
and rest under this tree.

Genesis 18:4

We are a tired people. No wonder; we rush around like rats on a wheel and never stop. Think about it. We enroll our children in programs as early as three years old. We sign them up for any and every activity under the sun because we don't want them to get behind or, heaven forbid, bored. What's wrong with us? We are doing this to ourselves!

Be brave, moms! Be brave and say NO! Be secure within yourself to not conform to the crazy scheduling. It wears you out. You will be too tired to handle the important things like disciplining and teaching moral truths. Let's get real: when you're exhausted, who has the energy to discipline a five-year-old or a teenager?

Put limits on your schedule. Don't say yes to everything. Make sure what you are saying yes to is worthy, because there will be an area that suffers or is sacrificed because of it. Sometimes it's worth the sacrifice, but make sure it is. Sometimes the whole family needs to hit pause and just rest for a season.

Father, give me courage – courage to say no
to the pull of culture that is always baiting my family
and me to do more. I need to be confident enough to say no.
Reveal to me what is most important and what will make
a difference in the long run in my children's lives. Amen.

Rest in Jesus

Then, because so many people were coming
and going that they did not even have a chance to eat,
He said to them, "Come with Me by yourselves to a
quiet place and get some rest."

Mark 6:31

Jesus knows the importance of rest. He knows that when you are giving of yourself all day long, constantly being tugged on, you become physically and emotionally exhausted. What's the remedy for exhaustion? Rest. It's that simple. When was the last time you got away by yourself to a place of peace and quiet and just rested? You as a mom need to get into the habit of forcing yourself to leave the chaos of your family and get away to find a place of rest.

The reason rest is so important is because you can't be the best mom you can be if you are running on fumes. If you are empty, you have nothing to pour out on others. Listen to Jesus calling you, "Come with Me by yourself to a quiet place, and get some rest." When you go, soak in His goodness, His love, and the fact that He cares about you and wants you to find your peace in Him.

Don't be a martyr telling yourself you can do it all without a break. Admit that you're not Wonder Woman. You are a woman with limits. You are a woman who needs rest. Take Jesus up on His offer to give you rest.

Father, thank You that I don't have to be Wonder Woman,
that You accept my weaknesses. Thank You for taking care of me,
even before I realized I needed to be taken care of. God,
give me the courage to get away, even if it's for only two hours.
During my time away, I pray that I would allow You
to fill me with Your love and Spirit. Amen.

Restoration and healing

In that day "I will restore David's fallen shelter –
I will repair its broken walls and restore its ruins –
and will rebuild it as it used to be.

Amos 9:11

Sometimes you feel hopeless about the future. These feelings can be about your job, your marriage or your finances. Or maybe a wayward teenager has broken your heart. But be encouraged! God is a God of restoration and healing. No situation in your life is beyond God's ability to fix.

Cry out to Him today. Ask Him to bring His healing to you and your family. Tell Him that you are willing to do whatever He asks of you. Let Him know that you are broken, that you are solely dependent on Him. God will restore you.

No matter where you find yourself today, know that God brings miraculous healing to anyone who will allow Him to work. Are you open to the idea of God healing your life, your family and your relationships? Go before God today and boldly ask Him to rebuild your life.

Father, only You know how to restore lives and make broken things new again. I am broken. My life is a mess and I need You. Please restore my life. I am willing to do whatever You ask of me, and I am placing all my faith and trust in You. Amen.

Revive me

The Spirit of God has made me;
the breath of the Almighty gives me life.

Job 33:4

Start your day by asking God to breathe His life into you … to revive you … to make you whole. Being a mom is tiresome. We give until we are empty. Who is breathing fresh life into you? Are you an empty cup, looking for something or someone to fill you up? We all get empty and search for ways to be filled, either through our husbands, money, friends, accolades or even our children. Those things will eventually leave us empty. God can fill you up to overflowing. Ask Him to fill you with His Spirit and breathe His life into you today.

You have an Almighty God living inside of you – all of His power, His glory and His love. We should all be asking daily for Him to fill us up. Tell Him you are empty and weak. He is waiting for you to cry out to Him, and He is ready and able to fill you and revive you. Get into the habit of asking for a fresh breath every day. You want to be 100 percent dependent on God, because only then will you find refreshment.

Father, I am tired and weary. I love my job as a mom; I wouldn't trade it for anything. But to be honest, my children suck the life right out of me. I need You to breathe new life into me. Amen.

Roll out the welcome mat

*"And whoever welcomes one such child
in My name welcomes Me."*

Matthew 18:5

We often believe our duties as moms are unimportant. We tell our-selves, "There has to be more to life." God, however, does not diminish your importance. He takes it very seriously. God knows that the work you do every day – the work that often goes unnoticed – makes a huge difference in your child's life.

If you fill your home with love and compassion, it is more than likely that your child will grow up to be a caring person. If you inspire your child to be responsible, it is more than likely that your child will grow up to be a leader. If you discipline your child with love and pa-tience, it is more than likely that your child will not feel entitled or be spoiled and will have self-control.

Today, as you wipe tears, realize that you are wiping the tears of Jesus. As you clean up spilled apple juice calmly, realize you are serving Jesus. As you discipline your children in love so they will learn what is right and wrong, know that Jesus is proud of you. The way you love your little ones is a direct reflection of your love for Him.

*Father, create in me a servant's heart toward my children.
Fill me with Your love, Your patience and Your grace.
God, when I begin to feel sorry for myself, thinking no one
is noticing or cares about all my hard work, remind me
that You care and that my work has eternal value. Amen.*

Run your race

Therefore, since we are surrounded by such a great cloud of witnesses, let us throw off everything that hinders and the sin that so easily entangles. And let us run with perseverance the race marked out for us.

Hebrews 12:1

What does your race look like? What are your goals for you and your family? Whatever your race, you must stay focused on your race and yours only.

A racehorse wears blinders to keep him focused on "his" lane and to keep him from being distracted by the other horses. We need to put on blinders too. There are a lot of distractions in our world, like social media, that can easily pull us away from our goals. Before we know it, we will be running someone else's race and never know how we got off course.

Persevere in your race. Be steadfast and determined to not veer to the left or to the right. You will notice other families running their races, but stick to yours and finish well. Finish the race that God has set before you.

Father, I am easily distracted. I confess that once I start looking at other people's lives, I become covetous of what they have and begin to want what they have. God, I pray this morning that You would make clear Your direction for my life and for my families' lives. Once my path is clear, I pray for steadfastness and boldness to stay the course. Amen.

Satisfaction in a job well done

Whatever you do, work at it with all your heart,
as working for the Lord, not for human masters,
since you know that you will receive an inheritance
from the Lord as a reward. It is the Lord Christ you are serving.

Colossians 3:23-24

I cleaned out my pantry recently and I felt so good about myself! It wasn't a hard job. It didn't take that long. Yet I felt like I had accomplished something big. How can doing something so small make a person feel so good?

When my children were young, I always had that same feeling of accomplishment when I cleaned out my Tupperware cabinet. Kelsey loved to play with Tupperware. Each night, I would give her a wooden spoon and she would sit and play happily with the Tupperware and her spoon while I cooked dinner. And every once in a while, I would take the time to reorganize my Tupperware cabinet. I felt like I had accomplished something amazing.

What in your life gives you that sense of accomplishment? Cleaning out your pantry, your closet, your junk drawer, your car? Whatever it is, go do it! Clean it out, stand back and look at what you have accomplished. I know it's small, but moms rarely get to see a project completely finished. Ah! That's it! In a short amount of time, we are able to start and finish something.

Father, thank You that I can find a sense of accomplishment
even in the smallest things. Help me to see the world as You see it,
not that one job is more important than another,
but that I should do my best in everything. Amen.

Saying no

From one man He made all the nations, that they should inhabit the whole earth; and He marked out their appointed times in history and the boundaries of their lands.

Acts 17:26

God places boundaries on the nations, on nature and on men. He appoints our days on this earth; he sets in motion where we end and someone else begins. Boundaries are good and if they are set in healthy ways, they bring peace and security. Don't be afraid to set boundaries in your life today.

Setting a boundary can be as simple as saying no to a play date with friends because you don't have margin in your life. When we don't set boundaries, we feel stressed and taken advantage of by people. Many times we feel guilty for saying no because we feel as if we are being mean. But in reality, saying no makes you a nicer person because you are not stressing yourself out by trying to please everyone around you.

Learn to say no to things that will bring harm to you and try not to feel guilty. That is no way to live. Sometimes it's healthy to say no.

Father, I give You this day and all that it brings. As I go about my day, show me any area where I need to set boundaries. Whether it is with my children, my husband, my family or friends, give me the strength to set appropriate boundaries and help me to do it in love. Thank You for showing me that boundaries are good. Amen.

Seasons of life

He has made everything beautiful in its time.
He has also set eternity in the human heart; yet no one can
fathom what God has done from beginning to end.

Ecclesiastes 3:11

A mom will experience every season of life with their child – from a newborn baby, to the toddler years, on through elementary age, pre-teen years, teenage years and into adulthood. Each season brings new challenges, sorrows and joys. Keep in mind as a mom that God will make everything beautiful in its own time. You may be in a difficult season right now, but one day you will see how God used these hard days to build strength and endurance in you and your child.

Try to enjoy the season of life you are experiencing right now. Ask God to show you how to take the challenges that are ahead of you and make them into a learning time both for your child and you. God wants to teach all of us how to grow and depend on Him through every season of life.

A lot of the time God will use our children to teach us moms some of the biggest lessons in life. What is God teaching you in your life right now? Is it patience, grace or self-control? We need all these characteristics in the journey of motherhood.

Father, help me enjoy each season of life I am in and not rush forward or wish for days gone by. I pray that I will look to You when life gets hard. I need Your wisdom and guidance concerning my children. Thank You for always being there for me. Amen.

Secure in God

I keep my eyes always on the Lord.
With Him at my right hand, I will not be shaken.

Psalm 16:8

———

What shakes you? Is it when you don't get your way? You want certain material things and you can't imagine being happy until you get those things? Or are you shaken when your husband or your children don't behave the way you want them to? Maybe it's sickness, divorce or financial disaster? These things have a way of shaking up our worlds and sending us reeling. How do we walk through these difficult times?

When our trust is in God, we will go through difficult times but we won't be shaken, because our faith is not in our children, our marriage, our finances, our material things or our health – our faith is grounded in God.

When our eyes are set on God, we realize that this world is broken and so we don't put our hope in it. We wait for a better world, a new world, with God. When Jesus returns, this world will pass away and all the pain and suffering will pass with it. Jesus will bring the new world and when our eyes are on Him, we will look forward to the new world and to God to get us through this world.

———

Father, I am guilty of putting my eyes on the things of this earth. I see others and secretly wish I had their lives. I know that's wrong. Forgive me. I want to start today anew and put my focus on You alone. I want to set my gaze on You and to stand firm and secure in You. Amen.

Seek Him

*"The gatekeeper opens the gate for him,
and the sheep listen to his voice. I am the good shepherd;
I know My sheep and My sheep know Me."*

John 10:3, 14

In order to hear God's voice, you have to seek Him and then listen. You will learn His voice just like you have learned the voice of your child. For example, if you are at a playground with a lot of children and you hear, "Mommy," you know your child's voice over all the other children's voices. You have spent time with your child and you are able to recognize his or her voice.

If you are seeking God, He will find you and He will show you how to parent your children the way they need to be parented. God knows everything about your children; He created them. He knows things even you don't know about them. Trust in Him. By trusting in your heavenly Father, your faith will grow and you will find peace.

*Father, I want to be able to distinguish Your voice above
all other voices. I want Your voice to be so clear in my soul
that there is no doubt in my mind who I am listening to. God,
give me courage to step out in faith when I hear Your voice.
You are my Shepherd and I am Your sheep. Lead me. Amen.*

Serenity and peace

A heart at peace gives life to the body,
but envy rots the bones.

Proverbs 14:30

This verse is soothing to my soul. Who doesn't want peace? There is nothing better than sitting at the beach in the late afternoon listening to the soft, gentle break of the waves. As you sit there, your mind slowly drifts away and you find yourself calm.

God tells us in this Scripture that a calm and undisturbed heart is the life and health of the body.

Many of us ignore God's teaching and choose the other path – envy, jealousy and wrath. It's so easy to envy other women, to be jealous of their houses, their husbands and their relationships with their children. If we allow them to consume us, envy and jealousy will eat away at us, and we will become angry and dissatisfied.

God teaches us to calm our minds and to be content with where we are. He will work it all out.

Father, I want to run far away from envy,
jealousy and anger. Show me how to seek a calm mind.
Teach me how to be content with where I am and with what I have.
I realize it's a choice, but sometimes I feel so drawn to compare
myself with others. I need You to gently remind me
when I start doing this. Thank You, Lord. Amen.

Sibling rivalry

Now Cain said to his brother Abel, "Let's go out to the field."
And while they were in the field, Cain attacked
his brother Abel and killed him.

Genesis 4:8

Sibling rivalry has been around since the very first set of brothers and will be around until Jesus returns. As moms we can teach our children about jealousy and the devastating effects jealousy has on a family.

In my family, I would call jealousy out and I even named it. We called jealousy the "green monster." So when my children were fighting over toys, envying the other sibling's newest gadget or clothes, I would say, "What's on your back?" My children would usually reply, "The green monster." I would say, "Get it off your back and address your jealousy or it will take hold of your life. You need to celebrate your sister and be happy for her. Your day will come."

Jealousy is a natural emotion that we struggle with. It is a huge tactic Satan uses to divide and destroy our families from within. Be wise and attack the source of the problem. Dig deeper and address the root of the problem. Get your children to see where the jealousy comes from; only then will they begin to recognize what's going on and be alert enough to change.

Father, my children do struggle daily with jealousy.
Teach me how to teach them to love, respect and celebrate one
another. God, I pray that I will be loving in my instruction
and not get angry. I pray that I will teach this principle
in a way my children can understand. Amen.

Silent but present

O God, do not remain silent;
do not turn a deaf ear,
do not stand aloof, O God.

Psalm 83:1

God is always at work in our lives, even when He is silent. We may pray for a situation to change, a person to change or our burdens to be lifted. If those prayers are not answered, we tell ourselves either God doesn't care or He isn't listening to us. Neither one is true. He does care about all of us and He is always listening.

God sees the big picture. He alone knows what is coming in our future and He alone knows what we need today to get us through to tomorrow. We must trust God during the times when we hear His voice clearly and when He is silent. Sometimes our faith grows the most during the silent times.

The Israelites were slaves for 400 years and cried out to God. He heard them and delivered them. But God was silent for a reason. He grew a nation so they would be able to take over the land He promised them. It took 400 years to grow that nation. Trust God. He has a plan and His plan will come to fruition.

Father, help me see You even during the silent times.
When I feel darkness all around me, I pray I will cry out
to You for refuge. I trust in You and in You alone. I choose
to trust that You are always here for me and are always
working on my behalf, even when I can't see it. Amen.

October

Simple truth

Jesus answered, "I am the way and the truth and the life.
No one comes to the Father except through Me."

John 14:6

❧ ——— ❧

We live in a complicated world. Nothing is easy anymore. We live in a day and age where you never really know what to do, because once you decide to go a certain way, you find ten articles on the Internet that convince you that way is wrong. As moms we can get so confused.

God is not a God of confusion and His ways are simple. If we want life, we must go to Jesus. Through Him we find God. The beauty of finding Jesus is that when we do, He will take care of everything else. He will guide you, direct you, give you wisdom, take away your anxiety and be your provider. It's so simple.

If you miss everything in motherhood, don't miss this one truth: Jesus is the way, the truth and the life. He is the answer. As you teach your children manners, their ABCs and their 123s, don't forget the most valuable lesson they will ever learn – teach them about Jesus. If they have Jesus, they won't need anything else.

••• ——— ❧ ——— •••

Father, our world complicates life, but You keep it simple.
Thank You. Give me courage to push past the confusion
and to trust in You. Thank You for Your Son, Jesus.
Without Jesus, I could never have a relationship with You.
I am so grateful for this simple, amazing truth. Amen.

Slow down

Be still before the LORD and wait patiently for Him ...
Psalm 37:7

When was the last time you were still before God? Not thinking about your grocery list, your errands, the ball practice you need to get to, the meal to cook, the cleaning that keeps calling your name – just still. It's hard to be still. It takes discipline and effort to clear your mind. We must train ourselves to be still, to sit quietly before God and to just "be" with Him. By doing this one small act, you are showing God that He is worth slowing down for.

Think about it: we slow down for people all the time – school zones, crosswalks, railroad tracks, shopping centers, neighborhoods, etc. Why not slow all the way down for God and learn to be completely still before Him? It will be worth the effort. It takes away all the stress we have, because we learn to leave the stress in His hands – His very capable, loving hands.

Father, I want to be still before You and to be patient with You.
I need You to teach me how to do this; it doesn't come
naturally to me. Show me how to clear my mind and be still.
I want that more than anything. Help me get out of the
go-go-go mentality and rest. I want to be completely
and utterly dependent on You for all things. Amen.

Song in my heart

Sing to the LORD, praise His name;
proclaim His salvation day after day.

Psalm 96:2

❧ ——— ❧

From the minute your eyes open in the morning until they close again at night, make sure that your heart sings unto God. Before you step out of bed, thank God for your day. Thank Him for the birds singing outside your window. As you go about your day – getting ready for work, taking children to school, staying home to clean the house – thank God for every aspect of your day and the things going on in your life. Even if life is throwing you a curve ball right now, you can still choose to sing unto the Lord. If you are going through a hard time, ask God for His protection, His mercy and His love to get you through the day.

Thanking God and having a heart of praise for Him is one aspect of the Christian life that we sometimes forget, but it is necessary. When we remember to praise Him, we are also reminding ourselves that we are not God. We are not in control, but there is One who is in control and who is holy. Sing your praises to God and acknowledge that He is holy and worthy of your praise.

•••———❧❧❧———•••

Father, I will sing praises to You all day,
whether my day is good or bad. I will keep my eyes on You.
I praise You for all the blessings in my life and I praise You
for the hard times. In those trying times, my love grows deeper
for You as You faithfully carry me to the other side. Amen.

Source of peace

"Peace I leave with you; My peace I give you.
I do not give to you as the world gives.
Do not let your hearts be troubled and do not be afraid."

John 14:27

As moms we can fear so many things concerning our children. We fear they might get sick, that they might not progress at the same rate as other children, that their peers in school will not like them, that we will not be good moms and that we will not be able to provide for them financially. These fears are real and they press down on us to a point of paralysis at times.

So what do you do? You can place your trust in the One who is trustworthy and faithful. When we place our trust in Jesus, He will give us peace. Through His amazing Word, God will give you peace, even during stressful times. Even during uncertain times, God is still God and He will never leave you nor forsake you (see Deuteronomy 31:6). He will give you a peace that goes beyond understanding (see Philippians 4:7).

Look to Jesus, not your circumstances. In Him you will find peace.

Father, You are the God of peace. You are my Redeemer,
my Lord and my Savior. Thank You for Your Son, Jesus,
and that through Him, I can have peace. I pray that I will
take my worries and concerns to You each day
and trust in You concerning my children. Amen.

Sovereign God

God has not allowed him to harm me.
Genesis 31:7

———

God protects His people. In the story in the Bible of Jacob and his father-in-law, Laban, Laban was trying to cheat Jacob. But despite Laban's efforts, God continued to bless Jacob. Jacob did not get caught up in the family drama, but stayed focused on his true Father, the God of Israel. He did not get caught up in fear or worry; instead, he stayed true to God and His principles.

Is there family drama going on in your life today? Do you feel that your in-laws are out to get you? Are you afraid that your friend or boss has a vendetta against you? Push against the fear and lean toward trust. God is trustworthy.

Jacob's story reminds us that even though it seems at times like our "enemies" are winning, God always wins. Don't get tangled up in the way things seem. Keep your eyes focused on God.

———

Father, thank You for taking care of me.
I want to be able to see You in the good and the bad,
and I know that I have to push past my fear in order for that
to happen. I know You are still with me, even during the bad
times. Please remind me of that. I love You. Amen.

Stages of discipline

Discipline your children while you still have the chance; indulging them destroys them.
Proverbs 19:18 (The Message)

We only have a short amount of time to teach our children, so use this time wisely. By allowing children to do whatever they want, whenever they want, you invite destruction into their lives.

What stage of discipline are you in with your children?

0-5 years: Set the foundation for your children's lives, teaching them that you are the authority. This is the best stage to instill the concepts of authority and submission.

6-12 years: During this stage, you are teaching the "why's behind the no's." Your child can understand during these years that you still have influence. Use this time wisely, instructing your children in the "reasons" behind the discipline.

13-18 years: These are the coaching years. At this stage, allow the natural consequences to play out, whether good or bad. You are guiding your children at this point.

Take heart, moms. If you discipline your children, you are setting them up for success for the rest of their lives. What a huge gift you will be giving them.

Father, my motherly nature wants to give my children everything they want. Teach me how to provide what they need and to teach them to look to You to provide their wants. Amen.

Stand alone

Each of us will give an account of ourselves to God.
Romans 14:12

Mothers are nurturers by nature. We were created to love, nurture, provide for and encourage our children. However, we can, in fact, begin to manipulate and control our children's lives. When we do this, we can get into trouble.

We tell ourselves that our child will not make wise choices, so we need to "help" them. Children will make mistakes. They will make unwise choices, but they learn through failing. Allow them to experience the pain and consequences of bad choices. If your children never fail, they may never learn to stand on their own.

One day in heaven, "each of us will give an account of ourselves to God." One day, your child will stand alone in front of God and you will not be able to weigh in on your child's life. Are you preparing your child for that day? Are you teaching them today that their actions have consequences? That what they sow, they will reap?

Your job is a big one, but it's not to live your child's life for them. You can, however, instruct them on the way they should live. Then, step back and allow them to make their own choices.

Father, give me courage to allow my child to stand alone.
When I feel the urge to constantly correct and use teachable
moments, remind me that my child will one day stand alone
to give an account of his or her life. Lord, pursue my child
and draw them closer to You; teach them Your ways.
Give me what I need to be nurturing but not controlling. Amen.

Stay alert

Only be careful, and watch yourselves closely
so that you do not forget the things your eyes have seen
or let them fade from your heart as long as you live.
Teach them to your children and to their children after them.

Deuteronomy 4:9

Stay alert. Don't be lazy with your parenting. It is hard to stay on your A-game as a parent, because our children tend to wear us down. But we must be vigilant in our parenting. We are training up the next generation.

Every new season of life brings new challenges and hopes. Embrace each season and don't grow weary in your guidance. As your children grow, take what you have learned from them and apply it to the next season of their lives. Being a student of your children never stops, even as they grow into adulthood. Continue to ask God for His infinite wisdom.

Ask God to equip you with what you need for each season of life. God knows your future. Ask Him to prepare your heart for the days ahead and to give you strength and courage when you need it.

Father, I pray that I would not grow weary
in my role as a mom. So many days I feel discouraged
and wonder if I'm doing a good job. Instill in me confidence
in You and endurance to keep pushing forward. I want to stay
alert and finish strong; I acknowledge I can only do that
through You. Thank You for meeting my every need. Amen.

Steadfast in the Lord

*At my first defense, no one came to my support,
but everyone deserted me. May it not be held against them.
But the Lord stood at my side and gave me strength.*

2 Timothy 4:16-17

We go through times when we feel as if no one truly understands our position in life and we believe we are completely alone. The times we feel most vulnerable are when we are at our weakest points. Maybe your husband is traveling this week, your children have the flu and you feel completely alone. Or maybe you are a single mom and the weight of the bills, home maintenance and yard work is beginning to be too much to bear.

Maybe you are physically sick, going from doctor's office to doctor's office and no one can find what's wrong with you. You feel all alone. No matter your circumstances, be encouraged; you are never alone if God is part of your life. God stands by us and fills in the gaps. Whether we "feel" Him or not, He is there.

God will give you strength when you don't have any left. He will hold you up when you feel like collapsing. God will never leave you.

Father, give me eyes to see You even during the dark and difficult days. Give me faith to take You at Your word and not to doubt that You are standing beside me. I want my faith to be so strong in You. God, I love You and trust You. Thank You for Your patience with me and Your never-ending grace. Amen.

Stop performing

But when the kindness and love of God
our Savior appeared, He saved us,
not because of righteous things we had done,
but because of His mercy.

Titus 3:4-5

In a world where we are constantly performing, constantly striving to be the best and to be acknowledged for our merits, it's refreshing to know our heavenly Father doesn't expect or want us to perform. He accepts us and loves us not because of what we do, but because of His love and mercy toward us. We are loved just because we are His.

As you go about your day and feel the pressure to perform within your circle of friends or at work, remind yourself that God accepts you and there is no performance needed. Even with your family, when you fail to get everything done and you feel like you didn't measure up in mommy world, remind yourself that you do measure up and God loves you regardless of your performance. If you are working on a project, either at work or at home, and it fails, don't for a second think that you are not good enough. You are accepted and loved by God.

In a performance-driven world, give yourself a break and walk in freedom. You are accepted and there is no performance required.

Father, thank You for Your mercy and love.
Thank You that I don't have to perform to be loved and accepted,
but You accept me just the way I am. Your love is so great
and I accept it with open arms. When I begin to perform
throughout my day, whisper in my ear, "It's not required." Amen.

Strength of the Lord

Look to the LORD and His strength; seek His face always.
Psalm 105:4

———

Being a mom is not for the faint of heart. A mom needs to be strong and bold. Our children look to us to provide security and answers. But our strength will eventually give in to weakness. We begin to doubt our abilities. Some days we just want to stay in bed, pull the covers over our heads and tell the world to go away. We want to announce to everyone, "I don't have the answer; go away and ask someone else!"

There is good news! You don't have to be a mom in your own strength. You don't have to have it all together. God has it all together. He is your strength and, unlike you, He never grows weary. He has all the answers and He is ready to give those answers to you – but you must ask Him. You must seek His face and stay focused on Him.

Learn to rely on God and look to Him for your strength. Today, if you are growing weary, cry out to God and tell Him you need His strength. He will answer your cry.

———

Father, thank You for always listening.
Thank You for always being there for me
and for Your endless love and strength. God,
I do grow weary as a mom. I am so thankful that I
can look to You for strength. Your love is never-ending
and for that I am grateful! Amen.

Submit to authority

Therefore, it is necessary to submit to the authorities, not only because of possible punishment but also as a matter of conscience.

Romans 13:5

In our culture today, there is a growing trend in the younger generation to not submit to authority. You see it in the work force, in the schools and in our homes. In the minds of the youth, the rules don't necessarily apply to them.

But that's not how God works. Jesus, who is God, obeyed the rules on this earth and paid taxes. He taught His disciples to submit to the authorities placed over them. This honors God.

In teaching your children to submit to the authority of their elders, they will more than likely push back and say that their elders don't know what they're talking about. One response to such an accusation is, "Sometimes you must respect the position, if not the person."

We need to get back to treating all authorities in our lives with respect and submission out of obedience to our heavenly Father.

Father, change my heart toward the authorities in my life that I push against and help me teach this God-given principle to my children. Help me understand that it's important for my children to see me model submission. Amen.

Teaching love to siblings

*"He committed no sin, and no deceit was found in His mouth."
When they hurled insults at Him, He did not retaliate;
when He suffered, He made no threats. Instead He
entrusted Himself to Him who judges justly.*

I Peter 2:22-23

If you have two children, you will have sibling rivalry at some point. Children are around each other day and night, so fights, disagreements, and jealousy are bound to appear. No mom wants to hear her children fighting. It's stressful and disheartening. We want our children to love one another and to have close relationships.

How do we teach that to our children? First, we teach our children to love others by loving others ourselves. Your children are not going to listen to you if they don't see you living out what you are teaching. Second, look to Jesus as your example. He is the perfect example of how to treat others. He did not retaliate. He made no threats. Instead, He trusted in God, that God would work it all out. If you are a Christian, you have Jesus living inside of you – all of His power, love and self-control are in you, so lean into Him. Show your children how to do the same.

Can you imagine if even one third of Christian families would start to embrace this way of thinking? We could change the world.

*Father, thank You for sending Your Son, Jesus,
as the perfect example of how to love others. Please give me
what I need to teach my children and myself how to rely on Jesus
100 percent of the time. Lord, I acknowledge that I am weak in
this area, but I also acknowledge that Jesus is living inside of me
and through Him, I can do all things. Thank You! Amen.*

Teamwork

*"You see the trouble we are in: Jerusalem lies in ruins,
and its gates have been burned with fire. Come, let us rebuild
the wall of Jerusalem, and we will no longer be in disgrace."*

Nehemiah 2:17

Every family should operate as a team. No matter what the size of your family, whether you are a single mom with one child, or married with five children, your family is your team. Loyalty, unity and respect are three characteristics of great teams.

Loyalty: Teach your children that your family will pull together to protect, guide and support one another.

Unity: Teach your family the motto, "All for one and one for all." There are times when certain family members will be asked to sacrifice for another family member — sitting through multiple sports practices, for example. Teach your children that sacrifice is given out of love and dedication to one another. Remind your children that we all sacrifice at one time or another.

Respect: Family members should respect one other and themselves. Even you, the mom, should show your children respect and not demean them in any way or embarrass them. Respect is needed throughout the team in order for the team to be successful.

Father, help me to model loyalty, unity and respect within our family. I want our family to be close-knit and to love one another. I believe that is possible with Your help. Guide and direct me to instill these qualities in my children. Amen.

Thankful hearts

With praise and thanksgiving they sang to the LORD.
Ezra 3:11

We need to cultivate thankful hearts. Have you ever noticed people who seem to be in a good mood no matter what circumstances they are going through? They have usually chosen to trust God even through the difficult situations.

To choose to be thankful can take on many forms. If you are a working mom, thank the people in your life that are taking care of your children while you are at work. Thank God for giving you a job to provide income for your family. Thank God for the blessing of your children and the joy they bring to your life. Remember to thank God for even the smallest things we usually take for granted … like electricity, indoor plumbing and even fully-stocked grocery stores.

Thank God for the relationships in your life. Tell your friends how grateful you are for their help and friendship. Become a person who is known to have a cheerful heart and a thankful attitude. It will not only change your world, it could also change the people around you.

Father, thank You for this day. Thank You for the sunshine and the rain. I need to always remember that You go before me and You alone orchestrate my days. You provide me with what I need when I need it. Help me to always be thankful and never to take anything in life for granted. Amen.

Thanksgiving

Enter His gates with thanksgiving and His courts with praise;
give thanks to Him and praise His name.

Psalm 100:4

There is nothing worse than children who constantly complain. It is frustrating on many levels, but mainly because they are usually complaining about something that you can't change. For example, when a child says, "I'm hot!" what can you do about the weather? When children complain about being bored, what can you really do?

Teach your children how to choose to be thankful and praise God for what they do have in life. Teach them to thank God for the day – the sunshine, their food and the shelter over their heads. Point out the things God has blessed your family with, such as health, love and even their siblings.

As always, you need to teach them by showing them what it means to show gratitude. Do this by constantly reminding yourself of the many blessings that surround you.

Father, thank You for all the blessings You give me
every day. I take so much for granted – my health
and my children's health. Today, I want to praise
Your holy name. Thank You for Your Son, Jesus.
He is enough! Amen.

The art of resting

Then God blessed [spoke good of] the seventh day
and made it holy, because on it He rested from
all the work of creating that He had done.

Genesis 2:3

Holy simply means "set apart." To set aside a day for rest is quite foreign in our fast-paced, drive-thru society. However, our God in all His glory and majesty, took a day to rest and He said it was a good thing.

Take some time to rest and reflect on the good that you are creating. Carve out consistent time to rest. Perhaps take a baby step such as deciding you will not do laundry on Sundays. When your family asks you why, tell them, "Rest is good for God and it is good for me."

We need to look to God for our example and follow His lead. If I want to be a mom who is engaged with my children, attentive to them and loving, but in order for me to do that, I need to rest every now and then. God wants you to take care of the body He has given you, so don't feel guilty.

God, please give me the strength to follow Your example
of resting. I don't want to be so busy that I forget to rest
and take care of myself. Gently remind me throughout
my week to take time to rest and help me honor You by setting
aside a day to reflect on Your goodness and provision. Amen.

The art of waiting

LORD, I wait for You; You will answer, Lord my God.
Psalm 38:15

Are you good at waiting? We all must learn to wait in life.

There are different types of waiting:

Sometimes we wait and there is nothing we can do to speed up the process. It's just slow, like your teenager child growing out of their rebellious stage. During the waiting, the best thing to do is to enjoy the ride. Don't rush to the next stage; it will get here soon enough. Each has its own special treasures, so take the time to soak them all in.

Sometimes we have to wait because of something we have caused – like getting out of debt. This type of waiting is hard because we tend to beat ourselves up in the process. Be diligent in paying off your debt and learn from your mistakes. God is a gracious and forgiving God.

Sometimes we wait on the Lord. We wait for Him to perform a miracle, to teach us an important lesson or we wait for God's timing. During these times, we need to trust God. Trust that He has a reason, whether you can see it or not. Trust that He wants good things for you.

Father, I want to wait on You in all areas of my life,
whether with my children, my walk with You or the problems
I created myself. I want to learn to trust You in all things.
Give me a desire to slow down and learn the art of waiting. Amen.

The bridge

But now in Christ Jesus you who once were far away
have been brought near by the blood of Christ.

Ephesians 2:13

———

If you stood on the widest side of the Grand Canyon and you were told to throw a rock to the other side, would that be possible? Of course not. That was our relationship with God until Jesus died for our sins. There was no way we could ever reach God or have a relationship with Him, because He is holy and we were not.

Then Jesus came and shed His blood on the cross so we could have an intimate relationship with God. Jesus is the bridge from us to God. Now, when God looks at us, He sees the blood of Jesus and we are washed clean from all of our sins. We are clean, pure and holy in God's sight.

Begin to see yourself as God sees you – holy, righteous and redeemed. Jesus paid a tremendous price to bring you to God; don't dismiss what He did on the cross. As you go about your day today, remind yourself that you were far away from God, but now you are near. You are dearly loved.

———

Father, words cannot express my gratitude for what
You did for me. You sacrificed Your one and only Son
to redeem me from my sins. Thank You! Your love is so great
and unconditional, it is hard to grasp. I step out in faith and
embrace all that You have to give. I love You. Amen.

The brokenhearted

*The LORD is close to the brokenhearted
and saves those who are crushed in spirit.*
Psalm 34:18

Life can deal some hard blows. Sometimes our pain is so great that our spirits are crushed. The deaths of loved ones, terminal illnesses or tragic accidents can leave us numb and seemingly without hope. God understands. When we are in these situations, God draws near to us.

Maybe you know of someone who is going through one of these times right now. That person may not even be able to cry out to God because they are so heartbroken. You should cry out to God on their behalf. Ask God to wrap His loving arms around your friend so that they will feel His presence.

Ask God to carry them in His arms until they are able to walk again. Ask Him to put soothing ointment on their wounds and restore them back to life. Your prayers could bring your friend out of the darkness. You may not see the results on this side of heaven, but don't ever doubt the power of your prayer.

Father, thank You for being such a loving God. You truly understand our pain and You are a compassionate God. Help me to focus on You during the difficult days and to realize one day You will wipe away all my tears. Amen.

The choice is yours

This is what I have observed to be good:
that it is appropriate for a person to eat, to drink and to find
satisfaction in their toil some labor under the sun during
the few days of life God has given them – for this is their lot.

Ecclesiastes 5:18

We all struggle to be satisfied with our circumstances. In order to be content with where you are in life, you need to keep in mind that contentment does not come natural to any of us. In our flesh, we will always yearn for more: more money, more material things, better status, more time for ourselves, more of everything. The "more" philosophy always leaves us empty. Push against Satan's trap of greed. At the end of the day, that is what being discontent is all about – essentially it is greed and wanting more.

The key to being content is to trust in Christ and His strength. Allow Him to live through you, and keep your eyes focused on Him and not the "things" of this world. Remind yourself throughout your day about the difference between "want" and "need." We all want things, however, we should ask ourselves if we truly need them. If we just stick to that simple rule, our lives will be less frustrating and we will find more contentment.

Father, I want to be content. I want to learn this very hard lesson.
Teach me how to find satisfaction in You. As I go about my day
and I look at all the pretty things life has to offer, help me decide
what are needs and what are wants. Give me the discipline
to resist the never-ending lust for more. Amen.

The choice to forgive

"For if you forgive other people when they sin against you,
your heavenly Father will also forgive you."

Matthew 6:14

Forgiving is not always easy. Sometimes, we feel like the person doesn't deserve to be forgiven. The wrong that has been committed is too great for us to forgive. However, Jesus is very clear about forgiveness. He says throughout the Gospels that we must forgive because Christ forgave us. It's that simple.

Because He forgave our sins, we are to forgive others. We don't deserve to be forgiven, yet we are forgiven. Therefore, since we are forgiven, we must forgive in return.

Once we decide to forgive someone, even if we don't "feel" like it, the emotions will eventually catch up. Initially, it is a choice that we have to make. Unforgiveness has the power to grow in us and destroy us. Allow God to take care of the vengeance. Simply obey Jesus and choose to forgive.

Father, I choose to forgive, because You have asked me to.
My human nature resists forgiving. I pray that You will give me
strength to forgive. I put my trust in You, Lord, not in myself.
I am obeying You and choosing to forgive. My prayer is that You
will take care of the rest of my feelings and emotions. Amen.

The delight of the Lord

The LORD delights in those …
who put their hope in His unfailing love.

Psalm 147:11

Have you ever tried to coax your child to jump into the deep end of the pool with you treading water waiting for him to jump? What convinces the fearful child to jump? Trust – trust in you, his mom. Doesn't it make your heart soar when he finally jumps and is so happy and proud of himself? Our heavenly Father feels the same about us.

How many times do we stand on the sidelines of life, waiting to "jump" in, but we are too afraid? We convince ourselves that God may not catch us. We need to remind ourselves that God loves us and delights in those who trust Him completely. Are you willing to put your hope and faith in His unfailing love? Do you really believe that the God of the universe, the Creator of all things, loves you?

My prayer for each mom today is that you would remember that God loves you and you can trust His love. He is there for you.

Father, give me confidence to jump! As I stand on the diving board of life, help me see that You are with me and You will catch me. I want to put all my faith and hope in You and I want You to be delighted with me. Thank You for Your patience. I'm going to jump into Your arms today and go "all in." Amen.

The fear of change

He changes times and seasons;
He deposes kings and raises up others.
Daniel 2:21

Our world is always changing. Some people can easily roll with these changes, but others struggle and resist them. Whether you accept change or you fight it, you need to remember that God is in control. It's His decision as to what He will change and what will remain the same. Our trust is in God, not our circumstances.

The sooner we realize that God is in control, the better prepared we will be to walk our children through uncertain times. We as Christians do not need to place our trust in our circumstances; we need to learn to place all of our trust in God.

A mom can teach her child that even though the world is changing, God never changes. He will be with them during a move, when changing schools or during the loss of Daddy's job. God will prepare the path before the journey begins. Teach your child from a young age to look to God for protection, guidance and safety. He is the one and only thing that never changes (see Hebrews 13:8).

Father, I pray that I will not cling so tightly to the things
of this world that make me comfortable. Teach me how to
abandon myself to You completely. Lord, help me teach my
child to trust in You and not in ever-changing circumstances.
Thank You for the security and peace I have in You. Amen.

The fixer

Many seek an audience with a ruler,
but it is from the LORD that one gets justice.

Proverbs 29:26

When life throws us a curve ball, what do we do? We usually run toward the experts of the world to "fix" our problems. If we have medical issues, we go to a doctor. If we have money issues, we seek an expert on finances. If we have marital problems, we consult a counselor or lawyer.

These people are all needed in our society, but the first Person we should seek is the Lord. Only God can bring justice into our circumstances. Through God's magnificent character, He can calm our storms, even when the storms are still raging.

Think about it: experts can offer advice, do surgery or offer plans, but they can't bring peace into your life. God can even during the most difficult days.

Father, when tragedy strikes, my first inclination is to run
to people that can help me. Forgive me for not running to You
first. Give me the courage to look to You first. I need to look to You
in all things – not so that You will change my circumstances,
but so that You will carry me through to the other side. Amen.

The fruit of joy

But the fruit of the Spirit is … joy.
Galatians 5:22

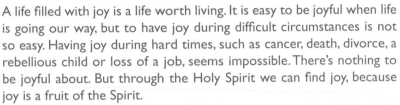

A life filled with joy is a life worth living. It is easy to be joyful when life is going our way, but to have joy during difficult circumstances is not so easy. Having joy during hard times, such as cancer, death, divorce, a rebellious child or loss of a job, seems impossible. There's nothing to be joyful about. But through the Holy Spirit we can find joy, because joy is a fruit of the Spirit.

In order to bear the fruits of the Spirit, you must be abiding with Jesus on a daily basis. Abiding means to rest in Jesus. Once we start doing that, Jesus, through the Holy Spirit, will fill us with joy regardless of our circumstances. We will begin to "see" this world through the lens of God. We will learn to seek God to fulfill us and to place our trust in Him, not in earthly things.

Your circumstances may not change, but your outlook will. You will exude joy during a time when you should not be joyful. You will instantly know that God is with you and you are bearing His fruit.

Father, fill me with Your Holy Spirit.
Fill me with Your joy. I want to "see" this world through
Your lens and not my own. I want to walk with Jesus every day.
To start or end my day without Jesus would be unfathomable.
Create in me a desire to long after You. I want to push
my desires aside and only seek You. Amen.

The fruit of love

But the fruit of the Spirit is love.
Galatians 5:22

Love … what is it really? We throw that word around, but do we ever truly think about what it means? The best example of love is from God: "For God so loved the world that He gave His one and only Son, that whoever believes in Him shall not perish but have eternal life" (John 3:16).

God loved and then He gave. He gave His most valuable possession – His Son. A mom gives all day long, so having love shouldn't be a problem. Unconditional love, however, is hard to give. It's easy to love a baby, because they are sweet, soft and warm. It's easy to love a toddler, because they are adorable and so much fun. But loving a rebellious child and showing unconditional love toward them is difficult. Loving a husband who ignores you is almost impossible. Loving your neighbor who is mean-spirited and vindictive seems downright insane.

We need God's love for these people. God's love is unconditional – He loved even though we were sinners, hateful, mean and full of envy. He loved and gave His Son to people who were not worthy, not deserving or even grateful. We need that kind of love.

Father, I want Your type of love.
I want to love unconditionally,
not worrying if I'm loved in return.
God, fill me with Your Spirit. Fill me with Your love.
Remind me throughout my day to seek Jesus. Amen

The hard task of discipline

Folly is bound up in the heart of a child,
but the rod of discipline will drive it far away.

Proverbs 22:15

Unfortunately, discipline is one job we have as moms that is not pleasant. It may not be pleasant, but it's needed. An undisciplined child will wreak havoc on everyone they meet.

Sometimes we get angry because they will not obey us. The Bible tells us that folly is bound up in a child. In other words, the child is behaving in the way that comes naturally to them. It's our job to teach them new ways to respond. Don't be surprised when your child rebels, but instead anticipate the rebellious behavior and discipline it.

Children will repeat what is rewarded. If your child is whining and won't stop, do you give them what they want just to quiet them? If you do, then you're rewarding bad behavior. Keep this verse in your mind as you go about your day today. When your child misbehaves, think what type of discipline would deter this behavior in the future and then do it. Folly has to be removed for a child to behave in an obedient and loving way.

Father, give me the courage to discipline my child the way
that I should. Help me to see that "folly" needs to be driven
out of my child and it's my job to do it. I don't like to be harsh
with my children, but I also don't want a disobedient,
rebellious child. Today, as I face my child, give me the strength
and love to discipline them the right way. Amen.

The heart of God

But You, Lord, are a compassionate and gracious God,
slow to anger, abounding in love and faithfulness.

Psalm 86:15

⋟ ——————◦—————— ⋞

We have preconceived notions about people we don't know very well. We prejudge them and say, "She's such a snob," or "He thinks he's better than me." Sometimes we "think" we know people, and then we spend some time with them and we realize we never really knew them at all. What is your view of God? Have you prejudged God? Do you see Him as a God that is far away, judgmental and ready to punish you the second you do something wrong? If that is your perception, then you have Him all wrong.

David writes about God's character in Psalms and says He is compassionate and gracious. He is full of compassion toward His children and gives us grace even though we don't deserve it. God is slow to anger. He is not looking for ways to punish you; He wants to keep you from harm. He is a God of love and faithfulness. He is always there for you.

Spend some time with God over the next few months and really get to know His character. Search in the concordance of your Bible how many times God talks about His love for you. You just might be surprised.

•••————————◦◦◦————————•••

Father, thank You for Your compassion, grace and love.
Thank You for always being faithful, even when I'm not.
I need to get to know You better by studying Your character.
Create in me a deep desire to learn more about You. Amen.

The heart that does not judge

God, who knows the heart …
Acts 15:8

Be careful not to judge another person's heart. Only God truly knows the matters of the heart. We as humans think we know what people are thinking or believe. We tell ourselves things like, "I know he or she thinks this way." Or, "I can tell they were talking about me and they don't like me."

The truth is though, we can't know what another person is thinking or believes unless he or she tells us. Only God knows what a person is thinking, so leave the mindreading to God.

When you find yourself in this predicament, take your angst to God. Share your thoughts with God: "God, I think this person doesn't like me," or, "She wants bad things to happen to me. But, Lord, I lay that at Your feet. Only You know her heart and only You can change her heart toward me." Get into the habit of taking your thoughts to God and allowing Him to work things out.

Father, thank You for Your endless love for me.
I try to understand the depths of Your love for me,
but it's difficult to grasp. I pray that I will not prejudge others
today, but instead will extend the love that You have shown
for me. Teach me how to love the way You love. Amen.

The illusion of control

*"You come against me with sword and spear
and javelin, but I come against you in the name
of the L*ORD *Almighty … for the battle is the L*ORD*'s …*

1 Samuel 17:45, 47

Moms control. It's that simple. We say we aren't going to, but we control because we don't trust. We don't trust that our children will make wise decisions. We don't trust that our children will act properly. And we don't trust that our children will be safe if we aren't watching their every move. This controlling behavior sends a very loud message to our children: "You don't measure up, so let me do it for you." The sad part is that in our hearts, we don't really believe that! We love our children and we do believe in them; we just have a hard time giving up control.

The reality is that moms aren't in control – God is. Do you trust God fully with your children? Do you trust that He loves your children more than you do and He wants the best for them? David had confidence in God. His trust was secure in the God of the universe. If you had that kind of confidence in God and you passed that confidence down to your children, imagine how confident your children would be.

*Father, You are in control. You are very capable of
protecting my children, guiding them and providing for them.
Remind me whenever I try to shelter and control.
I want to trust You with my children. Amen.*

November

The joy of the Lord

Nehemiah said, "Go and enjoy choice food and sweet drinks, and send some to those who have nothing prepared. This day is holy to our Lord. Do not grieve, for the joy of the LORD is your strength."

Nehemiah 8:10

God's joy is not determined by circumstances. He is good all the time, whether we can see His goodness or not. In knowing that, you have joy and begin to allow Him to be your strength. Think about it: Your strength doesn't come from money, marriage, relationships, children or prestige; your strength comes from something much bigger than any of those things – it comes from God.

As a mom you need strength – strength to get through your day, strength to stay strong and focused, and strength to parent wisely. Allow God to be your inner strength.

Ask Him to give you joy, even during the hard days. Ask Him to build a strength inside of you that will stand any test or hardship. He will do that for you. He wants to be your strength, the One you cry out to first. Trust Him today and allow Him to bring you strength and joy.

Father, thank You that I don't have to always have it together. Thank You that I don't have to always be strong, because, Lord, so many days I am weak. I'm putting my trust in You to strengthen me and bring me joy, regardless of my circumstances. Amen.

The Lord is my refuge

The LORD is my rock, my fortress and my deliverer;
my God is my rock, in whom I take refuge.

Psalm 18:2

Children need to know that regardless of their actions, they are always welcome in your home and that you will always love them and be there for them. But there is someone else who is even greater than you and is always there for them – God. Children need to learn at an early age that God loves them, wants to protect them and that they can count on Him.

You can't promise your children that you will be on this earth forever, but you can promise that God will be with them forever. What a huge blessing you will be giving your children, that they can trust God and rely on Him.

We all need someone or something to anchor our lives to. The anchor you choose needs to be solid, strong and secure. The psalmist says it so clearly: "My God is my rock, in whom I take refuge." God is your anchor and in Him you are safe. Your children will naturally look to you for security and love, which is a good thing. But let them know that you look to God as your anchor, your help in times of trouble. Encourage them to do the same.

Father, thank You for being my protector and my anchor in life.
The world tosses me back and forth, but as long as I can hold on
to You, I know I will be okay. Help me teach this important truth
to my children, so they will put their trust in You. Amen.

The Lord's day

*"If you keep your feet from breaking the Sabbath
and from doing as you please on My holy day ...
then you will find your joy in the LORD ...*

Isaiah 58:13-14

A day that is holy ... set apart ... a day of rest. That's what the Sabbath is to God. It's a necessity of life and one of the Ten Commandments. Even God took a day to rest after creating the world (see Genesis 2:1). How many times do we overlook our Sabbath day? How many times do we conduct life on Sunday like it's just another day?

Sunday is our Sabbath and we should honor God's request. He knows how important it is for us to rest. A mom, more than anyone, needs a day to rest. A day not to do laundry, a day not to worry about the dishes, a day not to clean, not to cook, not to labor over anything big or small.

A day set apart from the other days of the week to just sit and be still or to play a game together with her family. A day to go to church and be fed, instead of "feeding others." A mom needs that day. This week, start a new tradition in your family by allowing yourselves a day of rest.

Father, I have been remiss in not stopping all my activities and taking a day to rest. I need to honor You, Your Word and Your command. I know You will go before me and create more time for me to get my work done. I choose to obey You instead of doing it all on my own. Thank You for desiring the best for me. Amen.

The love of God

"Because he loves me," says the LORD, *"I will rescue him; I will protect him, for he acknowledges My name."*

Psalm 91:14

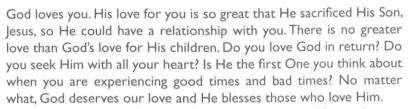

God loves you. His love for you is so great that He sacrificed His Son, Jesus, so He could have a relationship with you. There is no greater love than God's love for His children. Do you love God in return? Do you seek Him with all your heart? Is He the first One you think about when you are experiencing good times and bad times? No matter what, God deserves our love and He blesses those who love Him.

How do you love God? You love God by trusting Him and trusting His Word. The Bible says: "I will protect him, for he acknowledges My name." There are many of these truths throughout Scripture. Find them and hold on to them.

You can also love God by spending time with Him. Tell Him about your day, your struggles, your joys, your dreams and desires. Listen to God in return. Hit pause and rest quietly before Him. Take the time to know Him by reading His Word. God's character is revealed in the stories in the Bible.

Father, I do love You, but I know I could be more consistent in my love for You and I could trust You more with my daily life. It seems I trust You on the big things, but I don't include You in the little things. Lord, I want to love You more than anyone or anything. Please show me how to do that. Amen.

The need to please

*Am I now trying to win the approval
of human beings, or of God?*

Galatians 1:10

If you look up "people pleaser" in the dictionary, you will probably find a picture of a mom. Moms are always trying to please the people in their lives. There's nothing wrong with trying to make people happy, as long as we don't get out of balance.

It's easy to start to believe that it's our job to make our families happy and that their contentment depends on us. But it's not your job to "do" everything for everyone.

Being a mom is so much more than pleasing our children. We answer to a higher calling from God. He has entrusted us with these young lives and our first goal should be to push past the need to please them and to focus on doing what's best for them. You don't need their approval and you already have God's.

Father, show me if I have allowed my need to please my family to consume my life. If I have, Lord, please forgive me. I want to be a good mom, but more than anything, I want to follow You. Show me how to keep You first in my life and to only try to please You. I love You! Amen.

The peace of God

And the peace of God, which transcends all understanding,
will guard your hearts and your minds in Christ Jesus.

Philippians 4:7

God's peace is like no other. You can't explain how it happens, but it does. When God gives you peace, you can be in the most painful situation, yet somehow you know that God has it under control. When God takes hold of a situation, you can look death in the face and not be afraid. To be held by God and to know He has you brings a peace like no other.

Ask God for this peace in your life as you live out your days. One way of realizing such peace is to acknowledge that you can't attain this on your own. You can't buy it, manufacture it or give it to someone. It only comes from God and 100 percent abandonment to Him – realizing that God is in control, that He loves you regardless of the circumstances and He will deliver you – that thought alone brings peace.

Father, thank You for providing peace even when I am afraid
and full of doubt. Get me to the place where I am fully engaged
with You and trusting You. If my trust and hope is in You,
not in this life or my circumstances, then I will have peace.
I want this type of life – totally dependent on You for everything.
I give You my day, my desires and my life. Amen.

The perfect life

*For by one sacrifice He has made perfect forever
those who are being made holy.*

Hebrews 10:14

❧——————❧

So many times we strive as moms to live perfect lives. We work hard to create a perfect home filled with warmth and love, adorned with the perfect décor. We attempt to create perfect memories for our children with holiday traditions, perfect family vacations and perfect summertime activities. But so many times our perfectly orchestrated ideas fall short and we feel defeated.

Don't be defeated. Realize that perfection will only be achieved when we get to heaven. Life on this earth will never be perfect. Take heart, however, that we are made perfect in Christ. Because of Christ, His perfection and Him living in us, we are perfect.

We can achieve a small slice of perfection on this earth through Jesus Christ. As you go about your day today, change your focus from, "I must create the perfect home," to, "Our home is perfectly suited for us because Jesus abides with us here and through Jesus, we are made perfect." It will alter the way you view yourself. You will begin to exchange your feelings of inadequacy with feelings of confidence in Christ.

•••————————•••

*Father, thank You that in Jesus, I am made perfect.
Thank You, Father, for loving me enough to send Your Son
to pay for my sin so that I may have a relationship with You.
God, as I go about my day, help me to keep my focus
on You and not on my circumstances or failures.
Fill me with Your love, joy and grace. Amen.*

The perfect mom

*Your eyes saw my unformed body;
all the days ordained for me were written
in Your book before one of them came to be.*

Psalm 139:16

⇒———⇐

Being a mom is hard. Many days we feel inadequate and lost. Some days we even question if God knew what He was doing by giving us our particular child. We look around and think, My child would have done better in another home because there's a dad in that family and we don't have one in ours. Or we think to ourselves, I'm not strong enough to handle this strong-willed child. Those are lies. God gave you the child He did because in His wisdom He knew you would be the best mom for your child.

Never doubt God's sovereign plan. He ordained, before time, that your child would be with you. You may feel inadequate, which is precisely why you need a Savior. God is there to teach you, guide you and give you wisdom. Ask Him.

God knew exactly what your child would need in a mom and He gave your child you! God doesn't make mistakes. You may not be a perfect mom, but you are perfectly suited to be your child's mom. Absorb that thought and never let it go.

•••——⋙⋘——•••

*Father, thank You for my child. Thank You for perfectly
matching us as mother and child. God, there are days
when I doubt my ability as a mom. Help me remember
to call out to You. You have everything I will ever
need to be the best mom for my child. Thank You! Amen.*

The plan

"For I know the plans I have for you,"
declares the LORD, "plans to prosper you
and not to harm you, plans to give you hope and a future."

Jeremiah 29:11

❧ ——— ☙

We all have plans for our lives and God is the Architect of those plans. Whether life is good or bad for you at this moment, God is aware. He may not choose to remove the hard circumstances in your life, but He does promise to carry you through them and bring good from them. This takes a tremendous amount of trust in God.

In order to teach your children that God is in control of all, you need to believe it as well. Trust that God has a plan for your life and that He will lead you every step of the way.

Teach your children about God's sovereignty. Teach them about His great love for them, and His desire to prosper them and not to harm them. Think about it: if your children comprehend these truths, you will have given them a great gift – an eternal gift.

•••————⊰⊱————•••

Father, thank You for having plans for my life
and my children's lives. Thank You for allowing me
to play a role in my children's lives. I pray I will stay
close by Your side. Please remind me to always point
my children to You, teaching them of Your love for them. Amen.

The power of love

Above all else, guard your heart,
for everything you do flows from it.

Proverbs 4:23

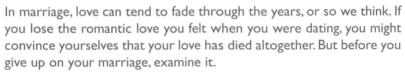

In marriage, love can tend to fade through the years, or so we think. If you lose the romantic love you felt when you were dating, you might convince yourselves that your love has died altogether. But before you give up on your marriage, examine it.

It's normal for the romantic part to die down. A couple can't maintain that level of excitement. However, in place of this temporary, romantic love, a deeper love begins to grow; a love that lasts through the good times and the bad times. This kind of love is so much richer than romantic love.

Today, it's so easy to look at your friends' marriages on Facebook, Instagram or Twitter and believe that their marriages are better than yours. Always remember that you are observing captured moments in time that may or may not be real. Pictures don't always show the whole story. You have to guard your hearts and minds; otherwise, Satan will take the opportunity to bring down your marriage. He loves to break up families.

Don't underestimate the power of enduring love.

Father, thank You for the gift of marriage ...
for the kind of love that endures through all things. God,
I pray that You would help me quiet the lies of this world that
create discontentment within my marriage. Remind me what
true love is ... the kind of love You exhibited on the cross.
Give me the courage to love my husband this way. Amen.

The prayer of a righteous woman

The prayer of a righteous person is powerful and effective.
James 5:16

❧ ——— ❧

Don't ever underestimate the power of prayer. Remember when Abraham prayed for Lot and pleaded with God to spare his life in Sodom and Gomorrah (see Genesis 18)? We find out in Genesis 19:29 that God spared Lot because He remembered Abraham's request. Abraham was a righteous man in God's eyes. He went humbly before God and begged Lot's life to be spared.

We cannot control our children, but we can pray for them. We can lift them up to their heavenly Father and ask God to work in their lives in ways that we as moms cannot. Pray that God will use the circumstances in your children's lives to draw them closer to Him. Pray protection over them from the wicked world.

If God allows your children to go through hard times, ask Him to equip them with strength and peace. Your prayers just might be the difference in how your children survive the storm. Abraham kept asking God to spare Lot's life; he was bold in his intercessory prayer. Don't give up praying after a few times; be diligent and keep going back to God with your requests.

••————————••

Father, thank You for listening to me. Thank You that I can approach Your throne and pray for my children. At times, I feel so helpless as a mom because I can't "make" my child do anything, but I know I can pray. Hear my prayers, Lord. Please act swiftly today concerning my child. Amen.

The Promised Land

"Leave this place, you and the people you brought up out of Egypt,
and go up to the land I promised on oath to Abraham,
Isaac and Jacob, saying, 'I will give it to your descendants.'"

Exodus 33:1

God promised Abraham and all of his descendants a land to call their own. God gave it to them, but Abraham had to trust God and walk in faith every day after the promise was given. God has also given you promises spelled out in His word.

Do you read the Bible and think to yourself that those promises are not for you? Do you tell yourself that those promises are for "good" people, people without a past, people who always do the right thing? Actually, God's promises are for all of His children.

Accept the promise that God will never leave you nor forsake you (see Hebrews 13:5), the promise that God has a plan for your life (see Jeremiah 29:11), the promise that God loves you and does not condemn you (see John 3:16 and Romans 8:1). These are just a few of the promises God gives to His children. Be a woman of faith and accept God's promises. Search the Bible and find all of the promises God has given to His children, and walk in faith daily with Him.

Father, I want to have faith like Abraham.
I want to not only read Your Word, but to believe it.
Help me to believe Your promises. Help those around me
to see my belief and to begin to believe Your promises too. Amen.

The right path

The ways of the Lord are right; the righteous walk in them.

Hosea 14:9

❧ ——————— ❧

In our world, anything goes. The lines of right and wrong and good or bad become blurrier each day. It's wonderful to know that in God's world, He is right all the time and His ways never change. For a mom, the idea that the Lord's ways are right should bring us comfort – God knows the way and all we have to do is to keep our eyes on Him and walk after Him.

He is faithful to direct our paths. There are so many paths to choose from, we can get confused as moms and get lost. God tells us not to be fearful (see 2 Timothy 1:7); He is the way and He will take care of us.

My goal as a mom is to walk after the Lord. Even though that sounds like an easy thing to do, it's not. The world is constantly trying to distract me and pull me off course. I must maintain my efforts to walk with the Lord and to stay fully engaged with Him at all times. Throughout your day today, remind yourself, "The ways of the Lord are right." Follow Him.

Father, You are sovereign and You are holy. Your ways are right, oh Lord, and You will guide my path. Give me the determination and discipline I need to stay focused on You. When the world pulls me away, give me discernment to realize what is happening so I will be able to correct my course and realign myself with You. Thank You for always guiding me. Amen.

The teacher

He guides the humble in what is right and teaches them His way.
Psalm 25:9

I want to be a "good" mom, but sometimes I don't know how. Luckily, God tells us that if we humble ourselves, He will be our teacher. He will show us how to parent each of our children the right way. But what does that look like in real life?

Reading the Bible: The Bible is full of practical advice and godly principles. If you don't know where to start, begin in Proverbs.

Mentor: Pray that God will bring a mentor into your life – an older woman who is a few years ahead of you in the parenting process, a woman that walks after God and lives a life worth following.

Pray: Too many times we forget this one easy step, but it's crucial in our walk with the Lord. Prayer connects you to God in a way that nothing else can. In prayer, you have the opportunity to share your heart with God. He already knows what's going on, but He's waiting for you to invite Him in.

Father, I want You to teach me Your ways. Today, I humble myself before You and ask that You make the Scripture clear to me. Give me a mentor and a friend – a woman that loves You and will guide me in my role as a mom. Father, I want to connect with You daily through prayer. Gently remind me when I forget to pray. Please continue to pursue me. Amen.

The ugly side of pride

Pride goes before destruction, a haughty spirit before a fall.

Proverbs 16:18

Pride tends to get in the way more often than not. Many times, I know that I acted wrongly, but because of my pride, I won't apologize. This can begin to destroy my relationship with my child and others. We as moms should humble ourselves and acknowledge when we are wrong. We should go to our children and say, "I'm sorry for …"

In humbling ourselves, we show our children that:

∗ We aren't perfect.

∗ We make mistakes and need to apologize, just like them.

By having humble hearts, we teach our children the correct ways to handle bad situations.

Don't ever be too prideful to not apologize. None of us are perfect. It's good for a child to see a parent own up to their mistake and make it right. You are the teacher. Teach your child the correct way to handle bad situations.

Father, I make mistakes as a parent every day. Give me a humble heart – a heart that is willing to apologize to my children and take responsibility for my mistakes. Father, I ask that as I lead my children, You would give me wisdom to parent with humility. In my own strength, I have a hard time doing that. Amen.

The ultimate teacher

Day after day, in the temple courts and from house to house, they never stopped teaching and proclaiming the good news that Jesus is the Messiah.

Acts 5:42

Moms have captive audiences every day and we should take advantage of that time to teach our children about Jesus. Children are eager to learn. The faith of a child is great. Leverage your time when they are young and teach them Jesus' ways.

Teach your children about the great love Jesus has for them, how He loved them so much that He sacrificed all for them. Teach your children about God's mercy and grace that He so freely gives to all. Teach them that there is no condemnation in Christ.

Make the most of your time with your children. While you are teaching manners, how to read, write and do math, don't forget the one value that is eternal – faith in Jesus Christ.

Father, I have lots of jobs as a mom: cooking, cleaning and caring for my family. Help me remember the one thing that is most important – You! Give me wisdom to know how to teach my child of Your love and Your ways. I will plant the seeds, but I need You to make them grow. Amen.

The waiting game

He waited seven more days
and again sent out the dove from the ark.

Genesis 8:10

Half of our lives as moms are spent waiting. We start our pregnancies waiting for the big arrival date. Then we begin to wait for our children to fall asleep for their naps, for our children to understand discipline; we wait in carpool lines, for our teenagers to get home from dates. Especially in the training and rearing of your children, there will be waiting. It's a slow, deliberate process that requires patience.

Children aren't going to learn to obey the first time you tell them no. It takes multiple times, with multiple discipline strategies, and then, over time, children will learn and choose wisely. We need to be patient in the process and not try to speed up their training.

Waiting is a learned skill and one that we need God's help in mastering. We want quick results, first-time obedience, but that rarely happens in the real world. Slow and steady wins the race. This needs to be our goal. As you wait, keep the goal in mind. It will give you the determination to "wait it out."

Father, waiting is my least favorite thing to do in life.
I like instant results and instant progress, but I know those
don't apply in raising my children. God, please give me the
determination to wait on You and then give me the patience
to wait on my children as they learn and grow. Amen.

Time management

Nevertheless, each person should live as a believer in whatever situation the Lord has assigned to them, just as God has called them. This is the rule I lay down in all the churches.

I Corinthians 7:17

Where has God placed you? Are you in the "infant" season, stuck in the house all the time, wishing your baby would sleep through the night and begin to interact with you? Are you in the toddler stage, where you wish your child would slow down and not get into everything around your house? Is your child in the busy years of elementary school, where you feel like a glorified taxi driver? Or is your teen driving themselves and you feel left out?

Whatever stage of life, "retain the place" you find yourself. Realize that there are only 24 hours in a day and not everything will fit. You will have to give up different things in different seasons of life. Your "time" as a mom is valuable. Decide the most important things you need to accomplish.

Whatever you decide, thank God for the season you're in right now.

Father, thank You for calling me for this season of my life. Please give me wisdom to know what's important and what can be set aside. Open my eyes to see my children the way You see them. Teach me how to parent them the way You want them to be parented. Amen.

Train up a child

Start children off on the way they should go,
and even when they are old they will not turn from it.
The rich rule over the poor, and the borrower is slave to the lender.

Proverbs 22:6-7

This sounds so easy, but in the "real world," it's hard. It's hard because when "life" happens, it's just easier to make our children's beds for them. It's easier to dress our three-year-old than to wait on him. It's easier to pick up our children's shoes or put away the toys or do that school project.

Verse 7 says, "The rich rule over the poor, and the borrower is servant to the lender." Why is that verse even included here? I believe if we do everything for our kids, they will be poor when they grow up. I know I just lost you because you passed out at the thought of your precious children not being successful, but please hear my heart.

How can your kids be successful if you do everything for them all their lives? When they hit the age of 21, a switch is not going to flip so that they suddenly become ambitious, hardworking, great money managers and leaders. These traits are learned and developed over time. You as a mom need to train up your children, and then when they are old, they will not depart from what you've taught them.

Father, please give me the discipline
to train up my children. Help me to see past today
and work for their futures. Thank You for the wisdom
in the Bible and for showing me how to parent wisely. Amen.

Transitions in life

He made the moon to mark the seasons,
and the sun knows when to go down.

Psalm 104:19

Transitions in life are normal. Whether or not you're prepared, change is always lurking. Some people handle change easily, while others resist it and fight to keep things the same. Change is inevitable. Look at your journey as a mom and how much change there is in your children. When your kids were babies, you thought you'd never get through that stage. Then the next stage came … and the next … and the next. Each stage brings its own set of challenges and joys.

Moms shouldn't fight these transitions, but embrace them. Celebrate the season that has just passed and remember the special times God gave you. Look forward to the next season.

What lies ahead for you? Is it the toddler years, elementary school, the teenage years, college or becoming an empty nester? Lean into God during these times. Learn to celebrate your children growing older and becoming more independent. Ask God for wisdom to handle each new season. Enjoy today.

Father, I want to transition well from one season to another.
I don't want to always be looking back, wishing for what I cannot
have and I don't want to always be looking forward to the future.
I need to be present with my children and enjoy life with them,
during whatever season we are in together. Amen.

Trials in life

Blessed is the one who perseveres under trial because,
having stood the test, that person will receive the crown of life
that the Lord has promised to those who love Him.

James 1:12

We rush in, as moms, always trying to protect our children from every hurt and hard situation. This is natural. However, as our children grow, we need to love them enough to allow them to experience hurtful situations and hard times. It is during these trials that our children learn and grow. It would be very sad for your kids to reach adulthood, never to have overcome a difficult circumstance.

How do we sit by and watch our children suffer? Learning to navigate trials in life is a process. Children don't come into the world knowing how to handle such things. Your job as a mom is not to fix them, but to teach your children how to work through them.

You need to empathize: "I know this is a hard situation. I remember a time when I was young and …" We need to listen. Listening is a powerful gift to someone who is hurting. We need to ask questions: "How do you think you should handle this situation?" Or, "What's your next step?" Or, "Have you prayed about this situation and asked God for His wisdom?"

Father, thank You for never leaving me
no matter how difficult life gets. I know my children will go
through hard times; I need Your strength and discipline to keep
me from jumping in and fixing their problems. God,
when I am tempted to "fix," remind me of James 1:12 …
that You have a crown for those who persevere. Amen.

True love

For God so loved the world that He gave His one and only Son,
that whoever believes in Him shall not perish but have eternal life.

John 3:16

One thing a mother truly understands in parenting is the deep love she feels for her children. There is nothing quite like it when your toddler can finally look up at you and say the words, "I love you, Mommy!" It melts our hearts every time. Even when our children disobey or do things that we don't approve of, we still love them. No one or nothing can ever break that love.

Did you know that your heavenly Father loves you so much that He gave up His only Son? Jesus gave His life for our sins, so we could be united with God forever. God is a holy God and the only way we could be united with Him was for someone to pay the price for our sins. That was Jesus – the perfect sacrifice.

Today as you hug your child and whisper those three words, "I love you," remember your heavenly Father loves you more than you will ever understand. He loves you whether you obey Him, trust Him or even know Him. He loves you! If you will accept His gift of love to you – Jesus – you will spend eternity with Him in heaven!

Father, Your love for me is so large, it's hard for me
to comprehend. But I trust You and trust that You love me.
Thank You for Your gift to humankind – Your only Son, Jesus.
God, I accept Your gift and look forward to the day
when we will be together forever in heaven. Amen.

True or false

Did God really say …?
Genesis 3:1

How many times do we as moms question the validity of God's Word? God's Word says, "He will not leave nor forsake you" (Hebrews 13:5), but how many times has Satan whispered in our ears, "Does God really mean He will never leave you? It sure feels like He has left you." Or in Jeremiah 29:11 when God promises us that He has a plan for us. How many times have I questioned His plan? How many times have I felt like the world was passing me by and there wasn't a plan for this stay-at-home mom?

Ladies, we need to realize that Satan is the author of all lies. Paul tells us the enemy is looking for someone to devour (see 1 Peter 5:8). Stand strong in God's promises.

When Satan whispers lies like, "Did God really say …?" your response needs to be bold and strong, "Yes! God has promised me these things. Get behind me, Satan."

Father, give me wisdom as a mother.
If I fall prey to Satan's lies, my children will as well.
Teach me Your Word and Your truth, so I may teach them
to my children. Your truth will set me free. Amen.

True worth

We are God's handiwork, created in Christ Jesus to do good works, which God prepared in advance for us to do.
Ephesians 2:10

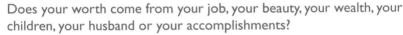

Does your worth come from your job, your beauty, your wealth, your children, your husband or your accomplishments?

You should base your worth on what God says about you, because God's mind is the only thing that does not change. The beauty of being a child of God is that when God looks at you, He sees His Son, Jesus. In Galatians 2:20 Paul writes, "I have been crucified with Christ and I no longer live, but Christ lives in me. The life I live in the body, I live by faith in the Son of God, who loved me and gave Himself for me."

Our worth is not determined by what we believe about ourselves; it is determined by what God says is true about us. God says:

* You are loved (see John 3:16).
* You are forgiven (see Acts 10:43).
* You are precious (see Luke 12:24).
* You are beautiful (see Isaiah 61:3).
* You are mine (see 1 Chronicles 29:11).

Moms, you need to learn God's truth about you and believe it with all your heart.

Father, thank You for loving me and for sending Your Son. Thank You that when You look at me, You don't see my sin; You see Your perfect, holy Son, Jesus. Help me to see my true worth and to believe what You say about me. Amen.

Truth

"Sanctify them by the truth; Your word is truth."
John 17:17

———

It's heartbreaking when you realize someone has been lying to you – a loved one, a politician or even a friend. But we also lie to ourselves on a daily basis. We tell ourselves that we aren't good enough, we don't measure up or we can't find peace. Those are all lies that imprison us. But Jesus wants to break that bondage and bring you freedom.

Jesus said, "Truth will set you free" (John 8:32). What is truth? Jesus is truth. Jesus said, "I am the way, the truth and the life" (John 14:6). Through Jesus, you can find truth and that truth will set you free from the bondage and chains that bring you down.

Did you know that the Bible says you are a child of God, holy and blameless (see Ephesians 1:3-6)? Did you know that? Did you know that your sin has been forgiven and removed forever (see Psalm 103:12)?

There is no reason to drag your past regrets and guilt around with you. They're gone. Quit believing lies that only bring you down. Embrace Jesus and His truth. The truth will set you free.

———

Father, I'm blown away that in You I can find freedom and know that I am truly loved. Thank You for giving me truth – Jesus. Sanctify me through Your truth and Your Word. God, I want to live a life full of freedom and love. Amen.

Uganda

*Keep your lives free from the love of money
and be content with what you have, because God has said,
"Never will I leave you; never will I forsake you."*

Hebrews 13:5

A life free from the love of money is a wonderful life. In Hebrews, Paul teaches us that we need to be content with what we have. Recently, I went to Uganda and experienced firsthand what Paul was talking about in this verse. The people in the village we visited were content with what they had and they didn't have much.

Actually, they didn't really have anything. I was invited to several homes while visiting this village and none of them had tables or chairs. They had worn-out benches and straw mats to sit on. None of them had a kitchen, but a wood fire outside with one pot to cook with.

The willingness of the Ugandan people to trust Christ with their lives changed me forever. They realized that Christ is enough. They know that life is not promised to them, because so many of them have died from starvation, AIDS and other diseases. They know they are not promised great wealth or prosperity. Most of them were born and will die in that village. But they seemed to understand that God is enough and that His promise to never leave or forsake them is all they need.

*Father, give me faith like the people of Uganda.
I have so many material things and yet I still want more.
Open my eyes so that I might realize You are enough and that the
material items I seek will never make me happy. Create in me a
generous heart to give to others less fortunate than me. Amen.*

Unclean words

*Jesus called the crowd to Him and said, "Listen and understand.
What goes into someone's mouth does not defile them, but what
comes out of their mouth, that is what defiles them."*

Matthew 15:10-11

Our culture is obsessed with cleanliness. We use hand sanitizers to wash away germs. We pay so much attention to having a clean house, clean car and clean clothes, but do we pay attention to clean words? Our words are direct reflections of our hearts.

Matthew 15:19-20 reads: "For out of the heart come evil thoughts, murder, adultery, sexual immorality, theft, false testimony, slander. These are what defile a person; but eating with unwashed hands does not defile them." Jesus said this over 2,000 years ago, before hand sanitizer was even invented.

We toss questionable words around and think they make a story funnier or more interesting, and we never give a second thought that they are making us unclean.

Are your words slanderous and negative toward others, or do they encourage and build them up? If someone were to sit in a room with you and listen to your conversations with your best friends, how would that person characterize you? As clean or unclean? Think about this as you go about your day.

*Father, I never realized that I could be unclean
because of the words I use. I have never made the connection
that what's in my heart comes out of my mouth. I need to do
some housecleaning in my heart. Forgive me. Cleanse me
and teach me how to live a clean life. Amen.*

Unity of the Spirit

Be completely humble and gentle; be patient,
bearing with one another in love. Make every effort
to keep the unity of the Spirit through the bond of peace.

Ephesians 4:2-3

These verses sound so wonderful … until life hits. It's hard to be completely humble when you want to brag about your child or the accomplishments of your spouse.

Be gentle? Am I gentle when my husband frustrates me for the umpteenth time in one day. Be gentle? Am I gentle when my child is supposed to take out the trash, but leaves it on the garage floor, the dog gets into it, trash is strewn all over the garage and my dog throws up on the carpet?

Be patient, bearing with one another. Do I practice patience when I'm at the grocery store trying to check out in a hurry and the cashier is new and can't seem to get her act together?

Make every effort to keep the unity of the Spirit through the bond of peace. Do I make every effort to keep unity when holidays roll around and the house is filled with family and in-laws? Do I help bring unity or do I add to the tension? Do I keep peace or do I stir the pot? These are great questions I should be asking myself daily.

Father, give me what I need to be humble, gentle, patient and unified in Spirit. I pray there would be less of me and my way, and more of You and Your way. I pray that Your love would be exhibited in me daily. Make me aware of how I act in the moment. I pray I will choose to walk with You and not on my own. Amen.

Waiting on God

But those who hope in the Lord will renew their strength.
They will soar on wings like eagles; they will run
and not grow weary, they will walk and not be faint.

Isaiah 40:31

⋗————◦————⋖

We all want to be strong and endure well in these lives we've been given. But strength is only found in waiting, waiting upon the Lord.

Does God have you in a time of waiting right now? Are you waiting on your husband to understand your point of view about a situation? Are you waiting on your child to get through this season of life and outgrow a certain habit? Are you waiting on a health diagnosis? Are you waiting for your prodigal child to come home?

No matter what you are waiting on, God will meet you while you wait and He will strengthen you. Allow Him to establish His plan for you. Ask Him to reveal to you what He wants you to understand during this time.

•••————◦————•••

Father, I want to be strong and wait on You,
but I admit this is hard. I don't feel strong; I feel weak.
I am seeking You today, Lord, seeking Your will for my life.
Please give me strength as I wait. Amen.

Waiting patiently

Be still in the presence of the LORD,
and wait patiently for Him to act. Don't worry about
evil people who prosper or fret about their wicked schemes.

Psalm 37:7 (NLT)

To be still before the Lord and to wait patiently on Him requires one thing from me – discipline. In the fast-paced world we live in, it takes discipline to sit quietly before God. If I will train myself to wait upon God, then He promises to act on my behalf (see Isaiah 64:4).

Sometimes, I feel like the world is passing me by. I look around and see other moms advancing in their careers, accomplishing so much, and I think to myself, What am I accomplishing? God tells us not to fret, but to be patient and to wait on Him, His timing and His way.

Slowing down and waiting enables me to keep things in perspective and realize my needs will be met through God, not me. It's a gift from God and it takes so much pressure off my shoulders.

Today, take your cares and concerns to God in prayer. Ask Him to meet you where you are. After your prayer, sit quietly before Him and think about His greatness: He was the one who created the universe, humankind and all things great and small. He, in all His greatness, wants a relationship with you!

Father, thank You for being patient with me
and loving at all times. Thank You for wanting
a relationship with me and for knowing and
understanding where I am as a mom. God, give me patience
and give me discipline so I can be still and wait on You. Amen.

December

Walk of faith

It was by faith that Abraham obeyed when God called him to leave home and go to another land that God would give him as his inheritance. He went without knowing where he was going.

Hebrews 11:8 (NLT)

Do you ever feel like you don't know where you're going as a mom? We must be like Abraham and have faith. Faith is "being sure of what we hope for and certain of what we do not see" (Hebrews 11:1).

Our faith is in God, not in a plan or what we want to have happen in our lives. To have faith in God means to believe Him when He says that He loves us, will take care of us and will never leave us. The manifestation of faith is obedience: to obey what God tells us in the Bible and to trust in Him.

Obey God today:

* Wives, submit to your husbands (see Colossians 3:18).
* Train a child in the way he should go (see Proverbs 22:6).
* Love one another (see John 13:34).
* Trust in the Lord with all your heart and lean not on your own understanding (see Proverbs 3:5).

These simple steps of obedience will begin to change your perspective on life. Be bold today and take God at His Word. Do it and see what happens!

Father, I give You this day and all that it brings. I want to live a life of faith like Abraham, to go somewhere that is completely unknown. God, meet me where I am. It's scary for me to walk in faith, but I trust You. Please take my hand and lead me. Amen.

Walking daily

Commit yourselves wholeheartedly to these words of mine.
Teach them to your children. Talk about them when you
are at home and when you are on the road.

Deuteronomy 11:18-19

Your heavenly Father wants to be involved in every aspect of your life. The God that created the universe, the God that set the stars in the sky, the God that created the oceans and the mountains, the God that gave breath to every living creature, that same God wants to walk with you daily. He desires to be in every level of your life. Invite Him in – when you sit down, when you walk around, when you lie down and when you get up.

If the President of the United States wanted to be your friend, you would answer his call every time. Well, God wants a relationship with you and He is far greater than any president on this earth!

Carve out time in your day to spend with Him. Place verses around your house to remind you of His love, His majesty and His grace toward you.

Father, thank You for wanting to have a relationship with me.
Thank You for the Bible, so I can read Your Word and capture it
in my heart. Draw me ever closer to You, Lord. Amen.

War in the spiritual realm

*For we are not fighting against flesh-and-blood enemies,
but against evil rulers and authorities of the unseen world,
against mighty powers in this dark world,
and against evil spirits in the heavenly places.*

Ephesians 6:12

As moms we need to begin to realize whom our struggle is with and start fighting on the real battlefield – the spiritual realm. Jesus tells us in John 16:33: "In this world you will have trouble. But, take heart! I have overcome the world."

Instead of trying to fight my battles in my own effort, I need to start taking my struggles to God and asking for His protection, His Word, His wisdom, His self-control and His love. In Him is the only place I will ever find victory.

But as long as I continue to believe the lie that my struggle is against my husband or the teacher that is not being fair to my child, or as long as I believe my struggle is with my child and the two of us can't get along, I will always be defeated. Our enemy, Satan, wants us to focus on these things because he knows we will lose the battle if we do. However, our heavenly Father tells us that our struggles are spiritual and we need to fight the battles in the spiritual realm. Only then will we find victory.

Father, open my eyes and show me Your way. Open my heart to see the world as You see the world. Fill me with Your Spirit so that I may have love, joy, peace, patience, kindness and self-control. I can only fight this battle and be victorious through You. Thank You for overcoming this world and for giving me hope! Amen.

Wasted time

Unless the LORD builds a house,
the work of the builders is wasted.
Unless the LORD protects a city,
guarding it with sentries will do no good.

Psalm 127:1

Time is too precious to waste. Your job is too important to waste the time God has given you with your children focusing on things that are of no eternal value. If your work as a mom is not built on God, then all the work you do is wasted. As you go about your day, ask yourself two questions: Is God at the foundation of what I am doing? Does what I am doing have eternal value?

What does it look like for God to be at the foundation of what you are doing? Consider God when you are making your life plans. Ask Him for guidance and to give you wisdom. Whatever your plans are, keep your hands open toward God, always being willing to change direction if He wishes.

Does what I'm doing have eternal value? If you are focusing on material things, career advancement or building your finances, none of these things have eternal value. People are eternal and our relationship with God is eternal. Keep your eyes focused on what matters to God, not what is important in this world.

Father, I want to build my family on Your Word,
Your principles and Your desires. I don't want my time to be
wasted. I am devoted to You and doing my job as a mom to the
best of my ability. I want to include You in everything I do.
Teach me. Show me. I am willing to learn. Amen.

What about submission?

Wives, submit to your husbands,
as it is fitting for those who belong to the Lord.

Colossians 3:18

—

Submission is a difficult concept in marriage, but God is clear on this topic. He doesn't give us any wiggle room. He doesn't say, "Submit if your husband is a good man," "Submit if your husband has prayed over the decision and you both agree," "Submit if your husband is wise." The verse says simply to submit.

What I have had to do in my marriage is realize I am ultimately submitting to my heavenly Father, not my husband. I am choosing to submit to God and His command, and my trust is ultimately in Him, not my husband.

In telling us to submit to our husbands, God has really given us a gift even though we don't always see it that way. God is saying that the man is the leader and the man will be held accountable for the way he leads the family. My job as a wife is to submit and trust God. Even though I don't understand God's way of thinking all the time, I need to trust Him.

—

Father, I want to obey You and be a godly wife.
Submitting to my husband is not easy. I love You and,
because I trust You and Your wisdom, I will obey You. God,
I pray that You will honor my obedience and bless my family
and me. My prayer is that through my obedience, You will
guide me as I walk this road of submission. Amen.

What an exchange!

*Come to me, all you who are weary
and burdened, and I will give you rest.*

Matthew 11:28

Can you hear Jesus calling to you? He is. He says, "Come to Me, all you who are weary and burdened." Most moms are weary, if for no other reason than they haven't had a good night's sleep in a while. Most moms are burdened by worry for their children. Jesus is calling us to come to Him and His promise is that He will give us rest. What an exchange! I can exchange weariness for rest.

Jesus understands your weariness and your burdens. When Jesus walked the earth, He had people pulling on Him all day long, wanting things from Him. Sound familiar? Jesus offers us rest. Jesus understands burdens. He carried the weight of the world on His shoulders; He can handle your burdens too. Will you take Him up on His offer?

Today, make a conscious effort to lay your burdens at Jesus' feet. Jesus says He is gentle and humble in heart. Take the burdens in your life that weigh you down, lay them at the feet of Jesus and pick up His "rest" for your soul. What an exchange!

*Father, being a mom is the hardest job I have ever had
and yet the most fulfilling. I want to include You
in every part of this journey of motherhood and invite You
to bear my burdens each step of the way. Thank You
for sharing my highs and lows, and for Your promise
to be there for me. I give You all the glory and praise! Amen.*

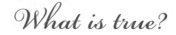

What is true?

I have been crucified with Christ
and I no longer live, but Christ lives in me.

Galatians 2:20

So many times we try to live the Christian life in our own strength only to fail miserably. We fail because God never intended for us to do it on our own. When we accept Jesus to be our Lord and Savior, it is He who is living in us and we need to learn to allow Him to operate freely in our lives.

It is imperative that we believe the truth that it is no longer we who live, but Christ now lives in us. Are we trying desperately to be patient, loving, compassionate and full of self-control? Only Jesus can do those things in us, and we must learn to allow Him to rule in our lives.

In order for us to live this truth out, we must die to ourselves. We must realize that we cannot be patient in our own strength – we need Christ. We cannot love compassionately without Christ or have self-control. As you go about your day today, remind yourself of the truth that Christ is now in control of your life and living in you. Fully surrender your life to Him and enjoy the fruits of the Spirit.

Father, thank You for sending Your Son, Jesus,
to die for my sins. Thank You, Father, that when He died,
I died with Him and now He lives in me. I pray that I will
learn how to allow Him to live His life through me
and I would enjoy His presence in my life daily. Amen.

What is your treasure?

For where your treasure is, there your heart will be also.
Matthew 6:21

It's human nature to "store up" things for ourselves (see Matthew 6:19). Our children are no different. Don't be surprised when your children are discontent, always wanting the latest and greatest gadget, toy, smart phone or computer. We need to teach our children that where their treasure is, their hearts will follow.

In order to teach this life principle to our children, we must first learn it ourselves. When our inner selves tell us that we must have the latest purse, the latest fashion trend, the club membership, a new car or a bigger house, we need to remind ourselves that none of those things will make us happy. Eventually, the new will wear off and we will still want more. Not that having a new purse is a bad thing, but do you want your heart to follow the desire of owning the best and looking the best? That desire will never fully be satisfied.

So, teach your children that it's okay to want these things but not okay to allow those desires to consume them. Teach them to give their requests to God, even the shallow ones, and allow Him to decide what they need versus what they want.

Father, You have given me so many blessings in my life and yet I still want more. I understand I will be battling these desires until I go to heaven, but I want to learn how to tame the beast. God, teach me how to be satisfied with what I have. Amen.

What's in it for me?

*Therefore, I urge you, brothers and sisters,
in view of God's mercy, to offer your bodies as a living sacrifice,
holy and pleasing to God – this is your true and proper worship.*

Romans 12:1

There is nothing better than being on a team and knowing that everyone is working together for a win. On a team, comradery is built, love is shared and sacrifices are made by all – not for individual notoriety, but for all. A slogan for many teams is: "All for one and one for all." Wouldn't it be great if your family took on this attitude?

This type of comradeship has to be nurtured. You as the mom need to weave it into the fabric of your family. Most of the time, children have the attitude, "What's in it for me?" Sometimes the answer is, "Nothing … except to sacrifice yourself, your time and your talents for the good of the family." Over time, the family bond will grow and a deep love will develop because of the sacrifices that are made on one another's behalf.

Think of your family as a team. For example: when one person is campaigning in a school election, what can the other family members do to support that person? When one person has a big athletic event, the other family members can cheer him or her on to victory.

*Father, give me wisdom to guide my children
and teach them how to sacrifice for their family.
I want our family to not just believe in You,
but to live it out. You sacrificed Your Son
and I want to model that love every day. Amen.*

What's my role?

He has shown you, O mortal, what is good.
And what does the Lord require of you? To act justly
and to love mercy and to walk humbly with your God.

Micah 6:8

The Bible is a Guidebook from God to help us live our lives. He sent His Son, Jesus, to pay for our sins so we could have a relationship with Him for eternity. God sent prophets to foretell the future and disciples to write about the life of Jesus so we would know how to live our lives until He returns.

Going to church once a week, hearing a great message and singing a few songs will not make us strong Christians. God requires that we act justly, love mercy and walk humbly with Him. To act justly means to do what is right. If you are a follower of Christ, your life should reflect His character; Jesus always did what was good. To love mercy means to show compassion and forgiveness toward all. Christians should be the most caring, accepting people of all, extending grace and love.

The last requirement is to walk humbly with God, never thinking that we have arrived, but realizing the more we learn and grow, the more we understand how holy God is, how anything we accomplish is due to Him alone.

Father, teach me Your ways. Give me the courage
to always do what is right, to love the way You love and to be
humble. I can't do any of these things without You. Please fill
me with Your Spirit today and guide my every step. Amen.

Who are you serving?

Respect the Lord your God and serve only Him.
You must use only His name to make promises.

Deuteronomy 6:13

In order for us to glorify God in all that we do, we must make God our number one priority in life. In our lives there are so many things pulling on our attention, time and service, that we need to focus on who and what we are going to serve. If I as a mom am going to be successful, then I need to serve only God.

One way you can keep God first is to focus on Him the moment you wake up in the morning. Before your feet hit the floor, train yourself to say, "Thank You, God, for this day. Thank You, God, for my marriage, my children and my job." As you go about your day, keep in mind that, as you serve your family, you can serve with a loving attitude and heart.

When your children are not thanking you for your endless acts of love, remind yourself that ultimately you are not serving them, but you are serving God. Your children are merely receiving the benefits of your love toward God.

God, as I go about my day, show me different ways I can serve only You. I want to be mindful of Your presence and commit my day to You. I do not want You to be an afterthought at the end of my day or feel guilty that I haven't talked to You all day. Thank You, Lord, for wanting to be in a relationship with me. Amen.

Wisdom

If any of you lacks wisdom, you should ask God,
who gives generously to all without finding fault,
and it will be given to you.

James 1:5

This verse includes a promise: if we ask, God will give, and He will give generously without finding fault. In a mom's world this is a home run. You can't lose if you follow this verse. "If" you lack wisdom – we are all learning in this realm of motherhood, so we all need wisdom – God promises us that if we ask, He will give generously without finding fault. So, at the end of the day God will not blame us for not knowing what to do, He will just lovingly give us wisdom.

In what areas do we need wisdom as moms? Discipline is a great place to start. Ask God to give you wisdom in knowing when to discipline and when to give grace. Also, God is the Creator of your children, ask for wisdom in how to best parent each child. God knows.

If we want the promise of wisdom to be granted, we must ask. Don't be afraid to ask.

Father, give me wisdom today as I parent my children.
Teach me how You knit my children together and how to
discipline each one. I want to honor You in all that I do
and the first step is to acknowledge that You are the Creator
and Lord of all. All wisdom comes from You. Amen.

Wisdom giver

*From all nations people came to listen to Solomon's wisdom,
sent by all the kings of the world, who had heard of his wisdom.*

I Kings 4:34

Solomon was known for his wisdom and the people around the whole world came to learn from him. How did Solomon become so wise? He asked God for wisdom (see I Kings 3:9). Solomon knew he could not lead the people of Israel in his own strength and the job of a king was too great for him to bear alone, so he asked God for help.

Do you feel that way as a mom? Do you feel overwhelmed with the burden and responsibility of leading your children? You may see all the other moms parenting the "right" way, and feel as if you are not equipped to do the job right.

Maybe you had a poor example and since you lacked a great role model, you feel as if you don't know what you're doing. Take heart! God is with you. Learn from Solomon and ask God for wisdom and discernment, and He will give it to you (see James 1:5).

*Father, I am asking You for wisdom. Most days,
I don't feel qualified to be a mom, but I know that
You are extremely qualified and I trust that You will give me
what I need. I am claiming James 1:5 right now …
that You give wisdom to those who ask. I am asking.
Thank You for listening and answering my prayer. Amen.*

Wisdom with money

The rich rule over the poor,
and the borrower is slave to the lender.

Proverbs 22:7

We teach our children many values during the 18 years we parent them. We should never overlook teaching the value of wise money management. We all like new "things," and children are no different. You have a wonderful opportunity to begin training your children how to attain the things in life they want, while at the same time not becoming a slave to the lender.

The best way to teach your children this very important principle is to not get into the habit of buying things on credit. Your children can get into a credit mentality, always telling you, "I'll pay you back." Teach them early on how to save for the things they want and then pay for it with cash. Help them to develop a game plan on how to accomplish their goals. In the end, they will learn several valuable lessons.

The Bible is full of truth and wisdom, and we will become wise moms if we take our direction from God's Word.

Father, I pray that You will guide and direct me
as I teach my children how to save money
and not be in debt. Our world thinks nothing of debt,
but I want a better life for them, not one where they
covered in debt. Give me strength not to give in to my children,
but to teach them how to be disciplined with their money. Amen.

Wise mom

Therefore everyone who hears these words of mine and puts them into practice is like a wise man who built his house on the rock.

Matthew 7:24

I want to be a wise woman and a wise mom. If I follow Jesus' command in this verse, I will need to hear His Word and then put those words into practice. It's a two-step process. So many times when I read the Bible, I fail to act upon what I read.

It's so easy to make excuses or justify what I'm doing when I don't do what God's Word says. One thing is for sure, the Bible is clear on so many topics. I must be wise, not in my own eyes, but in God's eyes. So many times, we can "think" we are being wise, but when we compare our thoughts to Scripture, they don't match.

Always go with what God says, even if the world tells you different.

Father, give me understanding when I read Your Word. Give me determination and discipline to apply Your Word to my daily life. So often, I am tempted to live life my own way, but I am acknowledging to You right now that I want to live life Your way. Thank You for Your patience with me and love for me. Amen.

With God, anything is possible

The one who calls you is faithful, and He will do it.
I Thessalonians 5:24

So many times as a mom, I try to produce patience, to love unconditionally, to not grow weary – all in my own strength. But God never intended for us to walk this journey alone. He actually doesn't want us to try to improve in our own strength; He knows it's an impossible task. He will do it for us.

I need to look to the source of my life – God. He is faithful; He will do all things through me. My role in our relationship is to abide in Him. If I walk with my heavenly Father daily, seeking Him to meet my needs, He will be faithful and He will provide.

He will also give me wisdom, unconditional love for my children, patience, strength and kindness. I want to be this kind of mom.

Father, thank You for Your faithfulness and Your love. Thank You that I don't have to perform for You, that You don't expect me to be perfect. So many times, I get confused and put all of the performance pressure on myself. God, help me to remember that only through You am I able to accomplish anything. Amen.

Wonderful Christmas traditions

So they hurried off and found Mary and Joseph,
and the baby, who was lying in the manger.
When they had seen Him, they spread the word concerning
what had been told them about this child.

Luke 2:16-18

Christmas is such a wonderful time of year, especially when you have small children in the house. Children get excited about the decorations, traditions and especially receiving gifts.

We all have our Christmas traditions, but don't forget to celebrate the birth of Jesus. What a glorious event! Jesus became human to build a bridge so that we could have a relationship with God.

We as moms can easily get wrapped up in the Christmas frenzy, getting all the presents for the family, creating the perfectly decorated home and baking the best cookies that will be the envy of the Christmas gathering. In the midst of this, we can easily forget that without Jesus' birth, Christmas would be just another holiday.

Without Jesus, we wouldn't be able to have a relationship with our heavenly Father.

Father, thank You for Jesus. Thank You for giving us such a wonderful gift of salvation. God, I pray that I don't forget the real meaning of this Christmas season. I pray I will be bold like the shepherd and spread the good news about Your Son. Amen.

Wonderful seasonal treasures

But Mary treasured up all these things
and pondered them in her heart.

Luke 2:19

This holiday season, take some time to treasure things in your heart. Take a few minutes each day and thank God for each family member in your home. Starting with your husband, thank God for him – really pray for him. Then move on to your children and lift each one up to your heavenly Father, asking for blessings over their lives and guidance and direction.

When you finish with your own family, move on to your in-laws and then your friends. On Christmas Eve, devote that day of prayer to Jesus and thank God for the wonderful gift He is to our world.

Don't let this month go by like every other month of the year. Treasure your blessings and give thanks to God. December can be the busiest month of the year, but purposefully slow down this year and reflect on everything God has given you, including His precious Son, Jesus!

Father, I could never imagine giving my child up for anyone.
But God, You loved the world so much that You sacrificed Jesus,
Your only Son, so we could have a relationship with You.
Thank You for Your endless love and grace. I pray that I will
discipline myself this month to reflect on the blessings You have
given me, especially the biggest blessing of all – Jesus. Amen.

Words that count

Do not let any unwholesome talk come out of your mouths,
but only what is helpful for building others up according
to their needs, that it may benefit those who listen.

Ephesians 4:29

Our words are powerful. Words have a way of staying with someone – even after time passes, the details fade, but the words remain. Therefore, make your words count, especially with your children. Paul tells us that our words should be "building others up" and that these words should "benefit those who listen." These marching orders can be very trying for us moms. Our children tend to push us to our breaking point, but remember that you as the mom have a tremendous amount of influence in your child's life, so your words are extremely important.

Today and every day, when you are teaching your child, think about your words. Ask yourself two questions: Do my words build or tear down? Are the words I say benefiting the receiver? Sometimes we speak brilliant, wonderful and uplifting words, but our children are not listening and, therefore, not benefiting from them. Ask your child to turn off the TV or to put the cell phone down and listen to you. Use that time to invest in your child with words. Even if you need to correct your child, you can use encouraging words while you teach. Make all your words count.

Father, it's amazing how powerful words can be,
both positive and negative. I want all my words to be uplifting.
I realize that by using these criteria, I won't be talking as much,
which may be a good thing. Gently remind me on a daily basis
that my words should be benefiting those around me. Amen.

Working unto the Lord

*Whatever you do, work at it with all your heart,
as working for the Lord, not for human masters,
since you know that you will receive an inheritance from
the Lord as a reward. It is the Lord Christ you are serving.*

Colossians 3:23-24

As a mom you do a lot of jobs that go unnoticed and unappreciated. It's hard to keep your attitude positive when you don't believe anyone notices the special touches you put on so many parts of your family's lives. But be encouraged: God notices.

He notices when you're making the beds, how you tuck that bottom sheet nice and tight so that when your children get in at night, it has a clean feel. God notices when you cook dinner that you go back and sample your cooking to make sure it's right.

God notices everything and He appreciates all the love you give to your children. He knows that because you love His children, they are more likely to accept His love for them. Take heart, moms – God knows! Keep serving and know that your heavenly Father is keeping score and you will receive your inheritance one day.

*Heavenly Father, I pray that I will have a good attitude
throughout my day as I serve my family. Please remind me
that I am ultimately serving You and that You do notice all
things. Thank You for loving me and I pray I will show that
love to my children on a daily basis. Amen.*

Worry that causes sleepless nights

Who of you by worrying can add a single hour to your life?
Luke 12:25

We worry in vain. Worry is a sign of a lack of trust in God. Our worrying doesn't change anything; it only makes us tired. So place your tired and weary soul into God's very capable hands.

If you're worrying about your child's health, will that change your child's health?

If you're worrying about your child's grades, will that change your child's grades?

If you're worrying about your child's rebellious heart, will that change their heart?

If you're worrying about your marriage, does worrying change your marriage?

If you're worrying about your finances, does worrying change your finances?

The answer to all these questions is no. Then why do we worry? We worry because it makes us feel like we're doing something. So let's do something that will make a difference: take your worries and lay them at God's feet.

Father, I do worry. I didn't realize that trying to control my circumstances or find an answer to my problem meant that I didn't trust You. I know that You have all the answers. The Bible says it's simple; still my brain likes to make it so complicated. Help me to live a simple life – a life without worry, a life that trusts You for all things. Amen.

Worry-free life

Therefore I tell you, do not worry about your life, what you will eat or drink; or about your body, what you will wear. Is not life more than food and the body more than clothes?

Matthew 6:25

The life of a mom can be filled with worry. We worry because we love our children so much. But Jesus tells us not to worry. Instead, He wants us to place our anxious thoughts in His hands and trust Him. In order for you as a mom to be able to exchange your worry for God's peace, you must trust God completely. You need to comprehend the endless love that God has for you and your children.

Where does worry get you anyway? By worrying, do you accomplish anything good for your family or yourself? No. One reason why worrying is unproductive is the fact that you can't change the outcome of your circumstances due to your level of worry. All you end up doing is working yourself into a frenzy. In the end, nothing has changed.

Instead of worrying, you need to take your concerns and fears to God and lay them at His feet. You need to ask God to either change your circumstances or give you what you need to get you through the tough times. It's up to God what He will do.

Father, in my human nature, I worry.
I try as hard as I can to stop worrying, but I always end up
thinking about my circumstances. God, I want a life that is
worry-free, but in order for that to happen, I realize I must
put my faith in You and not my circumstances. Teach me,
Father, how to do that. I am willing to learn. Amen.

Worthy of praise

Declare His glory among the nations,
His marvelous deeds among all the peoples.
For great is the LORD and most worthy of praise.

I Chronicles 16:24-25

Wake up this morning and sing unto the Lord! Thank God for all the blessings in your life, even if you're in a valley of difficulty. Soak in all the beauty that surrounds your home today – from the sunshine that warms your face, to the flowers that bloom outside your window, to the birds that sing you sweet songs throughout your day. Find a way to give God praise, no matter what circumstance you find yourself in today. Declare His glory; thank Him for providing for your needs, no matter how great or small.

We praise people all day long. We praise our children for making good grades. We praise our husbands for great work around the house. We praise our friends for being thoughtful toward us. But how often do we praise God? Do we "declare His glory"? Do we give God any glory for what's going on in our lives? He is worthy of our praise and He loves to be praised by His children. Don't you love hearing your children tell you that they love you? God needs to hear our praise. He, above all, is worthy of such praise.

Father, You are worthy of my praise! You bless me in so many ways – ways that I take for granted. Every breath You give me is a blessing … my children, my home, the beauty of nature all around me, the sweet rainfall and the birds outside my window. These are all such blessings. Today, I will declare Your glory and praise Your holy, holy name! Amen.

Wrestling with God

When the man saw that he could not overpower him,
he touched the socket of Jacob's hip so that his hip
was wrenched as he wrestled with the man.

Genesis 32:25

Have you ever wrestled with God? Have you argued with Him, thrown your arms up in the air or even screamed at God in exasperation, wanting Him to hear what you have to say? In Genesis, a familiar man from the Bible also wrestled with God.

Jacob wrestled with God all night long because he wanted God's blessing in his life. He didn't stop until he got what he wanted. God answered Jacob's request and changed his name to Israel, meaning "you have wrestled with God and with men and have overcome" (v. 28). God blessed Israel in a mighty way through his twelve children, who became the twelve tribes of Israel.

Sometimes it's worth it to wrestle with God, to stay in the fight until you believe God has heard your cry. Don't be afraid to push back against God and tell Him your desires. He already knows, but pursuing Him with such vigor only results in good. By putting your trust in Him and urging Him to hear you, you are growing your relationship with Him. Jacob was changed forever. His hip was wrenched, but in Jacob's mind, it was worth it. You may also be changed forever.

Father, give me wisdom to know when I should push
and when I need to submit. I know that wisdom will only come
from You. I seem to push for everything in my life, which I know
is not always good. God, thank You for loving me enough not
to let go of me, even when I am pushing against You. Amen.

You are not alone

And I will ask the Father, and he will give you
another advocate to help you and be with you forever.
John 14:16

Being a mom is an extremely hard job; there's no rulebook with step-by-step instructions on how to raise great children.

God has gone before you and made a way for you to parent with Him. God has given us the Holy Spirit, our Comforter and Counselor. He will guide us while we raise our children. Jesus knew when He left His disciples that they would feel very alone, so He provided the Holy Spirit.

The Holy Spirit lives inside of you. In Him, you have everything you will ever need to be a great parent. Most of us, however, never even think to ask Him for help. We try to figure everything out on our own. Jesus said He was giving us a Counselor that would stay with us forever. Why not use the Counselor?

Father, I feel lost at times as a parent.
Thank You for knowing my weaknesses
and providing help for me. I love You! Amen.

You go first

Do nothing out of selfish ambition or vain conceit.
Rather, in humility value others above yourselves.

Philippians 2:3

This could be a theme verse for all moms. We live lives of humility, beginning the day we bring our babies home from the hospital. There's nothing glorious about being a mom; it's a life of sacrifice, always putting others before you. How many times have you gotten out of bed when you wanted to sleep because you heard your child crying? How many times have you rocked them in the middle of the night trying to soothe them back to sleep?

We as moms live this verse out very well. She sits at the ball field, practice rink, rehearsal hall, golf course, tennis court or dance hall for hours on end so her children can practice. Moms usually push their needs a side. They give up the last bites of desserts, extra money for new clothes and so on. Their lives are defined by sacrifice.

Today, as you go about your day, realize this: your life matters to God and He always notices your sacrifice.

Father, thank You for the gift of being a mom. Thank You for the blessing of my children and what they mean to me. I pray today that I will be humble and self-sacrificing in my role and not grow resentful and bitter. I need Your love working through me to do this. Fill me with Your presence and Your love. Amen.

Your conduct

Whatever happens, conduct yourselves in a manner
worthy of the gospel of Christ.

Philippians 1:27

⋟———⋞

Regardless of where you find yourself in life, as a follower of Christ you are to conduct yourself in a righteous manner. So many times, we make excuses: I can't be loving toward my husband because he isn't loving toward me. I won't forgive my ex-husband because he doesn't deserve forgiveness. When my in-laws start treating me better, I'll start allowing them to see their grandchildren.

God doesn't operate fairly – or at least not according to our definition of fair. If He did, we would all be doomed. No, God gives grace where grace is not deserved. God forgives – always. God loves unconditionally. God expects His children (that's you!) to live lives worthy and reflective of Him.

Don't make excuses anymore. Love unconditionally, choose forgiveness and offer grace, regardless of your circumstances. Paul said to the Philippians, "Whatever happens …" Live free of excuses and allow God to sort out the fairness in your world.

•••———◦◦———•••

Father, I give into excuses regarding the way I treat others.
I tell myself, "If someone is mean to me, then I can be mean in
return." I'm realizing, as a follower of Christ, that this is wrong.
Please forgive me for treating people in such an insensitive
and unloving way. God, You're going to have to do this through
me. I can't do it on my own. Amen.

Your cup

Jesus commanded Peter, "Put your sword away!
Shall I not drink the cup the Father has given me?"

John 18:11

When God created the world, He created it perfect, without sin. But when Adam and Eve tasted the forbidden fruit, sin entered the world and the world has been broken ever since. We try to make this world perfect, but we are fighting a losing battle. It won't be perfect again until Jesus returns.

Oftentimes, our instinct is to run from pain, but no matter how far we run, we can't escape the hard times because of the world we live in. We often pray that God will take certain circumstances out of our lives so we won't have to experience the pain. Jesus acknowledged this. He knew His "cup" was to die on the cross and He accepted it, even though it would be painful.

It's okay to ask God to take away your painful circumstances. Jesus teaches us this so clearly when He asks God to take away the cross. But Jesus submitted to God's will and prayed, "Not as I will, but as You will" (Matthew 26:39).

What cup has God given you? If God is allowing you to go through something painful, then He will get you through it.

Father, we do live in a broken world and yet
I constantly try to make it perfect. Help me, Lord,
to see this world the way You see it, to realize that I'm
just passing through. Give me the strength to handle whatever life
brings my way and help me to accept what I can't change. Amen.

Your gaze

*… fixing our eyes on Jesus, the pioneer and perfecter of faith.
For the joy set before Him he endured the cross, scorning its
shame, and sat down at the right hand of the throne of God.*

Hebrews 12:2

Where is your gaze? What captures your attention? Is it your life, your problems, your circumstances? When there is a problem in your life, do you feel it's all on you to fix? It's easy to fix our eyes on just our problems. Even though we're inclined to hyper-focus on ourselves, that attention doesn't make our problems go away. It can even cause extra anxiety and worry.

A better option is to focus on Jesus. When you choose to keep your eyes fixed on Him, the problems of this world will fade away. When you think about the suffering Jesus endured and overcame, your problems will diminish. Your problems won't go away; they just won't consume you.

It's one thing to be consumed with a problem that you can fix, but most of the time, if you're like me, you are consumed with problems you can't fix – your husband, lack of finances, in-law problems or an illness like cancer. I can't cure cancer, but I can fix my eyes on God and draw my strength from Him while I battle the disease. With Jesus, I can find peace and joy in the midst of a situation that offers no peace or joy.

*I choose to fix my eyes on You, Lord. I want You to get bigger
in my life and my problems to grow smaller. You are the
ultimate Healer of all things. You alone know what I need
and when I need it. I will look to You always. Amen.*

Your nest

My Father's house has many rooms; if that were not so, would I have told you that I am going there to prepare a place for you?

John 14:2

A woman's house is an important part of her life. Where she lives, who her neighbors are, and whether she feels comfortable and safe means everything to her. Women want their homes to reflect their personalities, charm and warmth. This is a big deal for women, whether they live in a mansion or an apartment. They want to make their homes their own.

Many times, we get too caught up with the decorating and design, putting too much pressure on ourselves (and our husbands) to create the "perfect" home.

Jesus said He has gone to prepare a place specifically for you. When you get to heaven, God will have prepared your perfect home. Maybe it'll be on the ocean with beautiful views or maybe it'll be a cottage tucked away in the mountains. Inside, your house will be exactly what you love, because Jesus has prepared it just for you. Don't be discouraged in this world or put your family in debt trying to keep up with society. One day, you'll have the perfect place and you'll live in it for eternity.

Father, thank You! Thank You for knowing me so well and loving me so much that You are building my final home. You are filling it with special treasures that You alone know I will love. God, help me to stay content on this earth and keep my eyes focused on You and my ultimate home in heaven. Amen.

Your walk

*Noah was a righteous man, blameless among the people
of his time, and he walked faithfully with God.*

Genesis 6:9

So many times, we say we don't feel God's presence in our lives. We share with a friend that God seems to be distant; you cry out to Him, but He seems so far away. To be sure, there are times when God is silent. He is still with us, but He's silent and only He knows why. Many times when we feel distant from God, it's our own fault because we aren't seeking Him on a daily basis. We pray, "God, bless me and my family; God, help me; God, make this situation go away," but we must ask ourselves, "Are we walking faithfully with God?"

You play an important role in your relationship with God – you have to seek Him, learn about Him, listen to Him. Your relationship with God is no different than any other relationship you have. It's a two-way street. Are you doing your part? Are you spending quality time with Him? If you want to feel God's presence in an intimate way, walk faithfully with Him every day. When He's quiet, don't doubt Him; trust that He is still by your side. Ask Him, "What do You want me to learn during Your silence?"

*Father, thank You that I am able to have a relationship with You.
You are the God of the universe, the Creator of all things.
You alone are holy, righteous and worthy of my praise. God,
create in me a deep hunger for You and Your Word.
I want to know You and walk faithfully with You. Amen.*